INSIGHT

ST PETERSBURG

APA PUBLICATIONS
Part of the Langenscheidt Publishing Group

C000145092

ABOUT THIS BOOK

INSIGHT GUIDE
ST PETERSBURG

Editorial
Project Editor
Clare Griffiths
Editorial Director
Brian Bell

Distribution

UK & Ireland
GeoCenter International Ltd
The Viables Centre, Harrow Way
Basingstoke, Hants RG22 4BJ
Fax: (44) 1256 817988

United States
Langenscheidt Publishers, Inc.
46–35 54th Road, Maspeth, NY 11378
Fax: (718) 784 0640

Canada
Thomas Allen & Son Ltd
390 Steelcase Road East
Markham, Ontario L3R 1G2
Fax: (1) 905 475 6747

Australia
Universal Press
1 Waterloo Road
Macquarie Park, NSW 2113
Fax: (61) 2 9888 9074

New Zealand
Hema Maps New Zealand Ltd (HNZ)
Unit D, 24 Ra ORA Drive
East Tamaki, Auckland
Fax: (64) 9 273 6479

Worldwide
Apa Publications GmbH & Co.
Verlag KG (Singapore branch)
38 Joo Koon Road, Singapore 628990
Tel: (65) 865 1600. Fax: (65) 861 6438

Printing

Insight Print Services (Pte) Ltd
38 Joo Koon Road, Singapore 628990
Tel: (65) 865 1600. Fax: (65) 861 6438

©2002 Apa Publications GmbH & Co.
Verlag KG (Singapore branch)
All Rights Reserved

First Edition 1991
Fourth Edition 2002

CONTACTING THE EDITORS
We would appreciate it if readers
would alert us to errors or out-
dated information by writing to:
**Insight Guides, P.O. Box 7910,
London SE1 1WE, England.
Fax: (44) 20 7403 0290.
insight@apaguide.demon.co.uk**

www.insightguides.com

This guidebook combines the interests and enthusiasms of two of the world's best-known information providers: Insight Guides, whose titles have set the standard for visual travel guides since 1970, and Discovery Channel, the world's premier source of nonfiction television programming.

The editors of Insight Guides provide practical advice and general understanding about a destination's history, culture, institutions and people. Discovery Channel and its popular website, www.discovery.com, help millions of viewers explore their world from the comfort of their own home and encourage them to explore it first hand.

This book is structured to convey an understanding of the city and its people, as well as to guide readers through its sights and activities:

◆ The **Features** section covers the history and culture of the city in a series of essays.

◆ The main **Places** section is a complete guide to all the sights and areas worth visiting. Places of special interest are coordinated by number with the maps.

◆ The **Travel Tips** listings section provides a handy point of reference for information on travel, hotels, shops, restaurants and more.

The contributors

This edition of *Insight Guide: St Petersburg* was supervised by managing editor **Clare Griffiths** at Insight Guides editorial headquarters in London. The book has been com-

EXPLORE YOUR WORLD®
Discovery
CHANNEL

Map Legend

— · — · ·	International Boundary
⊖	Border Crossing
— · — · —	National Park/Reserve
— — — —	Ferry Route
Ⓜ	Metro
✈ ✈	Airport: International/Regional
🚌	Bus Station
❶	Tourist Information
✉	Post Office
† †	Church/Ruins
†	Monastery
☾	Mosque
✡	Synagogue
⚔	Castle/Ruins
🏠	Mansion/Stately home
⸫	Archaeological Site
⋒	Cave
⚱	Statue/Monument
★	Place of Interest

dubbed "the conscience of the nation", who wrote about the city's architecture. **Igor Zakharov** wrote about the city's colourful history and about parks and palaces in the suburbs. **Georgi Katayev** specialises in the city's cultural heritage and wrote the essay on The Hermitage, while **N. Zorkaya**, a leading Russian film critic, and drama critic **Andrei Karaulov** contributed to the essay on theatre and cinema. **Rowlinson Carter** wrote the new essay on religion, with additional work by **Robin Minney**, and the chapter on food and drink was revised by **Iain Law**.

Lidiya Ginzburg, who wrote *Notes of a Blockade Survivor,* died in 1990 at the age of 88 before the first edition of this book was published. The chapter on the "People of Peter" was written by **Fyodor Dmitriev**, who has lived in St Petersburg nearly all his life. The cultural aspects of this book were covered by various writers including **Elvira Kim** and **Olga Kalinina**, while **Leonid Ivanov** provided the detailed information in the Places section.

Like all Insight Guides, this book owes much to its striking photographs, many of which are by **Fritz Dressler**, **A Mockford** and **N Bonnetti** for Apa Publications and **Gudenko**.

The final touches were provided by **Bronwen Barber**, who proofread the book, **Isobel McLean**, who indexed the text, and **Sylvia Suddes**, who made the final checks.

Welcome, then, to the constantly changing St Petersburg. One thing that doesn't change is its spendour, and we hope you will be as captivated by it as our contributors were when compiling this book.

pletely updated and substantially rewritten by American-born journalist **John Varoli**. After living in Moscow for three years, Varoli moved to St Petersburg in 1995. He recently became the first Westerner to be granted permanent residency in St Petersburg since the collapse of the Soviet Union. Varoli writes regularly for *The New York Times*, *The Art Newspaper* and Bloomberg News.

This edition of *Insight Guide: St Petersburg* builds on foundations laid in earlier editions by **Wilhelm Klein**, who managed the original project. Original contributors to the book include **Yevgeny Yevtushenko**, the country's most outspoken contemporary poet, who wrote the introduction to the book, and **Dmitry Likhachev**, a native of St Petersburg

The main places of interest in the Places section are coordinated by number with a full-colour map (e.g. ❶), and a symbol at the top of every right-hand page tells you where to find the map.

CONTENTS

The Bronze Horseman, a statue of the city's founder Peter the Great

Places

THE RENAISSANCE CITY

As St Petersburg celebrates its tricentenary, the mood
in the city is one of optimism and renewal

After enjoying over 200 years as capital of the earth's largest empire, St Petersburg suffered horribly for most of the 20th century and sank into provincial obscurity. Today, however, St Petersburg is reclaiming its glory days, and the optimism is contagious as the city celebrates its 300th anniversary in 2003.

The city entered the new millennium triumphant on 31 December, 1999, when political power in the Kremlin finally passed back into the hands of a man from St Petersburg, Vladimir Putin. Since then, the Russian president has placed people from his home town into key positions in government ministries, as well as Russia's most powerful corporations, and often meets visiting foreign heads of state in his native city. Rivalry between Moscow and St Petersburg has always been intense on all levels but without exaggeration it can now be said that St Petersburg now rules Russia and Muscovites are gritting their teeth with contempt and jealousy.

Putin's presidency is now the defining influence on the city and as many political pundits believe he will hold office to 2008, if not beyond, the fortunes of St Petersburg look set to become golden for the next decade. Billions of dollars of federal money are needed to rebuild the city's infrastructure after decades of neglect by Soviet authorities and although the work has begun, such a $1 billion ring road around the city, most projects will take more than a decade to complete.

The tricentenary in 2003 is a celebration of one of Europe's largest, youngest and most important, yet least-known cities. Although it has been a decade since the end of the Cold War, many misconceptions about Russia and St Petersburg persist in America and Europe. First-time visitors often come with concern and even trepidation, but almost all leave with the joy of finding an undiscovered treasure.

Today Russians and foreigners (many of whom are joining the booming real estate market and taking up residence) are flocking to the city in search of better jobs. In tandem with the city's increased political clout, St Petersburg's cultural institutions, such as the Hermitage Museum and the Mariinsky Theatre, have once again risen to international pre-eminence. The city is also home to one of Russia's main centres of high-tech industry, as well as a renewed heavy engineering sector that is attracting interest from Asian countries.

The history of St Petersburg has been one of continued struggle, destruction and rebirth. Perhaps it is this constant tumult that generates the catharsis that has made the city a inspiration to some of the world's greatest cultural, scientific and business personalities. ❏

PRECEDING PAGES: the landing at the Spit during St Petersburg's heyday; the Fontanka, early 19th century; a view of the Academy of Arts in 1802; the Decembrist Uprising of 1825.
LEFT: Church on the Spilled Blood at night.

Decisive Dates

1703 St Petersburg is founded when Peter the Great builds the Peter and Paul Fortress. A year later the Admiralty shipyard is built. Work on Letny Sad (the Summer Gardens) begins.
1710 Alexander Nevsky Lavra is founded.
1712 St Petersburg becomes Russia's capital.
1714 The Kunstkamera, Russia's first museum, is founded and the first stone buildings are built.
1715 Russia's first Naval Academy is founded.
1718 Peter the Great executes his son Czarevich Alexei, in the Peter and Paul Fortress, which now

becomes a prison for enemies of the government.
1721 Peace is made with Sweden, ending the long Northern War. Peter takes the title emperor.
1724 The Academy of Sciences is founded. The remains of St Alexander Nevsky are moved from Vladimir to the Alexander Nevsky Lavra.
1725 Peter the Great dies, and his second wife, Catherine I, ascends the throne. The population of St Petersburg is about 40,000.
1728 Peter II, Peter the Great's son, becomes emperor and moves the capital back to Moscow.
1732 Under Empress Anna, Peter the Great's niece, St Petersburg comes capital again.
1736–37 Fire destroys downtown St Petersburg.
1741 Elizabeth Petrovna, Peter the Great's daugh-

ter, seizes power after deposing the child emperor, Ivan VI, ruler for less than a year.
1750 The city population reaches about 100,000.
1754 Francesco Bartolomeo Rastrelli begins building the Winter Palace.
1757 The Academy of Arts is founded.
1761 Elizabeth dies, Peter III becomes emperor.
1762 Peter is deposed by his wife, Catherine II (Catherine the Great).
1767 Catherine begins buying art collections, laying the foundation of the Hermitage museum.
1777 The city is hit by flooding.
1782 The Bronze Horseman monument is unveiled.
1785 The Marble Palace is built by Catherine II for her lover Prince Orlov and she purchases Diderot's library for her collection.
1789 The Tauride Palace is built by Catherine II for her lover, Prince Potyomkin.
1795 The Imperial Public Library is founded.
1796–7 When Catherine dies, her son Pavel begins his short rule. Construction on the Mikhailovsky Castle begins. The Russian-American Company is founded to administer Alaska, a Russian territory.
1799 Pavel is assassinated in Mikhailovsky Castle, and Alexander I, later known as Alexander the Great, becomes emperor.
1811 The Kazan Cathedral is completed.
1812 Napoleon invades Russia.
1816 Russia's first stock exchange opens on the Spit of Vasilievsky Island.
1823 The Admiralty building is completed.
1824 Flooding in the city.
1825 Alexander I dies, and the Decembrists rise up when Nicholas I ascends the throne.
1826 Five of the Decembrist leaders are executed at the Arsenal (now the Artillery Museum).
1832 The Alexander Column is erected.
1834 The Senate and Synod buildings, designed by Carlo Rossi, are finished.
1837 Russia's leading poet, Alexander Pushkin, is killed in a duel. The first Russian railroad opens between St Petersburg and Tsarskoe Selo. The Winter Palace burns down, and is rebuilt nearly a year later.
1850 The Annunciation Bridge, now Lt. Schmidt Bridge, opens as the city's first permanent bridge.
1851 The Moscow–St Petersburg railroad opens.
1853 The city's population is over half a million. Nicholas I dies. Alexander II ascends the throne.
1858 St Isaac's cathedral is finished.
1860 The Mariinsky Theatre is opened, and the State Bank of Russia is founded.
1861 Serfdom is abolished.

1863 A central water supply system is opened.
1869 Medeleyev, a professor at St Petersburg university, creates the periodic table.
1879 The first street lights appear.
1880 Alexander II narrowly escapes a terrorist bomb explosion in the Winter Palace. A year later he is assassinated and later the Church on the Spilled Blood is built on this spot.
1885 The St Petersburg sea port moves from the Spit of Vasilievsky Island to its current location in the city's southeast.
1890 Pyotr Tchaikovsky's *Sleeping Beauty* premieres at the Mariinsky Theatre. The city's population reaches one million.
1894 Alexander III dies. Nicholas II becomes tsar.
1898 The Russian Museum opens.
1903 The Trinity Bridge spans the Neva, spurring a building boom on the Petrograd side.
1905 Hundreds of peaceful workers and their families are shot by government troops on Bloody Sunday on Palace Square. A general strike begins, leading to a full uprising across the empire.
1906 As part of the government's concessions, the State Duma, the Russian parliament, convenes for the first time in the Tauride Palace.
1907 The Church on the Spilled Blood is finished.
1910 The city's population reaches over 2 million.
1914 World War I. The city is renamed Petrograd.
1917 Tsar Nicholas II abdicates in what is called the February Revolution. The Bolsheviks seize power in October. The city's population reaches its peak of 2½ million.
1918 The Bolsheviks forcibly dissolve the democratically elected Constituent Assembly, called just after the Bolshevik seizure of power to choose a new post-tsarist government. The Red Terror begins as anti-communist forces march on Petrograd. The capital is moved back to Moscow.
1919 Petrograd is under siege by the White Army. The population flees as food supplies are cut off.
1920 Only 700,000 people remain in the city, which is totally paralysed by the communist terror.
1921 The sailors of the Kronstadt naval base rise up against the Bolsheviks. All are massacred.
1924 Lenin dies; the city is renamed Leningrad. The third worst flood in city history strikes.
1929 Communist authorities begin pulling down churches as part of their anti-religion campaign.
1934 Sergei Kirov is assassinated in his office in

Smolny, setting off the Great Terror.
1939 The city population is 3.2 million.
1941 In June the Nazis invade Russia, and in September the Siege of Leningrad begins.
1944 The Siege is lifted. The city's population has declined to 500,000.
1948 The so-called Leningrad Affair begins, leading to the repression of local intellectuals.
1955 The subway opens.
1964 The Peterhof Palace opens to the public after restoration of damage caused by the war.
1979 Construction begins on the flood protection barrier in the Gulf of Finland.
1988 Fire rips through the library of the Academy

of Sciences, destroying thousands of rare books.
1989 UNESCO makes the city a world heritage site. The population reaches 5 million.
1991 Anatoly Sobchak becomes the city's first mayor.
1996 Vladimir Yakovlev becomes city governor.
1998 The remains of Tsar Nicholas II, his family and servants are interred in the Peter and Paul Cathedral. Financial crisis paralyses Russia.
2000 Former city deputy governor, Vladimir Putin, becomes Russia's president, and Yakovlev wins re-election as city governor. The city becomes the official capital of the Northwest Federal District.
2003 The city celebrates its 300th anniversary, marked by infrastructure projects. ❑

PRECEDING PAGES: Lenin calls for revolution.
LEFT: Peter I with his family in 1720.
RIGHT: a commander of the Red Army.

THE CITY WITH THREE NAMES

*Through a specially commissioned essay, the poet Yevgeny Yevtushenko
traces St Petersburg's changing identity through history*

The St Petersburg poet Georgi Adamovich found himself, after the Revolution, in one of the world's loveliest cities, Paris – yet he still used to sigh bitterly for the lost beauty of the city on the Neva whose beauty and spirituality he regarded even more highly:

On Earth there was but one capital.
The rest were merely towns…

None of the émigrés like Adamovich who tried to preserve this stone fantasy of Peter I in their memories ever called it Petrograd or Leningrad; when asked, they would always say they came from St Petersburg.

Of course, it was tragic – revolutionary Petrograd losing the essence of St Petersburg when raging crowds cleared the thoroughfares of the shadows of the Decembrist aristocrats in what was primarily a just, but also a filthy, stream. It was the Decembrists who, sipping French champagne, had once dreamed of embodying the ideas of pampered French liberalism. And it was tragic that Leningrad lost the essence of Petrograd where, in the Stray Dog literary café great poets like Blok, Mayakovsky and Mandelshtam could be seen sitting in the same room – true, usually at different tables – and where Chagall, who had not yet emigrated, used to decorate the streets during demonstrations, and where Gorky could still get Lenin to agree not to have some free-thinking intellectual arrested or shot.

Ever so, the City on the Neva became even greater "in light of the losses borne". There was the October Revolution, the sailor's gruff phrase, "The guard's tired", which broke up the Constituent Assembly. There was the terror of the 1930s when thousands of Leningradians were arrested and annihilated. There was the terror of the Fascist siege when people made soup from old belts or shoes. And all these tragedies made the city even greater in history. These three different names, it turned out, were not like the masks a resourceful actor could change with a magician's sleight of hand. On

the contrary, they proved to be three great roles which history had bestowed with cruel generosity upon an actor no less great.

Peter I

Pushkin, in his poem *The Bronze Horseman*, retrospectively eavesdropped on the secret

thoughts of Peter I, who had conceived the idea of building a new capital of Russia overlooking the world's open seas:

"By nature we are fated here
To cut a window through to Europe…"

Peter, the first Russian Westerniser on the throne, studied ship-building in Amsterdam and London, levied a tax on beards and forced all his courtiers to smoke tobacco; he could not have carried through his Westernising plans without a powerful port where, as Pushkin had him say, "ships of every flag" would indeed "come to visit us". Peter was compelled by another imperative, a psychological one, resulting in his urgent need to leave Moscow. In his

---

LEFT: the Mother of God icon.
RIGHT: the futurist poet Vladimir Mayakovsky in 1917.

childhood a frenzied, bloodthirsty mob had burst into the Kremlin, and he had been saved only by a miracle. Plots were constantly being hatched against him there. And what better place for rebellions and murders than Moscow's winding back streets?

The straight streets of the city on the Neva, on the other hand, were perfect for the promenades, parades and masquerades Peter enjoyed so much. The streets of St Petersburg looked just like a series of cuttings in the forest. They were so

HOISTING THE FLAG

The Russian naval flag – a dark blue cross on a white background – was first hoisted on the *Poltava*, the first battleship of the fleet, named after the town where Peter I had defeated the Swedish.

administrative élite established by Ivan the Terrible) but with the important difference that they not only tracked down and executed enemies of the state but also built St Petersburg alongside the Tsar.

In the Table of Ranks introduced by Peter, 14 rungs of the ladder separated the serf from the highest state officials, but Peter also made it possible for a person to climb to the top of the ladder in one go. True, this took a fair degree of good luck as well as a modicum of talent.

straight that it seemed they had been cut through the wooded marshes exactly as his eyes had directed, and not with axes. Fearless though he was in his battles against foreigners, Peter feared Moscow as he would fear an old witch with an evil eye. The marshes on which he built the new capital seemed firmer to him than the stone-patterned floors of the Kremlin.

While constructing St Petersburg, Peter was naturally afraid of relying on people who regarded Moscow as their hereditary nest. He made Alexander Menshikov his right-hand man; he, rumour has it, previously earned his living as a peddler of hot pies. The "birds of Peter's nest" were his *oprichniks* (the special

Peter's henchmen

Peter's companions helped him not only to chop off heads but also to hew the masts of ships and fashion the shape of the state. The Russian navy was built with Peter's own hands and it was no accident that the first battleship of this fleet was named The Poltava after the town where Peter had defeated the Swedish King Karl XII.

A dispatch from the British emissary, James Jeffreys, recorded the event: "They have launched a battleship with ninety cannons, ten ships are on the stocks… The ships are built here no worse than in Europe…" Jeffreys had forgotten that Russia was also Europe. But

Peter never forgot his first English boat which he had found in a barn and mended, and which, as a 15-year-old lad, he had learned to manoeuvre on the River Yauza. On his orders this boat, named The Grandfather of the Russian Fleet, was sent by cart from Moscow to St Petersburg. For 16 months it stayed on dry land until finally, in May 1723, it was lowered into the Neva. With an escort consisting of nine galleys plus the imperial yacht, Peter sailed the boat down the River Neva from St Petersburg to Schlüs-

PETER THE GREAT

Peter the Great was both a Spartan and an epicurean but he was talented and inventive, not senselessly oppressive, tasteless and dull.

clothes. Fever and disease claimed a great many lives. When a person died, he was wrapped in the matting in which he had just dragged earth, and was buried in the earth he had himself brought.

St Petersburg is a Russian pyramid. But Peter was a proletarian pharaoh who lost as much sweat as his slaves. He used to get up at five o'clock and spend half an hour walking about his room, thinking. Then for half an hour his secretary used to read him various business reports and hand him papers to sign. After breakfast, at

selburg. All the ships and boats on the river formed up and saluted The Grandfather of the Russian Fleet with gunfire, fanfares and fireworks. "From small causes may come great results" was written in blazing letters in the sky.

A city built on bones

St Petersburg is a marsh paved with human bones. As there was no suitable building land, the first migrants dragged earth from far-off places to the city bastions in old sacks, bark matting and even in the hems of their coarse hemp

LEFT: Schlüsselburg, where the city originated.
ABOVE: winter scene in Tsarkoe Selo (Pushkin).

six o'clock he would set off on foot or horseback for the wharf, Senate or Admiralty, work until late, and then celebrate with a feast.

Wishing to make St Petersburg a "paradise", Peter had palaces built in and around the city; he presented his wife, Catherine I, with the country house of Saaris Moisio (later renamed Tsarskoye Selo), his daughter, Elizabeth, with a palace at Strelna, and had Peterhof, with its famous cascade of fountains, built for himself where he greatly loved the small palace of Mon Plaisir. From the graveyard of its first builders, St Petersburg grew into a beautiful city. In the autumn of 1728 Moscow became the capital once again, and the Imperial Court moved back there. St Petersburg began to decline and its unfinished buildings started collapsing alongside the unfinished ships. Peter's stone fantasy, whose wings were made from the canvas sails of his ships, seemed to be doomed. After the deaths of Peter I and Catherine I, the remaining talentless careerists from abroad formed a foreign mafia around the Imperial Court later called the Bironovshchina, or the rule of Biron, named after the German favourite of Empress Anna.

CATHERINE THE GREAT

This German-born, French-speaking woman, who managed to make four mistakes in a three-letter Russian word, slipped into the role of an Orthodox believer like a gifted actress.

Anna and Elizabeth

In 1732 Empress Anna made St Petersburg the capital again but life in the city, which had once been so creative, now became parasitic. Peter had also been fond of fireworks but only when the smithies' fires were blazing nearby. Now there were again fireworks but the fires in St Petersburg's smithies – along with the fires in the torture chambers – were for forging tongs which, when white-hot, were used to tear apart people's nostrils.

St Petersburg became truly Frenchified when, in 1741 the palace guardsmen removed the regent Anna Leopoldovna, (who had ruled after Anna and Biron and was also pro-German) and placed Peter's energetic, fun-loving daughter, Elizabeth, on the throne. With her light feminine touch, Elizabeth wiped clean the window into Europe that had been smeared with Bironovshchina. The rights and liberties gained by the nobility were instantly transformed into palaces and country estates, no less magnificent than the Imperial ones, and into the exclusive Corps of Pages along with several other higher educational establishments.

The St Petersburg Academy of Sciences, which had been founded by Peter but which had then "stood idle" for some time, resumed its activities. The Academy of Arts was founded. The vast potential of the so-called "simple" Russian was seen in Russia's first academician, the illustrious Archangel *muzhik* (peasant) Mikhailo Lomonosov, who, in true Renaissance style, harmoniously combined the talents of a scientist, poet and artist. The Italian sculptor, Rastrelli, designed a bust of Peter while his son built the Smolny ensemble and the Winter Palace.

Catherine the Great

In order to change from the provincial Princess of Anhalt-Zerbst into the Empress of Russia, Catherine made a study of the Russian character. Subjected to the insults of her ruling aunt, Elizabeth, and her husband Peter, Catherine once even attempted to commit suicide but the knife caught in her corset; who knows, perhaps she was only play-acting.

With her intelligence and perseverance she eventually won Elizabeth's favour and this intelligence subsequently earned her the title of "Catherine the Great", an honour accorded to nobody else but Peter and herself, either in their lifetime or posthumously. Contemporaries noted that in her case ambition gave way to industry. With unequalled industry, for instance, she created her *Instruction*, a compilation of the works of Montesquieu and Beccaria and the first attempt at a Russian constitution.

Paradoxically, the deputies of the Legislative Commission to whose verdict Catherine had submitted her free-thinking work, began ruthlessly censoring the Empress's efforts, deleting with particular zeal all the parts dealing with measures to prevent the abuse of

Imperial power and suggested ways of emancipating the serfs.

The historian Kliuchevsky left this brilliant description of Catherine: "Autocratic power acquired a new aspect, as was her intention, and became something akin to individual constitutional absolutism. In a society which had lost its sense of the law, even such a fortuity as a monarch's felicitous character could pass for a guarantee." In her private life Catherine sought revenge for

> ### PETER'S STATUE
>
> Beneath your feet, there is a block of rock, a kind of underground monument to the ordinary Russian who, neither under the tsars nor under the Soviet regime, has ever had a monument erected to him above ground.

The bronze horseman

The rock for this statue was found seven miles from St Petersburg and nicknamed the "Thunder Stone". It weighed 1,600 tons, and a wide cutting had to be made for it through the forests. When it reached the Gulf of Finland several months later, it was loaded on board a scuttled barge. After the water had been pumped out, the barge rose to the surface and carried the rock the rest of the way. Thousands of spectators, including Empress

the many years she had spent living in obscurity at Elizabeth's court, and she tried to surpass her "dear aunt" both in lovers and feasts. According to some sources, she had 20 favourites during her 34-year reign from 1762 to 1796.

Catherine also devoted considerable time and attention to architecture, to which the city owes its inimitable beauty. A visit to the equestrian statue of Peter the Great by the French sculptor Etienne Falconet, is an essential sight, among others, if you are to understand what the original city was really like.

LEFT: a portrait of Catherine the Great.
ABOVE: the tsarina travelling during winter.

Catherine, watched in wonder as the rock was unloaded. Then the part needed for the pedestal was cut away. The block that was left was massive and a terrible eyesore.

Shortly afterwards a scruffy and, moreover, drunk peasant rolled up in a cart pulled by a scrawny horse to clear the block away. The crowd started jeering at him. He took no notice of them and started digging a pit with an ordinary shovel. He dug all day long, and all the next, and the next after that, carting the earth away to the Neva.

Then, on the fourth day, something extraordinary happened: the massive block rolled gently into the pit all by itself. Then the little peasant started chucking earth on top of it until the rock was completely covered. In his poem *The Bronze Horseman* Pushkin made this monument a symbol of the state in the shape of a massive horse, thundering on the heels of a defenceless man who is running away from it, and rearing on its bronze hooves over his head. These bronze hooves did not spare the prodigal children of the Russian aristocracy, the Decembrists, who organised an uprising against the autocracy in December 1825: they were

PETROGRAD

"Petrograd" lasted for only 10 years: from the start of World War I, when anti-German feeling instigated its renaming, until Lenin's death in 1924, when the city was renamed after him.

toyevsky's novel *Crime and Punishment*, the man who killed an old woman, no less unfortunate in her greed, with an axe, imagining himself to be Napoleon. All classical 19th-century Russian literature originates from St Petersburg's White Nights and dreams, swirling like the mystical vapours on the marshes that existed before the time of Peter I and which, it seems, had remained only hidden under the thoroughfares' cobblestones. St Petersburg is the birthplace of the Russian classics.

executed or exiled to Siberia. These Decembrists belonged to a generation who had been educated not by quasi-hairdressers and quasi-lackeys from France but by genuine French free-thinkers who had fled to Russia and instilled their heretical ideas in the children of the aristocracy.

In essence, all the great Russian literature initiated by Pushkin can be seen as the ordinary person's defence against the State's bronze hooves. These hooves loomed over Gogol's poor Akaky Akakievich who was stripped of his wonderful new greatcoat by thieves. These hooves did not spare the head of Fedya Raskolnikov, the murderer, and protagonist of Dos-

Petrograd

Petrograd's face was changed rapidly, not so much by World War I as by the 20th century which came crashing down on Russia like an avalanche. The city's landscape was definitely demeaned by the intruding factory chimneys, just as classicism in art was by decadence.

The latter coincided or, rather, was closely connected with the tremendous public outrage that followed the mass shooting in 1905 of a group of workers who were on their way to the Winter Palace with a petition. This day became popularly known as "Bloody Sunday" and very likely marked the beginning of the end of autocracy. Alexander Blok, who had an astounding inner sense of the destruction of St Petersburg's past, conjured up a vision of a Petrograd blizzard in which he saw twelve Red Army men as the Twelve Apostles, only with blood-stained hands, and Christ following behind like a white spectre.

Blok was prophetically right. The empire's weariness, coupled with weary liberal disillusionment, proved to be that fatal "couldn't care less" which resulted in the outbreak of World War I, and the Revolution was a direct consequence of the war. Before the war a foreboding of a world cataclysm, as of impending retribution, penetrated every corner of the capital like a disquieting draught before a storm.

Degenerate city
Count A.N. Tolstoy gave the following eye-witness account of Petrograd at that time. "During the past decade vast enterprises had been created with incredible speed. Fortunes worth millions had emerged out of nowhere. Banks, music halls, skating rinks and marvellous taverns had been built in cement and cut glass where people were held spellbound by the music, mirrors' reflections, scantily clad women, light and champagne. Gaming-houses, meeting houses, theatres, cinemas and amusement parks were hurriedly opened. On an uninhabited island not far from St Petersburg engineers and capitalists worked on a new construction project of unprecedented luxury. There was a spate of suicides. Debauchery was rife, and it spread like a plague to the Palace. And Rasputin, a powerfully built illiterate peasant with crazy eyes, gained access to the Palace and Imperial throne, and began ruining Russia's good name with his mockery and insults…

"Girls made a secret of their innocence, and wives of their faithfulness. Destruction was considered good taste, neurasthenia a sign of sophistication… People made up vices and perversions for themselves so as not to seem insipid. Such was St Petersburg in 1914…"

The words evoke the scene before the eruption of Vesuvius and subsequent destruction of Pompeii: life, already degenerate and totally out of control, with its masochistic, provocative coquetry actually bringing the volcanic lava upon itself from the fiery depths

into which it is so afraid to gaze. The eruption did not have to be prevailed upon for long, and the revolutionary lava came gushing out of the crater of war.

Kerensky, who represented the centrist liberals, made the unforgivable historical mistake of insisting that the war must be continued until victory was achieved. Returning from exile abroad, Lenin, previously little-known to the broad masses, won the workers', peasants' and soldiers' hearts with the slogans "Peace to the peoples", "Land to the peasants!" and "Factories to the workers", and was soon given a tumultuous welcome in the city of Petrograd.

Revolution
During this wave of social hatred the craze for creating new values was soon replaced by another for redistributing those already in existence. The idea of "constricting" the bourgeoisie resulted in the occupants of basements, sometimes several families at once, moving not only into the mansions of aristocrats but also the apartments of writers, composers, scientists, doctors and university professors. The slogan "Steal what's stolen" turned into an orgy of self-robbery on a hitherto unprecedented scale nationwide.

Here is what Maxim Gorky, a living witness and herald of the Revolution, wrote of this:

LEFT: a statue in the gardens of Peterhof.
RIGHT: outside the Smolny in 1917.

"People are stealing in a wonderfully artistic manner: there is no doubt history will describe this process of Russia's self-robbery with the greatest enthusiasm. Churches and military museums are being robbed and sold, cannons, rifles, quartermasters' supplies are being sold, the palaces of grand princes are being stolen, everything plunderable is being plundered, everything sellable is being sold…"

Petrograd lost the treasures of St Petersburg – not only from museums and churches but human ones as well. Gumiliev, the first chairman of the Union of All-Russian Poets, was executed. Many eminent representatives of the intelligentsia emi-

numerous young shoots, which then stretched towards the Revolution in spellbound wonder.

The writer Victor Shklovsky recalls how, in 1921, the composer Glazunov came to Gorky to ask his help in obtaining a bread ration for a musician. Gorky asked,

"How old is he?"

"Fourteen. He's a music teacher's son. Accompanies films in the Select Cinema. Recently the floor caught fire under his feet but he went on playing. He's brought me his compositions."

"Any good?"

"No, awful. It's the first music I can't hear

grated while they were still able, and a miniature St Petersburg was formed in Paris.

There were also many who stayed behind, including, for instance, Gumiliev's first wife, Anna Akhmatova, the great St Petersburg poet, who said that she clamped her hands over her ears when she heard a voice urging her to leave. Those who had stayed behind tried to preserve St Petersburg in their souls but it had vanished like Atlantis. It would be unfair, however, to say that the Revolution merely annihilated everything within its reach. Such was its dual effect that, while irrationally uprooting mighty age-old trees of culture with its feverish breath it also raised from the depths of the earth

when I read the score."

"Why have you come to me, then?"

"I don't like it but that's not the point, the age belongs to this young boy, not me."

"What's his name?"

"Shostakovich."

Boris Pasternak, who attended the First Congress of Soviets in revolutionary Petrograd, gave this eye-witness account of Lenin:

And suddenly he loomed on the rostrum,
Loomed, even before he had appeared
And I thought of the origin
Of the age of shackling burdens.
A genius comes, a portent of privileges,
And avenges his departure with oppression.

Peter's creation was renamed Leningrad after this man. Once Lenin had gone, everything turned out to be as aggressive and vengeful as the poet had predicted.

Leningrad

During the relative economic liberalisation of the NEP (the New Economic Policy that Lenin introduced in 1921 to revive the collapsed economy), it seemed as though old St Petersburg might yet return to Leningrad: private shops, restaurants and variety shows were opened. Once again the streets resounded with the clip-clop of the hooves of dray-horses

when he read his scores, was now turning into a giant of world music. He had no idea then that the floor was going to catch fire under his feet again.

Who could have foreseen then that the intelligentsia would be split, and that not all of its members would be able to withstand the test of fear in a dignified manner?

Whereas the authorities of Tsarist St Petersburg had dealt with free-thinking writers on an individual basis (Radishchev had been exiled to Siberia; Dostoyevsky had been sentenced to hard labour), in Soviet Leningrad reprisals were meted out wholesale. The 30-

which had miraculously not been made into sausage-meat during the Civil War.

The cinemas were showing films starring Adolfe Menjou and Douglas Fairbanks, as well as films by experimental Soviet directors in an entirely new idiom. Censorship in the 1920s was relatively lax, and did not apply to the form of works, as it did later. In Leningrad avant-garde artists still held exhibitions, cooperative publishing houses put out the works of Formalist authors and the skinny youth Shostakovich, whose music Glazunov could not hear

year-old writer Boris Kornilov was one of the numerous victims of the Revolution which devoured its own offspring. Hailed by Bukharin at the First Congress of Writers as the hope of the nation's poetry, Kornilov was later shot as an enemy of the people in 1938.

Kornilev's former wife, the poet Olga Bergholts, also had a tragic life. She was pregnant when she was arrested and was beaten so badly during the interrogations that she suffered a miscarriage. Later, during the Fascist siege of Leningrad, she read her poetry over the radio and appealed for courage, in the process becoming one of the city's best-loved heroines. She is the author of the austere lines

LEFT: the 1917 October Revolution.
ABOVE: Gorky and a group of literary friends.

engraved in the granite and marble war memorials in Leningrad and many other Soviet cities: "No-one is forgotten and nothing is forgotten." This great woman was subsequently denounced during the witch hunt in the 1930s that flared up after the murder of Kirov, the leader of the Leningrad Communist Party, in 1934. The murder had been organised on Stalin's secret orders to justify the mass terror which followed. Stalin stood by Kirov's coffin and shed crocodile tears, and Zhdanov was elected instead of

proud bearers of insolence and ignorance. With deadly precision Zoshchenko had showed how pathetic and miserable these people really were.

CHILD LABOUR

Children worked at factories to get worker's ration cards. Many were so weak with hunger that they were tied to the machines to prevent them from collapsing.

The war years

The human species was being destroyed. But then World War II, which in Russia is known as The Great Patriotic War, demonstrated the phenomenal moral resources of those Russian people who had miraculously survived the relentless war being waged against them by Stalin and his stooges. Besieged Leningrad

Kirov – Zhdanov who in 1948 was to become the infamous author of the report in the journals Zvezda and Leningrad, sanctioning the Party diktat in art and ridiculing the top writers, Akhmatova and Zoshchenko. His choice of these writers for reprisals was not accidental. The old St Petersburg aristocratic poetry of Akhmatova had infuriated the plebeian ideologists for some time, just as the aspect of an old cathedral infuriates rampant atheists. Zhdanov also had a special account to settle with Zoshchenko.

In his satirical short stories Zoshchenko had depicted the new masters of old St Petersburg as triumphantly self-assured nonentities and the

became the centre of this morality. The significance of the 900 days and nights of the Leningrad siege was far greater than the 10 days which shook the world in 1917.

A doctor by the name of Samovarova recalls: "They ate all the cats and whatever dogs there were. Men died first because men are brawny, and do not have much fat. Women – even small ones – have a thicker layer of fat. But women also died, even though they were tougher. People turned into old folk because their layer of fat had been destroyed and all their muscles and veins showed through, and they were all terribly flabby. You could tell the cannibals by their glowing pink faces."

A Bechstein piano could be bought for a few loaves of bread. There was no firewood and so people sometimes heated their apartments with antique books and valuable Empire furniture. The maximum daily bread ration was 125 grammes (4 ounces).

Here is the menu of a Leningrad workers' wartime canteen – in summer, what's more, not winter: "Plantain soup; nettle and sorrel puree; beet-leaf rissoles; goose-foot rissoles; cabbage-leaf *schnit-zels*; oil-cake liver; fishbone-flour sauce; casein fritters; yeast soup." When people could stand it no longer, they made soup from wallpaper, leather belts and gloves.

The diary of Yura Ryabinkin, a young Leningrad boy who died of hunger and cold, makes sad reading: "The cold... is driving us out of this room. But there used to be a stove here on which we cooked omelettes, sausages and soup... Sometimes the gramophone would play, and there'd be joyful laughter, and we'd have a huge New Year's tree, as high as the ceiling, and we'd light the candles..."There'd be piles of sandwiches on the table (with all kinds of fillings!) and lots of sweets and spicy biscuits hanging on the tree (and nobody ate them!)... The flat's empty now. And completely silent. It seems to have frozen and turned into an icicle, and it will only melt in the spring..."

Perhaps, if Yura Ryabinkin had survived, he would have become a fine writer – perhaps even a contributor to this book. The survivors tried to support each other by sharing their last crumbs of food and their hopes. Out of these hopes grew Shostakovich's celebrated symphony which was first performed in the besieged city and was named *Leningrad*.

Old employees of the Hermitage have this almost incredible but actually true story to tell. When the museum's main paintings were evacuated, the empty frames were inscribed with the artists' names and the titles of their paintings were left in the halls to make it easier to set up the displays again after their return. Servicemen, many of whom were not from

NEVSKY PROSPEKT

Gogol has described Nevsky Prospekt thus: "There is nothing better than Nevsky Prospekt, in St Petersburg at least: it is everything for it. What isn't this street, our capital's pride, blessed with?".

Leningrad, came to see this wonderful museum before they left for the front. Though the priceless works of art were gone, guides still took visitors around the freezing cold halls and, in front of the empty frames, did their best to describe the beauty and grandeur of the paintings which had hung there before the war.

Despite the Fascist bombings the Way of Life was opened across the icebound Lake Ladoga and lorries, often sinking through the ice, brought bread to their besieged compatri-

ots. As soon as Hitler, whose idea it had been to destroy the city on the Neva, was forced to lift the siege, the outcome of the war was decided. St Petersburg's Piskarovskoye Cemetery is a gigantic memorial to the victims of the siege.

Europe without St Petersburg is unimaginable. As Dostoyevsky wrote of Moscow and St Petersburg: "What, indeed, would seem more contradictory than St Petersburg and Moscow? From a theoretical viewpoint, St Petersburg was, in principle, founded, as it were, in contrast with Moscow and its entire concept. And yet these two centres of Russian life essentially constitute a single centre..." It could scarcely be better put. ❑

LEFT: Shostakovich working on his Seventh Symphony in besieged Leningrad, 1941.
RIGHT: selling tickets for the premier of Shostakovich's *Leningrad* symphony in 1942.

FROM ST PETERSBURG TO LENINGRAD – AND BACK

Although St Petersburg is only three hundred years old, it experienced
tremendous upheaval in its short history before taking on its present form

St Petersburg, built by Peter the Great in the northwest corner of the country, was conceived as – and indeed became – a window into Europe. A window is a dwelling's eye; and the eye is in the head. Hence St Petersburg is the head and the mind, while Moscow is the heart and the soul of Russia.

Russia, as one contemporary writer put it, is for the most part a land of "dissipated being", an endless expanse. Suddenly, almost three centuries ago, it was given this uncharacteristic city of stone (*petra* means stone in Greek; *burg* is German for fortress).

St Petersburg became the fist, the swordpoint, the transceiver tuned in to Europe and the waves of Western influence, the collector of raw Russian power, which civilisation harnessed and communicated to the world at large. This, by the way, is the reason why the Revolution could only have started here – as a response to the West.

It would be wrong to think of St Petersburg, either then or now, as being synonymous with Russia. Yet the rest of the country would not be Russia without St Petersburg. Russia, as the author Georgy Gachev remarked, "is realised as a permanent dialogue between St Petersburg and Rus".

An ancient trade route

The Neva was Russia's traditional outlet into the Baltic. A thousand years before the city was founded, Lake Nevo (Ladoga) was the northern border of the territories of the Ilmen Slavs, the tribe that lived on the banks of the River Volkhov, Lake Ilmen and the rivers that flowed into it.

The Volkhov, which connected Ilmen and Ladoga, was the main route from the Varangians, also known as Vikings, to the Greeks in

Byzantium; the route that started on the Neva and ended in the mouth of the Dnieper, on the coast of the Black Sea. Along this route Vikings, Slavs and Finns co-existed in trade and politics.

Though scholars still hotly debate the origins

of Russia, evidence tends to support the idea that the Vikings gave rise to a unified Russian state in the 9th and 10th centuries, with centres in Kiev in the south, and Novgorod in the north. Kievan Rus, as historians now call it, had borders from the banks of the Neva to the rapids of the Dnieper.

Nevsky's times

With time, the ruling Viking elite became assimilated into the culture of the Eastern Slavs, who by the 13th century found themselves at war with their Scandinavian neighbours; a conflict which would continue for the next seven centuries, with success passing from side to side

---

PRECEDING PAGES: the devastation after an air raid in 1941.
LEFT: the bronze head of Peter the Great.
RIGHT: Alexander Nevsky, the ancient hero of Rus.

(the final war ended in 1809 after Russia annexed Finland). The first famous battle took place 750 years ago on the Neva; Birger, the earl of Sweden, was routed by Alexander, the prince of Novgorod, who is known in the country's history as Alexander Nevsky ("of the Neva").

Villages in the delta

To undermine the resistance they encountered from Novgorod, the Swedes built the Landscrona fort on the Neva in 1300. The Russians destroyed it and built, in 1323, a fort of their own – Oreshek. After Moscow annexed Novgorod in 1471–78, the fort, which stood

(1558–83), the northern forts were claimed by Sweden. On the site where Landscrona once stood, the Swedes built a new fort, Niensants.

War with Sweden

By the end of the 17th century the Swedes controlled the Baltic Sea. This irritated Russia and contradicted the interests of Denmark, Poland and Saxony. In 1700 a war against Sweden was declared. The goal of Peter the Great's Northern War was to reclaim the lands of the "fathers and grandfathers", the old Russian forts and outlets to the Baltic. Undaunted by early defeats, Peter proceeded to renovate old forti-

further inland on the Neva, was part of the northern defensive chain together with Ivangorod, Ladoga, Yamburg and Koporye.

By the 16th century, there were several dozen villages (over 1,000 houses in all) in the delta of the Neva. The village of Spasskoye stood where the Smolny Palace was later built; the village of Palenikha was situated where Liteyny Prospekt runs today. There were two villages on the bank of Bezymenny Erik (Fontanka) – Usadische and Kalinkina (the latter gave its name to Kalinkin Bridge); further up the river Neva lay the villages of Verkhny and Nizhny (Upper and Lower) Dubok. After Russia, under Ivan the Terrible, lost the war of Livonia

fications, replenish the armed forces and create an artillery force almost from scratch. In November 1702, Noteburg (Oreshek) fell to the Russians after a 30-hour assault. Peter gave the fort a new name, both sufficiently belligerent and understandable to his enemies – Schlüsselburg (Key Castle). On 1 May 1703, the Russians took Niensants. They now controlled the entire length of the Neva: Russia held the "key" and the "lock" to the Baltic Sea. But to "stand on shore with steady foot", these forts were clearly not enough. In the search for a new and more reliable stronghold, the Tsar explored the isles in the Neva. A site was chosen in the delta, on the small Hare Island.

The founding of the city

Here, on 16 May 1703, Peter founded the new Russian fort, which he named Saint Peter Burgh. That autumn, over 120 cannons were installed on its bastions. In November, the first peaceful merchantman sailing from the Netherlands visited the fort.

From the beginning, Peter wanted his creation to be grandiose and glamorous. In the autumn of 1704, he wrote to his closest friend and advisor, Alexander Menshikov, that he was going to call his "capital" Piterburgh. Meanwhile, the Swedes still threatened the fortress from land and sea. But not for long: several years before

struction workers. Peter issued a decree concerning the "eternal settlement" of masons, bricklayers, carpenters, metalworkers, joiners, tailors and bookkeepers in St Petersburg. These workers were given houses and vegetable plots. Roughly 1,500 of them came every year; in the end, they formed the basis of the city's working population. There were also hired hands, soldiers and Swedish prisoners-of-war.

In the beginning, construction was headed by the first governor of St Petersburg, Alexander Menshikov, and the city's first architect, Domenico Trezzini, from Switzerland. In 1710, building work began on the Church of Isaac

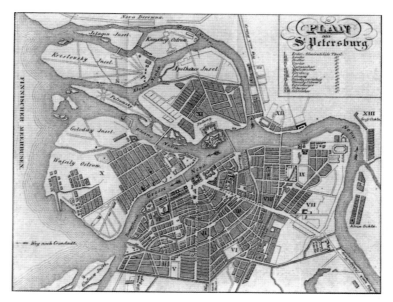

the end of the Northern War, the Russians seized all lands to the north and west of the fortress within at least a 100-km (60-mile) radius. From the sea, the mouth of the Neva was protected by Fort Kronshlot on Kotlin Island (later to become the sea fortress Kronstadt).

The early years

In the autumn of 1703, the number of workers sent to St Petersburg from various Russian towns reached 20,000. This figure doubled the following year. But the city needed trained con-

LEFT: Ivan III and the Tartars at the court.
ABOVE: a plan of St Petersburg, early 1800s.

THE BUILDING OF THE ADMIRALTY

The Admiralty was finished in 1705. Its shipyard became the first enterprise in St Petersburg and the birthplace of Russia's first "seagoing" battleship, the 54-cannon *Poltava*. It became the gravity centre for urban construction, which started with 100 *izbas* (cottages) for naval officers. On the right bank of the Neva, not far from the fort, was Peter's log cabin (built in 1703). Not far away, in Troitskaya Square, the builders erected a wooden cathedral. Several hundred wooden stores made up the Gostiny Dvor. The first streets of the city's early settlements (Pushkarskaya, Ruzheinaya, Grebetskaya and Rybatskaya) were oriented towards the fortress.

Dalmatsky. That same year, the Alexander Nevsky Monastery was founded. The opening cut in the woods between the Admiralty and the monastery was called Great Perspective (later to be called Nevsky Prospect). In 1712, Trezzini started work on the stone Peter and Paul Cathedral inside the fortress. As the cathedral rose above the ground, the fortress gradually became known as Peter and Paul.

Next came the turn of private residences. Menshikov ordered a magnificent three-storey stone palace with a large garden on Vasilievsky Island. The Summer Palace was built on the left bank of the Neva for Peter himself. The

verdant Summer Garden surrounded the palace.

On the same bank, but closer to the Admiralty, a winter palace was built for the Tsar (not to be confused with today's Winter Palace which houses the Hermitage). Further upstream, there was the Foundry (now Liteyny Prospect) – St Petersburg's second largest industrial enterprise. To the east of the Foundry lay the Tar Yard (now the Smolny), which produced tar for the Admiralty.

The capital of the north

St Petersburg officially became the Russian capital in 1712, when the Imperial Court moved from Moscow to the banks of the Neva. Several

months later, the Senate too moved there (the Senate was a collegiate body that succeeded the Boyar Duma). Young Russia celebrated victories not only on the field of battle, it also carried out fundamental internal reforms which ushered in a new era of development.

Construction was booming. Peter himself presided over construction work on the Vyborg Side, Vasilievsky Island and at Peterhof and Oranienbaum (his summer palaces and parks). In 1714, almost 10 million bricks were produced for the city. Yet more building material was needed, and Peter banned construction in stone all over the country with the sole exception of St Petersburg. Masons and other "artists of the building trade" were sent to work on the new capital by force.

Many foreigners were invited: the architect Jean-Batiste Leblond, the stucco-moulder Bartholomeo Carlo Rastrelli, the oak-carver Nicolas Pinaud, the fitter Jean Michel, the caster Pierre Sauvage, the metal-worker Theodore Belen, masons Bethalier and Cardasier, and many others. Each of them was given a shop with 10 Russian apprentices. This turned St Petersburg into a unique training centre for builders, who were shown the most advanced methods and absorbed the latest word in their trade.

Progressive ideas stood behind the general plan of the city, notably the master layout of the "House of Nobles". Stone edifices designed by Leblond (which have mostly been redesigned since then) are still regarded as the architectural backbone of many of the older quarters, which still retain their matchless rhythm and harmony of proportions.

The Northern War ended in victory for the Russians in 1721. It lasted for over two decades and cost Russia the lives of 40,000 soldiers and at least 70,000 civilians. But the country did not pay this terrible price in vain: the gap between the Middle Ages and the new times was bridged. Russia emerged as a developed and mighty European power.

Industrial development

With St Petersburg providing access to the Baltic Region, Russia gained the right to join the circle of northern countries, traditional exporters of timber, leather, lard, fish, grain and iron. Peter's Persian War (1722) strengthened Russia's presence on the Caspian Sea, with its trade routes connecting Central Asia and Western Europe. But exports and the transit of oriental goods were not the only factors of the economic boom in Russia. The country now had a well-developed industry. The number of industrial enterprises grew more than tenfold during Peter's reign and most of these innovative and previously unheard-of factories were concentrated in St Petersburg.

The scale of reform, which Peter implemented with utter ruthlessness, bred a new ideology, created new economic and political needs and promoted the dynamic development of education, science and culture – primarily

well as calendars, manuals and translations from foreign languages.

Many hitherto unknown things came to Russia: new uniforms and new firearms for the regular army regiments, huge naval vessels, libraries, a public theatre, museums and the Academy of Sciences, parks and park sculpture, fountains and canals, "exemplary houses". In the avenues of St Petersburg there were new clothes, new manners and a new style for daily intercourse, amusements and festivities. It seemed only natural that all these novelties were more concentrated in the new capital than at any other place in Russia.

in the new capital.

In 1711, the first print shop was opened in St Petersburg, producing the country's first newspaper, Vedomosti. Peter's library was moved to St Petersburg from Moscow, and it was opened to the public (albeit noble classes). Next door, a collection of rarities was on display – the first museum in town (the Kunstkammer).

The volume of printed matter grew 20 times in Peter's lifetime. Ninety percent of this output was secular literature concerning navigation, ship-building, mathematics and medicine, as

LEFT AND ABOVE: portraits of three of the architects of St Petersburg: Rastrelli, Quarenghi and Rossi.

THE POST-PETER YEARS

Unfortunately, many of Peter's projects fell under the shadow of oblivion with his death in 1725. In a little more than 14 years, Russia had four monarchs: Catherine I (Peter's last wife), Peter II (his grandson), Anna Ioannovna (his niece) and the infant Ivan Antonovich (Anna's nephew). Every time the throne stood empty, political rivalry split opposing groups of gentry. At one point in 1728 the capital was transferred from St Petersburg back to Moscow by Peter II– but for a short time only. Then the officers of the Guard put Peter's daughter, Empress Elizabeth, on the throne and the capital was moved back to St Petersburg.

The rise of the gentry

Meanwhile, the gentry was expanding its influence, particularly its right to own estates and serfs, and concentrated on ridding itself of the rigidly prescribed duty (in accordance with Peter's decree) of state service. The gentry won the day: On Bestowing Liberty to the Gentry of Russia, the manifesto signed by Elizabeth's successor, Peter III, finally freed them of state duties. This essentially turned the gentry into a class of parasites, which controlled the entire

THE FIRST BRIDGE

The first floating bridge across the Neva was put into place in 1727; several decades later, the city had 40 bridges spanning its assorted rivers and canals.

A centre of art and science

As Russia's capital, St Petersburg became the country's centre of financial capital, wealthy clients and the "educated class" of the imperial court. This offered a unique opportunity for architects, artists, actors and scientists. The court orchestra appeared in 1729; many aristocrats kept orchestras and choirs of their own.

In the 1730s, an opera and ballet theatre was put together in the imperial palace. In 1738 ballet-master Jacques Landais opened a ballet

might of the empire's military-bureaucratic machine. Their position grew stronger with each new military success: the war for the Black Sea with Turkey in 1735–39, the war for Finland with Sweden in 1741–43, the Seven-Year War with Prussia in 1756–63.

By the middle of the 18th century the population of St Petersburg reached the 100,000 mark (fewer than 40 percent were women). There were 2,000 aristocrats, as many merchants, and entire quarters filled with foreigners – Englishmen lived on the Neva behind St Isaac's Church, Germans and Frenchmen on Vasilievsky Island, and Italians between Sadovaya, Nevsky and the Fontanka.

MIKHAIL LOMONOSOV

In the middle of the 18th century, Mikhail Lomonosov, the "father of Russian science", reached his prime. He was a professional chemist, mathematician, physicist, geologist, astronomer, botanist, philosopher and historian. He made important discoveries in metallurgy, mining and the production of glass, porcelain and dyes. He was the author of *Russian Grammar*, the mastermind behind "Russian classicism". He and his supporter, Count Ivan Shuvalov (who helped Lomonosov found the Moscow University in 1755), created a new centre of education and the arts, the "Academy of the Three Noblest Arts" – painting, sculpture and architecture – in St Petersburg.

school which founded the famous Russian tradition of choreography. In 1756, there appeared The Russian Theatre for Comedies and Tragedies (it was founded by actor Fyodor Volkov and its first director was Alexander Sumarokov, the famous poet and playwright).

Catherine the Great

In 1762, Peter III was removed from the throne after another palace coup. The reins of power passed into the hands of his wife, Catherine II, the daughter of an insignificant German landowner. But Catherine went on to rule Russia for a third of a century. She presided over the conquest from Poland of the territory which is now Belorus and Ukraine, and waged war with Turkey to conquer the Crimea and the northern coast of the Black Sea. Georgia and Armenia asked for Russia's protection, and entered the empire, which soon spread over 17 million square kilometres, and a population of 28 million.

New enterprises were under way – Berd's Iron Foundry, Potyomkin's Glass Factory, the Admiralty's giant Izhorsky Complex. The number of hired workers grew, even though a third of the population of the capital was made up of bureaucrats and army and navy officers. The growing might of the state was adequately represented by the majesty of monumental architecture. Cultural life, science and education thrived. In 1764, the country's first educational establishment for women, the Smolny Institute, was founded. In 1774, the Mining College, one of the first in Europe and which was crucial for expanding Russia's industry and hence weapons manufacture, was opened.

New educational establishments, academies, theatres and libraries all required buildings which would reflect the ideals of the "enlightened monarchy", notably its devotion to "universal well-being". The stern and majestic classical architecture which replaced mid-century baroque, expressed these socio-aesthetic ideals with the utmost elegance and simplicity.

Stone embankments were built on the Neva and the Fontanka. The Hermitage went up next

---

LEFT: the facade of the Kunstkammer, from the German *kunst* (art) and *kammer* (chamber).
RIGHT: a portrait of Peter III.

THE CITY GROWS

St Petersburg, the political centre of Russia, was turning into one of its largest cities. By the end of the 18th century, its population was 220,000, equal to that of Moscow.

to the Winter Palace. Creations by Yury Felten, Antonio Rinaldi, Jean Batiste Vallen de la Mothe and Giacomo Quarenghi were numerous and pleasantly different. In 1782, St Petersburg got what is probably its most famous masterpiece – the *Bronze Horseman* (the statue of Peter the Great).

In this way, the end of the century produced the unique, majestic and beautiful city that people began to call the Northern Palmyra, in homage to the great city of antiquity renowned for its harmony in architecture.

The new century

Emperor Pavel ascended the throne in 1796, and with it began one of the shortest but most controversial and colourful reigns in Russian history. Pavel was both an extraordinary visionary and pedantic reactionary.

When Napolean disbanded the Maltese Order in 1798, Pavel gave the Order refuge in Russia, and later on that year the Maltese knights living in St Petersburg elected him Grand Master. For three years, St Petersburg was the capital of the Maltese Order, and an Orthodox tsar headed the oldest Roman Catholic order in what scholars now consider one of the first and most significant ecumenical gestures between the two religions. During his short reign, he made spasmodic attempts to restore the austere might of Peter's epoch in new social conditions, to transform the gentry into a mechanically exact, powerful apparatus, which could successfully face a revolution comparable to the one that had taken place in France.

The gentry responded with yet another conspiracy: no sooner had the emperor moved to his new, impenetrable Mikhailovsky Castle than he was assassinated on 3 March 1801. His son, Alexander, ascended the throne as Russia was entering the 19th century.

The liberalism and reformist intentions of

Alexander's first decade on the throne and his profound belief in the firmness of the Russian monarchy were reflected in an architecture of grandiose proportions and serene beauty.

Outstanding architects, with their new understanding of the city ensemble, aimed for openness and organic harmony with the city's layout. St Petersburg gained the ensemble on the tip of Vasilievsky Island (Thomas de Thomon), the new Admiralty (Andreyan Zakharov), and the Kazan Cathedral in Nevsky Prospekt (Andrei Voronikhin).

It was from this monument to Russian military glory that on 11 August 1812, Count Mikhail Kutuzov, who had been appointed commander-in-chief, left to join his army at the front; it was here that the remains of the great general were buried after the war with Napoleon had been won.

Mirror of the tsars' might

The 1812 war, in which a 14,000-strong volunteer corps from St Petersburg took part, unleashed an unprecedented wave of patriotism. The victory over Napoleon, the triumphant march of the Russian army, and the taking of Paris boosted Russia's international prestige. Growing national sentiment marked the new phase of construction in St Petersburg. It was the time for "High Classicism", the art which, as the greatest master of the school, Carlo Rossi, put it, "was designed to leave everything that Europeans of our era created far behind in its majesty".

The city that elevated all spheres of human endeavour to unprecedented heights now expressed itself in the perfect harmony of architectural masterpieces. The rare compatibility of expanses of water and open spaces, the balanced novelty of architecture and the unforgettable light of white nights made St Petersburg, the world's northernmost capital, one of the most beautiful cities ever seen by the human eye.

The city reminds you of its might with every step you take. Helmets, shields and javelins are ubiquitous ornaments on the innumerable walls of palaces and administrative buildings. They are repeated on the rich facades of private mansions. Laurel wreaths and military symbols are often incorporated into iron grilles. St Petersburg would allow no one to forget that it was the capital of the empire, the seat of the all-powerful sovereign.

And if a foreigner chanced to find himself in this Russian city and marvelled in awe at the poverty of the serfs who wore straw *lapti* on their feet, there were usually clever people to tell him, "Don't be fooled, stranger! These poor serfs will take to the axe if another Napoleon tries to burn down their wooden huts again. Don't be fooled, stranger, when you admire the nature of Russia, don't be fooled by the slow, unhurried flow of Russian rivers, by the eternal calm of the endless Russian steppe…"

St Petersburg is the mirror of the tsars' might. Canals cross its straight paved streets, and the waters of the Neva wash the granite of its quays. All this gives the city the appearance of a northern Amsterdam, the only difference being that there are no windmills, no ephemeral European-ness of scenery. Frequent rains wash the walls of the luxurious palaces, arranged into architectural ensembles as if by someone's divine hand. Low clouds hang over the city like a threatening omen.

The city is rich, proud, haughty in the Tsar's way. The iron grilles, lace made of metal, illustrate the skills of the people who made them. Yet they speak nothing of freedom and airiness. The entrances to many edifices have stone arches, yet their only purpose is to commemorate a military or triumphal peace.

Austerity, geometric harmony and military might are the distinctions of this city. This frowning force cannot be made friendlier even by the domes of innumerable cathedrals, resplendent in their gold attire. Poets and dreamers have not found life comfortable here. They have looked at the city with a stranger's eye, listening to the wind howl around the spacious parks and seeing relentless Father Time march by.

Social contrasts

There was no other place where social contrasts were felt so acutely. In the golden epoch of aristocratic culture, the apex of clamour and splendour, protests thundered in St Petersburg, voices which condemned the evils of serfdom and monarchy, voices which brought the Revolution to life. In 1816, the "Union of Salvation" was founded in St Petersburg by radical officers, veterans of the 1812 war. The goal of this small secret society was to destroy monarchy, adopt a constitution and eliminate serfdom.

Two years after that, there appeared the "Union of Prosperity", which had as many as 200 members. In 1820, after riots in the Semyonovsky Regiment and the government's vicious reprisals, the leaders of the union dissolved it, and formed a secret society in its place. The "Northern Society" was set up in St Petersburg in 1821, and its counterpart, the "Southern Society", appeared somewhat later in the south of the country.

The Decembrists

Emperor Alexander died late in 1825. The members of both societies decided to play upon the indecision in the highest corridors of power concerning the nomination of a successor to the throne. The coup was planned for 14 December 1825. On that day, the Decembrists fired the first shot against tsarism in Senatskaya Square behind the statue of the Bronze Horseman.

They lost. The leaders were executed on the wall of the Peter and Paul Fortress on 13 July 1826 – Pavel Pestel, Kondratiy Ryleev, Piotr Kakhovsky, Sergei Muraviev-Apostol and Mikhail Bestuzhev-Riumin. That year, the

Emperor Nicholas created the ominous Third Department of his Chancellery; the gendarmes in its employment started their campaign of terror which struck against freedom of thought in Russia.

The total domination of the empire's military-bureaucratic machine, whose only purpose was to perpetuate serfdom, should have stopped the country's economic, political and cultural development. Yet it did not, in large part because the country's defence needs, as in the time of Peter the Great, demanded that the country strive to maintain par with other European powers. So, St Petersburg continued to act as the industrial centre of backward, feudal Russia. Its enterprises

LEFT: Napoleon occupies Moscow in 1812.
RIGHT: a portrait of the victorious Alexander I, who reigned between 1801 and 1825.

were frequently equipped to state-of-the-art level, manned by well-trained worker cadres and supervised by professional engineers.

The first steam engine was installed in the Admiralty in 1800. The first steamship, the *Yelizaveta*, came out of the shipyards in 1815. In 1801 the Kronstadt Iron Mill was transferred to St Petersburg. Later it became known as Putilovsky Works; in Soviet times and even today, it is called Kirovsky Works. The first locomotive was produced in 1845. St

LITERARY CRACKDOWN

In 1849 a mock execution was staged for the 21 members of Petrashevsky's circle. Among them was Dostoyevsky, who was condemned to forced labour.

airport) was opened in 1839. In 1842, there came another important scientific event – the foundation of the Depot of Standard Measures and Weights (where the famed Dmitry Mendeleev, the father of the periodic table, worked later). During these years, such greats as Alexander Pushkin, Mikhail Lermontov, Nikolai Gogol and Mikhail Glinka lived and worked in St Petersburg.

St Petersburg's magazines – especially *Sovremennik* and *Otechestvennye Zapiski* – printed heated articles by the new generation of revo-

Petersburg was also Russia's first city involved in the railroad business. The first railway connected the capital with the suburbs – Tsarskoe Selo and Pavlovsk – and opened in the autumn of 1837; in 1851, the Moscow to St Petersburg railway came into operation. At the same time, the city gained its first cast-iron bridge across the Neva (today the Nikolayevsky Bridge).

Industry and transportation required qualified engineers. In 1828, the St Petersburg Technological Institute opened its doors, followed by the Civilian Engineers' School four years later. The Academy of Sciences opened new branches. The Pulkovo Observatory (located near today's Pulkovov international

lutionaries, the men who founded the revolutionary-democratic movement in Russia: Vissarion Belinsky, Nikolai Dobroliubov and Nikolai Chernyshevsky. Literary criticism, which was a legal form of expression, was used, in effect, to criticise the social order. As new revolutionary ideas spread, underground circles appeared and the Tsar took action to suppress all criticism of this form.

By 1855, the losses in the Crimean War against the European powers showed Russia could not keep up. Shortly before the fall of Sevastopol, the largest Russian fortress on the Black Sea, Nicholas I died in his Peterhof residence. Before he died the emperor observed the ships of the British fleet which were anchored off of Kronstadt, on the horizon. Russia was about to lose the Crimean War – "payment", as Russian historian Sergei Soloviev put it, "for 30 years of lies, 30 years of suppressing everything that had life and spirit, of popular force."

Times of terror

A new stage of the struggle for liberty started in the 1850s and the 1860s. It was marked by mass activity, a change of leaders, from aristocrats to people of common origins, democratic-minded intellectuals and students. The government of Alexander II proceeded with reforms, which had the effect of opening the way for capitalist development in Russia yet preserving the foundations of absolutist rule. Serfdom was abolished; administrative management reorganised; self-management was allowed at grass-roots level; a judicial reform was carried out.

Yet society wanted more: the government lost popularity and appeared more and more conservative. Narodniks (populists) tried to provoke a peasant uprising through terrorism. In April 1866, Dmitry Karakozov, a student, attempted to shoot the Tsar near the wrought-iron fence of the Summer Garden. He failed in his assasination attempt, but there was now no stopping the revolutionary terrorists. This upsurge of tragic heroism was accompanied by the birth and gradual development of an organised proletarian movement.

The first worker leaders in St Petersburg did not yet dissociate their goals and means from the populists' terror tactics. In February 1880, Stepan Khalturin placed a bomb in the Tsar's apartment in the Winter Palace. The emperor once again, miraculously, escaped death. One year later, however, on 1 March 1881, the death sentence passed on the Tsar by the populists was carried out.

On the embankment of Ekaterininsky Canal (now Griboyedov Canal), he was mortally wounded in a bomb attack; the blast also succeeded in killing his assassin, Ignaty Grinetsky. From now on, all tsars and their high-ranking officials became targets and the

LEFT: the Neva embankment during the 1800s.
RIGHT: Alexander II, who was later assassinated.

LENIN'S FIRST STAND

Lenin emerged as a political activist in 1895 when he presided over the creation of the "Union for the Struggle to Liberate the Working Class", which became the Bolshevik's revolutionary party.

government found itself constantly at war with organised terrorism. Six years later, on 1 March 1887, conspirators preparing to assassinate Alexander III were arrested and executed. Among them was Alexander Ulianov, Lenin's elder brother.

Lenin himself first emerged as a political activist in St Petersburg in 1895, when he presided over the creation of the Union for the Struggle to Liberate the Working Class, which later evolved into the proletariat's revolutionary party.

The Revolution draws to a close

The defeat suffered by Russia in the war against Japan (1904–05) accelerated the Revolution. On 2 January 1905, the workers of St Petersburg's Putilovsky Works went on strike. This grew into a general strike by 8 January. On 9 January ("Bloody Sunday"), a peaceful worker's demonstration was met by gunfire. The first barricades appeared that same day. The first Russian Revolution had begun. It lasted for two years and covered the entire country. Nothing was gained.

Reaction and police terror set in. By 1913, the volume of industrial production had increased tenfold over the previous 50 years;

the city's 1,000 factories and plants employed half a million people, of whom 70 percent worked at enterprises employing more than 500 persons. St Petersburg produced 15 percent of the national industrial output. The capital had almost 600 banks; 40 percent of the capital invested there belonged to monopolies.

Art flourishes

Spiritual life was also full of contradictions and tension. It assumed a great many forms. The Russian Museum was opened in 1897. Its creative approach to the artistic heritage brought artists into the centre of public attention –

including the works of Alexander Benoir, Konstantin Somov, Yevgeny Lansere, Mikhail Dobuzhinsky. Traditional painting by Ilya Repin and Valentin Serov was still quite popular. The radical left-wingers rallied around the "Youth Union" and its stars – Kasimir Malvich and Vasily Kandinsky.

Plays by Anton Chekhov, Maxim Gorky and Leonid Andreev enjoyed immense popularity. The stage of the Mariinsky Theatre was graced by Fyodor Shaliapin and Leonid Sobinov, Anna Pavlova and Matilda Kseshinskaya.

Russian music was enriched by the works of Alexander Glazounov, Alexander Scriabin and Sergei Rachmaninov. The search for new forms

and decisions in modern-style architecture, and the development of the St Petersburg architectural tradition by the neoclassicists (which continued even after the Revolution) brought new architectural solutions, and these served to determine the image and layout of the city for the following decades.

World War I became history's great accelerator. St Petersburg was in the centre of things (it was then given the more Russian name of Petrograd). The ruling circles were losing their hold on power, workers and the other have-nots lived in want and the bourgeoisie got rich on manufacturing supplies for the military. The war took more and more lives, fuelling pacifist and revolutionary sentiment among the workers.

In 1916, the revolutionary movement in Petrograd became a tangible threat to tsarism; in 1917, Russia was caught in a nationwide crisis, which led to the democratic revolution in February when Emperor Nicholas II abdicated. But a single, effective government could not be created, and two entities, the moderate Provisional Government and the radical leftist Soviets of Workers, Soldiers and Peasants Deputies, ruled the country.

The Bolshevik coup

Lenin returned to the city in April, and immediately called the workers and peasants to struggle for a socialist revolution. The conditions for this revolution were ripe by autumn. On 24 October (6 November, according to the modern, Gregorian calendar), an armed struggle for power began. The Bolsheviks ordered soldiers and workers from the Red Guard to take control of bridges, the telegraph system, railway stations and the central power station.

The next morning Lenin, who headed the uprising from the Bolshevik headquarters in the Smolny Institute, and Leon Trotsky, the head of the Petrosoviet, ordered the State Bank and the central telephone exchange to be seized. A single shot from the revolutionary battleship Aurora on the evening of 25 October signaled the beginning of the attack on the Winter Palace, where the Provisional Government was in conference.

The palace was taken, and the majority of delegates to the Second Congress of Soviets, which convened in Smolny, adopted Lenin's Decree on Peace and Decree on Land. This congress also elected the new Executive Council and the council that was to govern the country – the Council of People's Commissars, chaired by Lenin. In January 1918, the Bolshevik commissars dispersed the Constituent Assembly, which was Russia's first truly democratically elected body, but which worked for one day only (the Bolsheviks did not have a majority there); the new state system was then legalised through force by the Third Congress of Soviets at the end of January, and the onslaught of the Red Terror.

On 6–8 March 1918, the Seventh Congress of the Communist Party convened in Petrograd. Lenin addressed the congress no fewer than 18 times. He managed to come out on top of the

and suffering. The communists soon began a reign of terror that drove most educated and propertied classes from the city.

Where there were 2½ million people in February 1917, only 740,000 remained in the city in 1920. The "best" elements of society were either deported by the communists or fled into exile abroad, and the city remained inhabited by an uncontrollable rabble.

The Soviets, however, acted quickly to reign in the chaos spawned by the abdication of the tsar. In January 1924, after Lenin's death, Petrograd was renamed Leningrad. As if to show its displeasure, Mother Nature wrecked havoc

heated debate: the Brest peace with Germany, Austro-Hungary, Bulgaria and Turkey, which was concluded on 3 March, was approved. This was the last party congress to take place in Petrograd – on 10 March the government and all central authorities moved to Moscow, which once again became the capital of Russia.

Soviet times

The city of three revolutions, Petrograd remained at the front edge of the revolutionary struggle, and paid the price in rivers of blood

on the city that year, with the waters of the Neva river pouring forth one of the most devastating floods in the city's history. Still, slowly the city's cultural and economic life began to flourish once again as a new generation arose to replace those who had left.

In 1925, Leningrad started producing the first Soviet tractors. The first generator for Volkhov Power Station, the first in the ambitious chain planned for the entire nation, was manufactured here. The Mariinsky Theatre saw some of the finest dancers and singers perform on its stage, while the Russian avant-garde artists such as Kandinsky and Rodchenko enjoyed great popularity before being outlawed in the 1930s.

LEFT: the last tsar, Nicholas II.
ABOVE: the ideological fathers of the USSR.

Times of war and suffering

In 1939, the population topped 3 million. But their peaceful labours were disrupted by war. In the winter of 1939–40 when the Soviet Union invaded Finland, Leningrad became a frontline town: a mere 25 km (16 miles) to the north lay the Finnish border. In March 1940, a peace treaty was signed with Finland, in accordance with which the border was relocated to over 100 km (62 miles) from Leningrad.

On 22 June 1941, Germany invaded the USSR, starting what is known in Russia as the Great Patriotic War. On 18 July 1941, the first Nazi bombs fell on Leningrad. The first

German artillery attack came on 4 September. On 8 September the blockade of Leningrad began, a 900-day struggle the likes of which history had not known.

Hitler's group of armies code-named "North" (30 divisions) stopped and formed a 200-km (125-mile) siege ring around the unbending, impenetrable city. The enemy dropped over 100,000 bombs and fired 150,000 artillery shells. The death toll was 16,747; 33,728 were wounded. Hunger killed 641,803. Another 716,000 were left homeless. But the foot of an enemy soldier never stepped into Leningrad. This thought gave strength to the exhausted people who, though hungry and cold, did not

stop working. The blockade was broken only in January 1943. Another year passed before the soldiers of the Leningrad front finally routed the Germans late in January 1944.

After the war, the people of Leningrad worked hard to quickly repair and restore the city. Sometimes their achievements were impressive, for instance, by 1948, the city's industry had reached the pre-war level, which increased 2½ times by 1955.

The Cold War era

Much of that production, however, were armaments to fight a new war, the so-called Cold War against western Europe and America. Indeed, Leningrad played a crucial role in the Soviet Union's Cold War plans. Besides numerous defence plants that were churning out ships, tanks and rockets, the city was home to dozens of scientific research centres, mostly working for defence needs.

If the city's population in the mid-1960s hovered around 2½ million, by the end of the 1980s that figure doubled to 5 million, with most of the newcomers arriving from neighbouring villages and towns, lured to the city to work in the city's growing defence industries of the late Soviet era.

If industrial production grew rapidly, the lot of the common worker remained abysmal. Until the mid-1960s, most of the city's population were living in cramped communal flats, which were (and still are) some of the most wretched slums in Europe. The Soviet housing boom in the late 1960s only took the people out of the gutter and onto the sidewalk. Workers were given small apartments, where one family lived in 30 sq. metres (323 sq. ft), about three times less than the West European average.

The only consolation was that, locked behind the Iron Curtain, Russians didn't know any better, and so, on the whole, remained content with what they had. But with the collapse of Communism across Europe, pent-up desires and ambitions were suddenly let loose. Russia is still trying to come to terms with the shock of living in a capitalist society where everyone must fend for themselves, and material enrichment is the goal of the game. ❏

LEFT: Stalin, the initiator of a reign of terror.
RIGHT: vegetables growing in front of St Isaac's Cathedral during the blockade of Leningrad.

NOTES OF A BLOCKADE SURVIVOR

These vivid recollections of the 1941–43 siege of the city are those of
the writer and historian Lidiya Ginzburg (1902–90)

There was no peace, ever. Even at night. Normally the body should calm down at night, but the fight for warmth continued even in one's sleep. It wasn't that people hadn't the means to keep warm – they certainly piled enough warm things over themselves before going to bed. But this made the body struggle –

all these heavy things were quite a load; what is worse, they slipped and constantly fell off. In order to hold the entire pile in place, one had to make insignificant yet ultimately tiring muscular efforts. One had to train oneself to sleep without moving, with one leg twisted in such a way as to hold the base of the pile. One could not afford to throw one's arms wide, or to lift one's knees beneath the blanket, or to turn and hide one's face in the pillow. This meant that the body never got a complete rest.

People fought for their lives in their own apartments just as polar explorers do in emergencies. In the morning they woke in a sack or in a cave constructed from every conceivable material they could pile up. People woke at four, at five. They managed to get warm during the night. Yet all around, there was cold, which continued to torment them all day long.

Still, people waited with impatience – not even for morning, because morning (light) came much later – no, they waited for a suitable reason to get up together with the beginning of the new day, 6am, when the stores and bakeries opened. This does not mean that everyone went to the baker's at six in the morning; on the contrary, many tried to stave off the moment for as long as they could. But the 6 o'clock mark was a comfort line, which brought awareness of new possibilities. In a way, it was the best moment: all the bread of the day is still ahead, yet it is not the reality of the day.

Hungry impatience got the upper hand over fear of cold. It pushed people out of their little caves, warmed with their own breath, into the coldness of the rooms. It was easy to get up, much easier than in the life where scrambled eggs were waiting for you and hardly required a second thought.

The typical day started with a visit to the kitchen or the service staircase, where firewood had to be prepared for the temporary stove. Night was only just starting to disperse, and the walls of the building opposite did not yet carry even a hint of their light yellow colour; they loomed darkly through the broken glass of the staircase window. So one had to work by touch, driving the axe at an angle to the wood, and then striking. Hands were the greatest problem. Fingers tended to close and remain in some chance position. The hand lost its ability to grasp. It could only be used as a paw, a stump or a stick-like tool. People groped in the dark as they collected splinters from the stone floor of the landing, lifting them between two stumps, and placing them in a basket.

The next thing to do was to bring water from the frozen cellar. Ice covered the steps of the laundry, and people slid down on their haunches. On the return trip, they went up with a full bucket, searching for dents in the icy surface to put the bucket in. A kind of mountaineering exercise. The resistance of each thing had to be negotiated with one's will and one's body, without intermediate tools or devices.

One could rest on the lower steps with full buckets. Head thrown backwards, people measured the height they were about to negotiate. Far away, a ceiling with an alabaster knob... head thrown backwards, people measured the rise of the staircase, through which they were about to carry the rock-heavy water using sheer willpower. The day would bring many more spaces. The largest was the space separating one from dinner. The best place for dinner was a departmental canteen, where porridge tasted more like porridge. People would run, spurred on by the cold, through the insultingly beautiful city, snow crackling underfoot. Alongside, other people would run (or crawl – it was always either/or) with bags, with covered dishes suspended from the ends of their stick-like arms. People would run in the cold, conquering space that had suddenly become material. In the canteen, it is so cold that the fingers that froze in the street will not open; people hold spoons between the thumb (the only digit that works) and the frozen stump.

Dinner itself is another hassle with space; the spaces of dinner are small yet agonisingly condensed with queues of people. A queue before the door, a queue before the inspector, a queue for an empty seat at the table. Dinner is something fleeting and ephemeral (a plate of soup, and so many grammes of porridge). Yet it was overestimated and decelerated in accordance with the classic canons of literary plotting. If asked what they were doing, the people would answer, "We are having dinner."

Then there was a period of successive air raids, which came one after another. On the way to dinner one had to hide in cellars or continue through the noise of the anti-aircraft guns and the whistles of the militia. People hated the militiamen, who saved them from the bombs, and thought of the bombing as of something that kept them away from dinner.

Some people left home at eleven in the morning and sometimes came back at six or seven in the evening. It was absolutely dark at home.

LEFT: relief commemorating victims of the Blockade at the Piskarevsy Memorial.
RIGHT: General Staff Building during the Blockade.

The stove was lit and, in its smoky light, the soup from the canteen was poured into a pot. Bread was cut into 40-gramme pieces. Then the person who came from the outside world, the world with dinner, moved closer to the stove and warmed frozen hands.

Until the day's supply of splinters burned out, nothing could tear that person away from this exquisite pleasure. In the room behind, cold was raging and darkness reigned. It was only near the small door of the stove that the life-giving circle of light and warmth shone. The circle of life. The only thing one could warm were one's palms. The palms absorbed the

flames. It was sheer ecstasy, which was invariably spoiled by the swift end.

It was waiting for the end and the realisation of the ebbing of our vital forces which spoiled any joy and the very sense of life. The blockade made this formula self-evident. What takes place is the displacement of suffering with suffering, the mindless sense of purpose of the doomed, which explains why people survive in an isolated cell, a forced-labour camp, in squalor and in the lowermost depths of humiliation. This is something that the more fortunate people find difficult to understand; it is people in comfortable cottages who blow their brains out without any apparent reason. ❏

MODERN TIMES

*After years of neglect, St Petersburg is rejuvenating through a
number of ambitious tricentenary projects and generous central funding*

During the hard-line communist coup of August 1991 the people of Leningrad massed onto Palace Square, in front of the Winter Palace, just as they did in 1917 when the fate of this immense country was decided on these same smooth cobblestones. But this time there was no government in the palace, either to defend or to storm. This time it was Moscow that was the scene of action.

One month later, the democratic forces, which had never really taken to being Leningraders, won the city's subsequent change of name back to St Petersburg. They pride themselves on their academic traditions and on speaking the purest Russian language anywhere. No wonder that the mayor at that time, Anatoli Sobchak, won thanks and sympathy from all who had been awaiting a real return to the romantic past.

Many of the democrats' hopes and dreams failed to materialise, however, and by the mid-1990s many were too consumed by persistent and overwhelming economic hardship to worry about high ideals. Survival in Russia's brutal capitalist world became the ultimate deadly game: businessmen had to dodge the bullets of organised crime, while workers were paid slave-like salaries, if paid at all.

The 1998 crash

By the end of the 1990s, after the August 1998 financial crash, St Petersburg's plight was abysmal and apparently hopeless. Receiving only 5 percent of all foreign investment (while Moscow gathered 80 percent), the city teetered on the brink of bankruptcy, the federal government shut down the city's only national broadcasting station; and the most talented people in town were fleeing for Moscow, Europe or America. This great, former imperial capital had been reduced to a crumbling, provincial town. That,

however, all changed in the course of one night, in August 1999, when Vladimir Putin, an obscure government official, was appointed Russia's prime minister. On 31 December of that year, he became Russia's acting president, and a few months later won the presidential election.

Today St Petersburg is a boom town, and

once again quickly becoming one of the most fashionable places in Europe thanks to its rich cultural, economic and technological potential.

There are plenty of stores with a wide assortment of goods and services. Though locals often complain how little they earn, they clearly spend beyond their means, which simply proves that most people are making their money off the books – tax evasion has become a national sport.

Take Marina, aged 30. Her official salary is $100 a month, but in fact she makes $1,500 working as a deputy director of a real estate company. Her money goes far in St Petersburg, and allows her to meet all her needs and that

---

PRECEDING PAGES: sunset over the Baltic from the sea terminal.
LEFT: art for sale on Aleksandrinsky Square.
RIGHT: advertising dollar exchange rates.

of her five-year-old son. Like most locals, she owns her flat, inherited from her grandmother, and her only expenses are food and clothing, both of which are not very costly as long as she doesn't indulge in luxurious imported goods. Foreign travel once a year is not a problem, with a trip to Europe costing about $800 for one week. The city's yuppie class is growing, with most employed in the new capitalist economy, in industries such as telecommunications, sales and trading, public relations and media, as well as banking and real estate. A decade ago, these sectors did not exist and most people were employed in the Soviet defence industry.

analysts, Putin is indeed the ultimate St Petersburg sphinx, combining two seemingly incompatible backgrounds: career KGB agent and top assistant to one of post-Soviet Russia's leading democrats.

Yet, the fact remains that with his ascendancy to the Kremlin, St Petersburg rules Russia. There is no reason to move the capital back to the banks of the Neva because, besides Putin, others from St Petersburg occupy most of the highest positions in his government, many of whom worked with the President in the early 1990s. Little wonder that the Russian government easily approved spending $1.7 billion –

The rise of Vladimir Putin

Most of the city's current prosperity is due to President Putin, who was born and raised in St Petersburg. Putin has made the city the official capital of the Northwest Federal District, one of the seven federal districts created in 2000 as part a plan to reform the country's government. The Northwest has one of the richest and fastest growing economies in the country, with its numerous ports, increasing foreign manufacturing, and the largest oil deposits in Europe.

Vladimir Putin began his political career in 1991, serving as Sobchak's deputy mayor until the latter's defeat in the 1996 mayoral elections. Considered an enigma by many observers and

POLITICAL RIVALRY

With the domination of St Petersburg over Moscow, many young St Petersburgers, mostly men in their 30s, are being drafted to serve in the ministries of the federal government. One Moscow joke has a Moscow porter coming up to a young man who has just got off the train from St Petersburg:

"Mr Minister, let me take your bags."

"I am not a minister, you must be mistaken," answers the young man.

"But you're from St Petersburg," insists the porter, "so it's probably only a matter of days before you're appointed."

a huge sum in Russia – over a three year period to rebuild Russia's Window on the West in time for the city's 300th anniversary in 2003.

Infrastructure projects

As part of the tricentenary projects, construction on the flood protection barrier, which began in the early 1980s, will require about $500 million to complete. While flooding is an annual occurrence, primarily in the autumn, three times in the city's 300 year history – in 1777, 1824 and 1924 – St Petersburg

NAME GAME

All Russian names have a diminutive form (Alexsander – Sacha; Maria – Masha; Viktor – Vitya). Many have several: Irina, for example, can become Irisha, Irishka, Irishenka and Irinuchka.

World Bank will loan the city about $150 million for the reconstruction of the historical centre. Part of that plan envisages giving a boost to the hotel and tourism industry. The city has few western-level hotels to accommodate the growing number of foreign visitors, which totalled nearly two million in 2000. Placed in perspective, such plans are a humble effort to rebuild a city centre, that has over 5,000 pre-1917 buildings, a large number of which are crumbling and dilapidated. About 15 percent

has been hit by devastating floods. Another project, the Auto Ring Road, at a cost of just under $1 billion, will allow vehicles to avoid the city centre when travelling between city districts, as well reroute heavy lorries between Finland and major Russian cities.

Rebuilding the city

Among the other main beneficiaries of federal largesse are the ongoing reconstruction of the Hermitage Museum, the Russian Museum, and the Mariinsky (the former Kirov) Theatre. The

of city residents live in communal flats in the centre, among the worst slums in Europe.

Wander through an archway into the courtyard behind some brightly painted facade and go into the entrance hall of some old apartment house. Inside, by the huge front doors of each apartment, are lots of bells, perhaps four, maybe even eight. Some have a grimy message telling callers to ring a signal of two long buzzes and one short for a particular person.

These are the communal flats with a separate family to every room, where they share a common bathroom and kitchen. Often in former extravagant tsarist-era quarters, the new Russian rich, as well as an influx of foreigners, now

LEFT: travelling across one of the city's many bridges.
ABOVE: strolling on the banks of the Neva.

covet these flats. One of these flats goes for about $50,000. Then one must pay to resettle the tenants, and fixing them up might cost just as much, if not more. Take St Petersburg newcomer, American August Meyer, 38. Two years ago, he quit his job as a deputy public prosecutor in San Diego. Now he is a real estate developer and aspiring innkeeper who bought six apartments in the historic centre to rent out to tourists and visiting business men.

"Where else in the world would I have this?" he asks, gesturing out the window of a 200-sq metre (239-sq yard) apartment on the Griboedova Canal. "The opulence you can acquire here is vastly cheaper; I fully intend dying here; just think how this city will be even more fabulous as it develops."

The crime rate

Like any big city, St Petersburg has its problems. The rise in the crime rate has been accompanied by an increase in corruption among the police force that has made them ineffective in protecting the citizenry, and sometimes even more of a threat than the criminals. The fear Russians have of their own police is shocking to Westerners. Russian police often extort, beat and harass people; locals say

THE RICH AT PLAY

In the long, northern, summer nights – the White Nights, as they are called here – St Petersburg is at its most attractive. After the busy rush of the day is over and the sun has at last set, the city's wrinkles fade in the half-light and its 19th-century beauty becomes apparent.

With over 600 palaces previously belonging to the tsars and aristocracy, St Petersburg provides the perfect backdrop and ample inspiration for hosting balls, and the city now stages about a dozen a year, most of which have been held annually only since 1999.

The demand for gala events is certainly there, and for many people "attending such a ball is the closest thing we

will ever get to being royalty," as one woman remarked.

Tickets sell from $800 to $1,500, but such events are not open to anyone from the public willing to pay. Organisers emphasise the balls' elite nature, and most guests are specifically invited.

"In the context of contemporary Russian society, balls definitely have a place as a wealthy class takes root in today's Russia," said Alexander Pozdnyakov, a St Petersburg commentator who writes about cultural and social affairs. "If before their only outlet was noisy and tacky nightclubs, now they want a more dignified venue to show off their power and wealth."

nothing like it went on in Soviet times. The police usually work well, if you're willing to pay them for an investigation. They too are capable capitalists who have basically privatised justice. Yevgeny is a successful businessman, and when some thugs came around demanding protection money, he turned to the city police's special forces unit. After promising the police a nice sum for their services, the thugs disappeared. Unfortunately the police sometimes work on behalf of criminal groups and the

CORRUPT POLICING

Over recent years St Petersburg's police department has been singled out repeatedly by the Interior Ministry as one of the most corrupt in Russia.

as a guard dog. Still, St Petersburg is safer than it was in the early 1990s. Most crime today concerns businessmen and rarely touches tourists, except for the pickpockets and gypsies who prey upon unsuspecting visitors in the summertime. As in any large city, it pays to be street wise in St Petersburg.

Modern women

Flaunting wealth is a Russian pastime, and Russian men know it is what most readily catches a Russian women's attention. Indeed,

likelihood of demands for more police protection money is high.

In times of distress, poorer Russians are loathe to call the police, so they rely on themselves and their friends for protection and to mete out justice. When Natasha's big, black, family dog had to be put to sleep, some people advised her to get a new puppy, but of a smaller breed, more suited to life in a crowded flat. Natasha replied that she wouldn't have a dog unless it was sufficiently large and fierce to act

LEFT: workers take a break from their work.
ABOVE: many old people in the city find it hard to make ends meet.

VLADIMIR PUTIN

Vladimir Vladimirovich Putin, the only son of Vladimir and Mariya Putin, was born on 7 October 1952 in St Petersburg. After graduating in law in 1975 he worked in the KGB's foreign intelligence service, mainly in East Germany. He left the state security service in 1990 and became an ally of Anatoly Sobchak, the mayor of St Petersburg. After Sobchak's failure to get re-elected as mayor in 1996, Putin moved to Moscow where he ended up as head of Russia's security council. After President Yeltsin's shock resignation, Putin was unexpectedly appointed prime minister in 1999. In March 2000 he was elected president of the Russian Federation.

most Russian females aren't interested in western ideas of feminism, but rather are on the look out for a successful husband to support them. And they do know how to snare their prey: indeed, the women of St Petersburg are considered to be the most beautiful in Russia. Little wonder that dozens of marriage agencies operate in the city, attracting Western men in search of the perfect Russian bride. This new phenomenon, the image of the Russian woman as sex-object has largely been prompted by the Westernisation of Russian society through advertisements and film. The battle to achieve real equality of status for women will be long.

The drinking revolution

More than 80 years on, a new revolution is brewing in St Petersburg. Of all the upheavals ripping through the fabric of Russian society in the past 15 years, one of the most significant is the rapid increase in beer consumption. It sounds like heresy to many older Russians, weaned on vodka and grain alcohol, but younger Russians are finding comfort in the better quality beers produced by almost a dozen domestic manufacturers that have appeared since economic liberalisation began in 1991.

Five years ago, Alexei remembers the small crowds, maybe a few tens of thousands, who gathered to sample Russian beers at the first St Petersburg Beer Festival. This year, however, organisers estimate that almost one million people came to the festivities, held in the area around the Winter Palace, the former imperial residence and the scene of the Bolshevik coup d'état in 1917. Home to the country's leading brewers, such as Baltika, Vena, Bochkarev and Stepan Razin, St Petersburg has been christened Russia's beer capital.

Besides beer, in the 1990s St Petersburg become Russia's tobacco capital, home to the country's largest factories such as Japan Tobacco (in fact, the largest cigarette factory in the world outside of the US), as well as that of Philip Morris.

Other industries

The city is also going back to what it does best – arms manufacture, especially naval vessels, and heavy engineering equipment for power plants and the oil and gas sector. China, India, and Iran are among the biggest clients. St Petersburg is also the Baltic Sea's largest and Russia's second largest port. Plans to modernise and expand the port will double capacity to 60 million tons a year and make it the largest port in the country.

But high-tech industries, especially those connected to computer programming and the Internet, are rapidly growing and showing the city the way to future wealth. With its enormous scientific potential and highly qualified workforce, St Petersburg has been named Russia's Silicon Valley. "St Petersburg is the intellectual capital of Russia, and software engineers in St Petersburg are superb," said Regina Velton, President and CEO of eVelopers, a privately-owned company based in San Jose, California.

Take Slava, aged 25. In the mid-1990s, many computer programmers were lured to America and Europe with big salaries, as part of a so-called brain drain. Now, Slava and many others are finding well-paid jobs at home, which suits them. Slava doesn't want to go abroad and leave his home. In St Petersburg, he may make only $600 to $1,000 a month, but can live quite well on that amount. Most important, says Slava, is to be home; to be home in his beloved St Petersburg. ❑

LEFT: accordian player.
RIGHT: stalls outside Kuznechny Market.

THE PEOPLE OF PETER

Despite its beauty, St Petersburg is a tough city in which to live,
but most of its inhabitants wouldn't want to be anywhere else

The city known as St Petersburg, Petrograd and Leningrad – over the approximate 300 years of its history years which have, nevertheless, absorbed entire epochs – has always been referred to as "Peter" by its inhabitants. Having once walked its streets and breathed its air, moistened by the closeness of the Baltic, it is impossible to shake the initial feeling that you are touching something eternal and holy, yet, at the same time, something earthly and fleeting.

St Petersburg is Russia's second largest metropolis. Its population is over five million; it has huge ports, factories, research institutions and educational establishments. Referred to as the "northern capital", St Petersburg has lost much of its former imperial glamour, yet much of it still remains.

In the early 1990s, commentators said St Petersburg was in the death throes of the last shreds of that very St Petersburg culture which, as the city's star newsman, Alexander Nevzorov, put it, was "violently interrupted in its development in October 1917".

One could go on forever about whether St Petersburg's culture has disappeared once and for all, about the fate of the city's famous intelligentsia, about the causes of the present plight of what used to be one of the world's most beautiful cities. As the people of St Petersburg realise with sinking hearts, one thing that is definitely not coming back is the old Peter atmosphere. But today the people are busy building a new St Petersburg, both to preserve and restore that which remains, and to build a modern city on this sturdy foundation.

The old and the new

The city of Peter the Great, as well as architects Rastrelli, Quarenghi, Rossi, Stasov and Voronikhin, lies elsewhere, behind the old gates. It is spread across 42 islands and the

mainland, crisscrossed by 40 rivers and 20 canals. There is the majesty of the Winter Palace, St Isaac's Cathedral and the austere beauty of the Peter and Paul Fortress. There are St Petersburg's 200 museums (of which the most famous are the Hermitage and the Russian Museum) and over 25 professional theatres,

including the world famous Mariinsky Theatre.

It is this incredible cultural milieu that insures that waves of immigrants from surrounding villages and towns, many of whom were peasants just yesterday, are assimilated into the haute St Petersburg type, proud to be educated and cultured. Once the metro, bus or tram takes St Petersburgers to their mundane "sleeping" districts, however, they leave the charms of the old city and become the "population", hurrying to identical, poorly-built apartment blocks with cramped living conditions. Indeed, the dichotomy between the old and new St Petersburg is startling but it is something that most tourists never see.

PRECEDING PAGES: a wedding party at the statue of the Bronze Horseman; a young St Petersburger.
LEFT: winter is frosty in the city.
RIGHT: waiting for the bus.

Housing

Life in the so-called sleeping districts is often frightful to most foreigners, especially those used to living in their own houses. Most of Russian housing is pre-fab, poorly built, dangerous, and with small apartments that are on average one-third the size of the average West European apartment.

Russians, however, are used to the conditions and don't complain. Many are thankful to have their own apartment, and often boast about the "clean air" in the housing projects. Indeed, most projects are towards the outskirts of town, but living there hardly feels like living in St

in the old city is not always much to write home about, either. Though the new rich are moving in, many inner-city residents still live in "communal" apartments (sharing kitchens and bathrooms with neighbours). And where students, artists and unrecognised poets find a certain bohemian charm in the corners, rooms or apartments they rent in the old town, the majority of native locals find them too "exotic" to live in.

Old people

St Petersburg is one of the oldest towns in the nation in terms of the age of the people: 1.2 million inhabitants are past retirement age.

Petersburg, Russia's cultural capital, with its superb pre-Revolutionary architecture. Such pre-fab districts can be found in any Russian city, and they are identical and soulless.

Katya, a mother of two, says that while she loves the city centre, it is too dirty for her children to grow up in. And when they want, they can easily make the 25-minute metro ride to the centre to visit museums on weekends.

For average families such as Katya's, housing is cheaper on the outskirts than in the centre. In the centre most land is bought by real estate companies, as well as wealthy Russians who enjoy the feel of living in the grandeur of a tsarist-era apartment. Come to think of it, life

OLD AGE IN ST PETERSBURG

Raisa, now 83, remembers working as a nurse during the fierce fighting on the Leningrad front. She likes to tell the story of how she met her husband. He was wounded by a shell and sent to her care. It was love at first sight. Today, frail and hardly able to move, she lives at home alone. She has no children, and social service workers must come to help her buy food and pay the bills which always seem to get more expensive while her pension remains about $40 a month. She has access to free state medical care, but it is abysmal: the wait for attention is long, though doctors are willing to serve you quicker if you bribe them.

The majority of them suffer housing problems. They are also burdened by food shortages and increasing poverty as inflation eats away at their livelihood. Senior citizens and people who are a generation younger still remember the war, the 900 days of the blockade, the bombs and shells which destroyed 3,000 buildings and damaged another 7,000. As they repeat the habitual "Let there be no war – that's the main thing", they still cherish faint hopes of someday living in apartments of their own, even in old age.

During World War II hunger claimed 650,000 lives; air and artillery raids another 17,000. Some have who seen frozen corpses in the

groupings – workers, peasants, intellectuals, and then the small, ruling Party elite which fed like hungry parasites on the labour of the previous three groups.

Today, Russia has a vast variety of social groups, and that is even more pronounced in major cities such as St Petersburg. While it is impossible to specify who is a typical St Petersburger, there are some dominant types who most likely define life in the city today.

Academics and students

St Petersburg was always known as an educated town, a town of good manners and culture.

streets and the lawns near St Isaac's turned into vegetable plantations are still alive. Come Victory Day (9 May), the veterans march along Nevsky prospekt. Every year, however, their column inevitably gets that much shorter.

The new Russia

Russian society was quite homogeneous in the Soviet period and even up to the early 1990s. Before, there were several major social

LEFT: many older inhabitants have experienced hard times.
ABOVE: some remaining war heroes commemorate the Great Patriotic War.

Refined intellectuals from "Peter" have at times been unfairly attacked by jealous rivals (especially from Moscow) as snobs. In fact the influence of Europe, which is right on the doorstep here, and the best kind of cosmopolitanism (even in the worst years of the Iron Curtain) gave local intellectuals profound foreign language skills and worldly knowledge.

Here, too, lie the roots of Russia's formidable culture of the 18th century – and succeeding centuries. St Petersburg gave us Alexander Pushkin, Nikolai Gogol and Fyodor Dostoevsky. It has heard the music of Piotr Tchaikovsky, Mikhail Glinka and Nikolai Rimsky-Korsakov. Moscow was the hotbed of

Slavophiles; St Petersburg was more open to Western influence and freely gave of its talents. It may be that the haughtiness one sometimes encounters in St Petersburg is fuelled by the old but not forgotten insult – taking away the capital status from a city of such wondrous history. But surely Dmitry Likhachev, Academy of Science Member, one of the country's foremost intellectuals and an impassioned fighter for Russian culture, and Iosif Brodsky, the Nobel Prize-winning poet who emigrated to and died in

LOCAL AILMENTS

Built on marshes and bogs the climate of the city is damp. Many locals suffer from chronic head colds, lung problems and other ailments arising from the damp and cold weather.

cost as little as $400. You can recognise a member of the student tribe anywhere – despite the varying quality of the clothes they wear, the students of St Petersburg resemble their peers from Paris, Boston or Stockholm. Well, perhaps St Petersburg students are paler and more prone to head-colds.

The businessman

The businessman is probably the most maligned and conspicuous new personage on the Russian demographic map. Often

America, could not be described as snobs.

There are many people who study in St Petersburg 40 colleges, institutes, and universities. Students get a small state subsidy but it is too small a sum to count, so many students work to support themselves, while the richer ones are supported by their parents. Easy-going academic terms are interspaced with excruciating exam periods with sleepless nights. Untold hours are spent in libraries (the city has several large ones and some 1,500 regular libraries). To make up for all the suffering, there are the long summer months – time to go on vacation to the Black Sea, either to the Crimea in Ukraine, or to Turkey where a vacation can

disparagingly referred to as New Russians by poorer Russians and those with Soviet political views, the country's businessmen are indeed accumulating great wealth, but their lives are far from problem-free.

Take Dmitri, 28. The son of factory workers, he dropped out of medical school seven years ago to start his own tourism company working with foreign visitors. Now, he owns several food-processing factories that make him worth almost $10 million. There are many tales of rags to riches in Russia today. Many young Russians, especially those who grew up in Soviet poverty, are hungry to make something out of their life. While much public attention for the past decade has been on the Robber Barons, the so-called oligarchs, since the 1998 financial crisis there are more and more businessmen like Dmitri, who are honest, hard-working people building a new economy, and basically a new country.

Like many Russian men, Dmitri married his high-school sweetheart at the age of 18. Russians tend to marry before the age of 25, but as more young people are focusing on their careers, some are putting off marriage. The city's young female population has two roads to choose from. Most would prefer to latch on to a successful businessman and stay at home with

wealthy businessman, but he thought that since he paid the bills he could control every aspect of her life. She left him and now is intent on building up her own PR company one day.

Post-Soviet working class

The post-Soviet working class hardly resembles what it was in Soviet times. Many factories, especially tied to the collapsed defence sector, have since closed or laid off more than half their workers. Many workers have degenerated en masse owing to the long years of idling, guaranteed wages and suppressed initiative. Those older than 40 or 45 are unable to

the children. But a growing number of young women realise that there aren't enough rich men to go around, and that they have to make their own career to make ends meet. These women are proving themselves not only capable, but tough in the rough, male-dominated Russian world of business.

Take Lisa, 22. She comes from a wealthy family and attends night classes studying public relations. She has already been married, to a

LEFT: a group of young people relaxing on the steps of the Kazan Cathedral.
ABOVE: playing volleyball on the beach at the Peter and Paul Fortress.

orient themselves in the new economy. Lacking skills that are now in demand, they just sit at home in despair, watching TV (at best) or drinking with friends at home or in the street, near a beer kiosk. Incidentally, these kiosks, where booze is cheap and plentiful, are regarded as one of the most sacred achievements of the revolutionary proletariat.

The criminal world

The large number of idle men in St Petersburg does not reflect growing unemployment. In fact, the new economy is in dire need of workers, but young ones, quick, smart, and educated. Those from the old economy can only make big money by turning to crime – apartment break-ins, petty theft and muggings.

Like many major cities, St Petersburg society has become dramatically stratified, with the rich tending to live in certain districts while the poor end up in less desirable areas. There are certain districts, such as the city's southeast, considered to be one of the most drug-infested in Europe, which you'd be better off avoiding all together.

Tourists have little to worry about. Street crime in the city centre is limited to pickpockets, as well as some street vendors who may short-change their customers. Beggars have

returned to Nevsky prospekt, with mothers in rags holding pallid, mute children. Child labour, which is nothing new in Russia's history, is also back on the streets as kids, usually from poor families, try to make some money to buy the expensive items they see for sale.

The Russian criminal world also demands people with skills. Organised crime has become more sophisticated and is more likely to use computer hackers, of which St Petersburg boasts the best in the world. For the most part, the mafia has gone legitimate and become part of the establishment. It's an open secret that many politicians are on their payroll, or in some cases mafia bosses are in public office. And

now they have legal control – obtained through violence, however – over the most profitable parts of the local economy.

Getting around

At least 20 years ago, Vladimir Vysotsky, the popular actor and singer, wrote a song about Leningrad taxis. Today, however, it is not easy to get a taxi. Locals prefer to ride with *chastniki*, private drivers making some extra money, and therefore many taxis have gone out of business. But it's their own fault. Taxi drivers can often be rude and charge exorbitant prices, especially if you're a foreigner. Most foreigners are afraid to try *chastniki*, but it is the cheapest and most efficient taxi service.

Most locals don't have the money for taxis, and rely on municipal transport, which is always crowded yet reliable. First and foremost, that means the Metro (built in 1955). Fares in Russia are still very cheap by comparison to the West, although the quality of service does leave something to be desired.

Yet optimism runs high in St Petersburg. There's more to life than everyday chores. Something new happens daily on the culture scene. St Petersburg offers more than any other Russian city to lovers of theatre, classical music, concerts and opera. Young people in particular tend to do their own thing, as demonstrated by the rave parties that regularly take place. Sports enthusiasts can watch their heroes – the Zenith football club and the Army hockey club. Local people love the countryside: St Petersburg has beautiful environs, made famous by the former residences of the tsars and pleasing to the eye by their forests and the lakes of Karelia, to the north of the city. And if there's no time to get away to the beaches of the Gulf of Finland, you can enjoy the sun right in the city limits, on the small beach near the Peter and Paul Fortress.

Making your way through the bustle of Nevsky, meeting the people, you realise the truth of what singer, Boris Grebenschikov said: "I do not see that the city is dying. I do not know what is wrong with it, true, but I have no tragic premonition. St Petersburg has suffered much. We must make life easier for the people, and the city will take care of itself." ❑

LEFT: an old woman begs for money.
RIGHT: two young sailors on the *Aurora* cruiser.

THE RELIGIOUS REVIVAL

*The relationship between Church and State has not been an easy one
and even today the relaxation on open worship has its opponents*

The gradual rehabilitation of churches since the late 1980s, together with the congregations they attract and the growing number of novices entering the priesthood, constitutes something of a religious revival in Russia. Some see it as a triumphant repudiation of the propaganda drummed into Russians over four generations by State organs such as the Society of the Militant Godless. Others draw comparisons with the rise of Islamic fundamentalism in the Asian republics of the former Soviet Union, a manifestation of confused societies dredging through their past for some kind of cultural anchor.

Religion in Russia should not be equated with, say, Roman Catholicism in Poland, itself undergoing a renaissance. The latter is a more political and intellectual force, at loggerheads with everything atheistic Communism represented. Russian Orthodoxy, on the other hand, was never intellectualised as Christianity in the West was by the likes of Thomas Aquinas in the 13th century. The Russian faith was and is rooted in worship, not scholastic theology, and it is not inconceivable that it could have contrived a modus vivendi with Communism as it did with tsarist absolutism.

Who goes to church?

Visitors to a Russian Orthodox service will be struck by the highly orchestrated ritual. There are no books in evidence, but almost everyone seems to know the procedure. Even those who don't can cross themselves and bow at almost any time. The air is thick with incense, the richly coloured icons hold pride of place, and there is close interaction between clergy and congregation, communicating with one another through the medium of splendidly sonorous chant. Those familiar with the Greek Orthodox liturgy will see their common Byzantine source.

Anyone who visited Russia in communist times will be struck not only by the large

number of churches open, especially in Moscow and St Petersburg, but also by the age range of the worshippers. One or two Moscow churches even provide a carpet and toys for young children. Even in less accommodating churches, people feel free to come and go.

Closer acquaintance will reveal that nearly

all middle-aged and younger Christians, at least in the cities, are well-educated, while poorer, working-class people are to be found only in the few churches that undertake serious social involvement, such as prison visiting and distribution of food and clothing. In addition, there are the sometimes bossy *babushkas* (grandmothers) and other elderly people who have maintained their faith through the decades of persecution.

Of course, the enthusiasm for getting baptised, a craze which started in the late 1980s, has produced many nominal Christians who no longer go to church; some of these, in particular, are inclined to look back to times before

LEFT: the golden spire of the Peter and Paul Cathedral.
RIGHT: a baby is baptised.

Bolshevism, with a view to reliving past glories of the Russian Empire. Russian culture is closely interwoven with Christian values and symbols, and even Communism could not conceal this. But nostalgic fantasy can lead to alarming ideas. One of these is a desire to restore an absolutist monarchy. A small minority of Orthodox church-goers are monarchists.

The role of Church and State

The Russian Church had a peculiar role in society, because it never went through the process which eventually separated Church and State to varying degrees in the West. Ivan the

GREGORIAN CALENDAR

The Russian Orthodox Church observes the Gregorian Calendar, known as "old style". This means that church festivals are 13 days later than in the West – so, for example, Christmas Day is on 7 January rather than 25 December. The Church Council of 1918–19 decided to follow the State and adopt the Julian calendar ("new style"). Obviously every diocese was to lose the 13 days simultaneously, but State persecution and the arrest of bishops prevented it from being announced. Recent suggestions for change have met strong resistance from the mass of churchgoers, but there can be no doubt that it will happen within a few decades.

Terrible directed arbitrary horrors against the church in the 16th century (for which he undertook exaggerated penances), but the Church was not finally subjugated until the early 18th century, as part of the westernising reforms of Peter the Great.

Peter abolished the office of patriarch, and made the synod an organ of State, presided over by a government official – not necessarily a Christian – who had power to appoint and move bishops, and parish priests were even required to report to the police some of the things heard in private confessions. When their time came, the Russian communists regarded themselves as the ultimate spiritual authority, in exactly the same way as they assumed command of the armed forces.

The messianic manner in which the Bolsheviks presumed to convert the whole world to Communism was uncannily reminiscent of the phenomenon of Moscow as "the Third Rome". (Constantinople became "the Second Rome" after Rome was overrun by barbarians in the early 5th century.) Although the Russian Church had progressively distanced itself from its Greek origins by adopting Old Slavonic for liturgical purposes (the Cyrillic alphabet was invented specifically to facilitate the translation of Byzantine Greek texts into Slavonic languages) and replacing its Greek bishops with native Russians, the bonds remained close, if only to counter the hostility of Western Christianity to the Eastern rites as a whole.

The fall of Constantinople to the Turks in 1453, just as Russia had emerged from the Mongol yoke, was therefore a devastating blow to the Russian Church, and Ivan III decided it was Moscow's sacred duty to become "the Third Rome", the beacon of the True Faith. This mission ultimately led to what were in large part religious wars with Roman Catholic Poland in which the latter was no less determined to win Russia for the Pope and Rome.

Old Believers

In the mid-17th century Russia was plunged into a religious dispute which, unlike the Reformation, was about ritual rather than doctrine. Nikon, a peasant monk who was a close friend of the Romanov Tsar Alexei Mikhai-lovich, became patriarch in 1652. He decided to bring Church ritual into conformity with contemporary Byzantine practice. In effect this meant people crossing themselves with three fingers rather than two and a few changes in verbal formulas. These proposals were opposed by conservatives within the Russian Church who came to be known as "Old Believers".

Nikon was an authoritarian and uncompromising character, and persecution was fierce and even cruel in some places. It continued into the reign of Peter the Great when the Old Believers refused to surrender their beards in the interest of bringing Russian society into line with Western Europe, where men were in the habit of shaving. Old Believers fled to remote areas rather than shave.

Colonies of Old Believers exist to this day, and have at least two active churches in Moscow. When official persecution ceased, many Old Believers chose to remain in their remote colonies. They became famous for their hospitality, although if the visitors were not Old Believers any plates or glasses they used had to be smashed afterwards. Guests were expected to leave money for replacements.

Monasticism

Russian monks could claim much of the credit for opening up vast tracts of the Russian interior. Taking after the desert fathers of Syria and Egypt, they went deep into virgin forests to find sites for secluded monasteries. The forest was their desert. The tireless energy with which they made these remote areas habitable was their undoing because they were trailed by peasants pleased to exchange their labour for the right to settle on the monastic lands as tenants.

These arrangements were preferable to serfdom, and led to the monasteries becoming the biggest and richest landowners in Russia. Many monks were content to capitalise on their enterprise and become landlords, but others preferred to push the frontiers ever outwards and start all over again. The cycle repeated itself until monasteries ringed the White Sea and encroached on the fringes of Siberia.

St Sergius of Radonezh (Sergei Radonezhskiy, 14th century) is the best known and most popular of the monks who simultaneously Christianised and colonised Russia. His tomb is revered at Sergeyev Posad monastery, 50km

LEFT: two elderly women sit in quiet contemplation in a church.
RIGHT: a monk reads from an ancient text.

(30 miles) outside Moscow, probably the holiest shrine in the country. It resembles a walled fortress and contains no fewer than seven churches and one of the Orthodox Church's theological seminaries. There is also provision for visitors, with a museum and shops.

The Church under Communism

The tsar's abdication in February 1917 was welcomed by the Church which saw its opportunity to break free from State control and to restore the office of patriarch after a gap of two centuries. Patriarch Tikhon, who had been metropolitan archbishop in North America, was

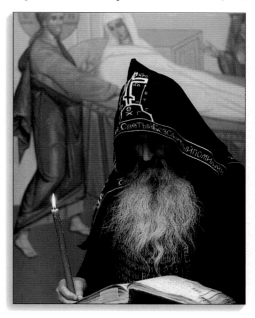

elected. Some people welcomed the Bolshevik revolution and Lenin's decree of 23 January 1918 which separated Church from State and schools from Church. This separation turned out to be rather one-sided, as the State took over all Church property and placed obstacles in the way of free association and travel.This was before serious persecution began. The famine of 1921–23 persuaded Patriarch Tikhon to hand over much of the Church's gold and silver plate, stipulating only that sacred vessels be melted down by Church authorities and handed over in the form of bullion.

This was done, raising enormous sums, but accounts show that all the money went into

Party funds, and none, apparently, to the famine victims. The Party, or often just local officials, wanted to take everything. Tikhon issued an appeal to resist the theft of Church property, and the result was 1,500 "bloody conflicts", followed by exile to Siberia or execution for the culprits.

Tikhon was also arrested and ecclesiastical communist sympathisers usurped his position. They declared the patriarchate void and called on "every faithful churchman… to fight with all his might together with the Soviet author-ity for the realisation of the Kingdom of God upon earth… and to use all means to realise in

day the suspicion that moves for change are tainted with Bolshevism.

Tikhon was arrested and urged to repent in order to resume his duties. "I was filled with hostility against the Soviet authorities," he said on his release in 1923. "I repent of all my actions directed against the government." Tikhon's confession reaffirmed the traditional solidarity of Church and State.

The Church moves underground

More serious was the statement made by Tikhon's successor, Patriarch Sergei, in 1927, although the content was very similar to that of

life that grand principle of the October Revo-lution." The faithful proved to be unmoved by the call and stayed loyal to the patriarchate rather than the alternative "Living Church" offered to them. The Living Church derived from sincere moves for reforms within the Church dating back to the 1880s.

There was a general desire for change, but little agreement on detail. Various groups amal-gamated and the communists saw this as an opportunity to split the Church. They favoured the Living Church with privileges, including free travel, while restricting everyone else. Gradually, believers saw through this trap and deserted the group, unfortunately leaving to this

Tikhon. Assuming that both these confessions had been made under duress, elements of the Church went underground. Taking their cue from the communist cell system, they used passwords to make themselves known to one another. Priests in plain clothes would pop up unannounced in villages, administer to the faithful, and as suddenly disappear.

In 1927, the year in which the first Five-Year Plan commenced, intellectuals and Christians were denounced as enemies of the revolution. Tax collectors swooped on churches and, if the sum demanded was not met, they were boarded up. Teaching religion to children under 18 was forbidden except in private houses and to groups of no more than three children at a time. Stalin relaxed the ban on Church activities during World War II in an attempt to lift morale. Everyone could see that the Germans were allowing churches to open in the territories they occupied, and after they withdrew the churches remained open by popular demand. When the war was over, however, controls were reimposed in the form of intense anti-religion propaganda in schools and general intimidation of anyone who aired religious convictions.

Under Khrushchev and Brezhnev, many believers served terms in prison for holding prayer meetings or conducting baptisms – not because they were crimes as such, but because they constituted anti-Soviet agitation. The few officially registered places of worship were infested with KGB informers. Bibles and other religious texts were unavailable except on the black market. Persecution intensified in the early 1960s, and more churches were closed under Khrushchev than had been under Stalin.

The communist state went to great lengths to discourage religious observance. For example, at Easter, the high point of the Orthodox calendar, state television would schedule a rare night of rock music. Those who went to midnight mass would encounter police and volunteer militia whose job was to stop anyone under 40 from entering the church. They were not actually forbidden to enter, but it was made clear that names of those attending "cult events" would be noted by the authorities.

When Gorbachev introduced perestroika in the 1980s, Christians of all denominations sensed freedom, and took every opportunity to come into the open. The millennium celebration of Russian Christianity, held in 1988, was a big, international event. The present Russian constitution makes a fairer separation between Church and State, but today's politicians like to appear in public from time to time with an archbishop somewhere in the background.

Other faiths and denominations

All religions suffered repression and persecution under communism. The Baptists, an active (though not so numerous) union of Protestants who trace their origins in Russia to 1870, were in turn tolerated and persecuted like the members of the Orthodox Church. Roman Catholics were totally suppressed. Islam had a marginally easier time because most Russian Muslims live in communities which are ethnically not Russian, and less easy to control from Moscow.

There are Buddhists here too, and a well-established Buddhist temple can be visited in St Petersburg in Novaya Derevnya. Today, there are Pentecostal churches in many parts of Russia, missions from Mormons, and other sects, mostly from Korea and North America. The scale of this theological invasion has

latterly begun to alarm both Orthodox churchmen and some politicians.

Under pressure from right-wing nationalists, and with some support from the patriarchate, Boris Yeltsin passed laws which curb the religious activity not only of sinister sects such as Aum Shinrikyo (which allegedly gassed the Tokyo metro in 1995). However, fears that the laws would damage established denominations such as the Roman Catholics and the Baptists have so far been unfounded. It seems, though, that the pendulum is swinging back again towards intolerance and persecution. Perhaps the struggle for religious freedom in Russia is not yet over. ❑

LEFT: religious freedom allows an Orthodox ceremony to take place outdoors.
RIGHT: a nun pictured in 1908.

FOOD AND DRINK

Traditional cuisine is making a comeback as Russian restaurants
compete for custom alongside multinational chains

The popular belief that Russians survive on a diet of potatoes and beetroot alone, with a healthy portion of *ogurtsi* (small cucumbers) and vodka to aid the digestion is not actually that far from the truth. These are indeed national favourites. However, with a little less prejudice and a desire to discover the truth, your stay in St Petersburg can be enriched and your palate educated by the wealth of cuisines on offer.

Foreign influences

From the Ukrainsky *borshch*, that infamous but delicious beetroot soup, normally served in a *gorshok* (deep clay pot) with *petrushka* and *smetana* (fresh parsley and sour cream), to the frozen *sibirskie pelmeny*, a small boiled pastry parcel of meat, mushrooms or potatoes, the national cookbook is as comprehensive as the country is big.

The years since perestroika have seen a renewal of the European influence in every walk of Russian life, including the kitchen. The sunny summer streets of towns buzz with café-life, and with trendy bars below street level. In addition to the foreign fads, there is a noticeable revival of traditional Russian restaurants catering for every pocket from the modest student stipend to the extravagant, no-holds-barred, *novy-Russky* (new-Russian) cash-filled handbags for men.

In the 19th century, Russia was in thrall to all things French, and borrowed from Paris not only its food, but also its theatre, poetry, architecture and fashion in hats. The French influence is felt in the penchant for thick sauces for meat, in the love of complicated salads, and in the huge variety of cream-filled tortes to be eaten at the end of the meal with *chai* (tea). One such cake is the *ptiche moloko* (bird's milk), so called because it is supposed to be so fine that it cannot possibly be created by humans.

LEFT: a section of a tile mural showing the food and drink of 19th-century rural life.
RIGHT: *solianka* (stew) and *borcht.*

Tempted by *zakuski*

The glory of Russian cuisine is the genuine desire of the host to see his or her guests fed and watered to absolute capacity – a desire that springs from the quintessence of the Russian soul: generosity and pride.

It is the tradition to load the dinner table in

advance with a vast variety of delicious *zakuski* (hors d'oeuvres). The *zakuska* plays an important role in the process of dining in Russia, and can save the inexperienced from certain disaster when drinking with the locals. Russians may have a big heart, but their capacity to consume alcohol is tremendous.

As a guest in a private home you will be treated in style to the best your host has to offer.

However, don't expect any leniency when it comes to drinking, you will have to imbibe your share. Toasting is as important, and here, too, you won't be let off the hook with a moderate "cheers". Toasts can last for minutes and are a science of their own. The formula to remember is your host, the women present and the spread in front of you. In fact, the *zakuski* are the main event of the meal, and it is an experience as daunting as it is appetising to look on a table laden with red and black caviar, a selection of cold meats, garlic sausage, smoked sturgeon, salmon, the array of potato salads, mushrooms in sour cream, bowls of pickled cabbage, beetroot vinaigrette, goat's cheese, as well as the usual liquid ensemble of deep-chilled vodka, *shampanskoye*, and syrupy Georgian wines.

Every hostess will confide in you her secret recipes and claim that nobody beats hers. Pop-ular favourites include *seledka pod shuboi*, literally "salted herring in a fur coat", which is a delicious combination of fish, beetroot, boiled (and grated) egg and mayonnaise, and *domashni piroshki* (homemade pies), which can be stuffed with a variety of cabbage, meat, mushrooms or apricots. By the time the second course arrives, most diners are already too replete to lift a fork.

Asian specialities

Russians can also call on the spicy southern, almost Mediterranean traditions in food. The cuisines of Armenia, Georgia and Azerbaijan,

as well as Uzbekistan, Kazakhstan and Kyrgizstan – which make liberal use of typical Asian ingredients such as coriander leaf, fruit and meat cooked together, walnuts, vine leaves, chillis, beans and flavoured breads – can be found in the Russian home as well as on the menu in restaurants.

Meat in these Asian countries will more often than not be boiled – with the tasty exception of *shashlik*, which is normally made from sheep and grilled over hot charcoal. This favoured dish is known throughout the

CAVIAR ON THE MENU

Beluga, osetrina and *sevruga* are translated as one, "sturgeon", and produce black caviar. Red caviar comes from salmon.

All of these are found on the *zakuski* section of the menu, and the most expensive restaurants will have them waiting on the table when customers arrive.

Other *zakuski* include *zhulien* (julienne), thin slices of smoked and non-smoked red and white sturgeon, and *kolbasa* (salami-like spicy sausages). *Salat* (salad) is often simply a mixture of tomatoes and cucumbers, but green salads comprise *travky* (literally "grasses") which in reality can be a refreshing plate of fresh basil, dill and other green herbs.

Russian Federation, and the chef, normally the man of the house, will be passionate about the preparation and cooking of what some may simply call a barbecue.

The *pelmeny* puts in an appearance wherever you are in or around Russia: you'll find it smaller than usual in Siberia – but made in vast quantities for the winter; it comes large, flat, fried and known as *cheburek* throughout Central Asia and the Transcaucasus, or *manti* in Kazakhstan; the more wholesome version in Georgia is known as the *khinkali*.

LEFT: celebratory pie; barbecue time.
ABOVE: Caucasians enjoy the local produce.

Traditional dishes

The Russian cookbook may now be as cosmopolitan as any other, but the traditional meals as eaten during the reign of the tsars would have been very different. *Kisel* (blancmange), made from oatmeal, was the basis of most meals and was eaten with savoury and sweet foods alike. *Shchi*, a soup made from *kislaya kapusta* (sauerkraut) and meat or fish, would probably feature in every main meal of the day. The fruits of Russia's abundant forests have long been harvested. Berries such as *brusnika, chernika, klyukva, zemlinika, golubika, malina* and *yeshevika* (foxberry, bilberry, cranberry, wild strawberry, blueberry, raspberry and blackberry) were gathered and used to make preserves, jams, desserts and drinks – as indeed they are still today. Vegetables such as *brukva*, (swede) *redka*, (radish) *markov* (carrot) and *chesnok* (garlic) were staple foods, too.

What remains traditional today is the *blin* (pancake), which is eaten both as a savoury and sweet dish. *Bliny* with lots of honey, *smetana* and red caviar are natural choices of filling for hungry Russians. *Bliny* are eaten at *Maslinitsa*, the week leading up to the *veliki post* (great fast of seven weeks) before Easter, which in turn is celebrated at the end with a *kulich*, a light, Easter cake similar to the Italian Christmas

panettone. A delicious sweet dish, *paskha*, synonymous with the celebration of Easter is prepared from *tvorog* (curds) with dried fruits and sugar added for sweetness.

The upper echelons of society would have known a different menu, one which shocked many visiting dignitaries with its richness and quality. Carp in *smetana*, baked *osyotr* (sturgeon) and *okorok* of ham (baked leg of ham in pastry with fruit and spices) were some of the dishes served to important visitors and the ruling class. Great pies of fish and meat, *zapikanky* (bakes) of rice, *smetana*, eggs and sugar and *kulebyaki* (more pies) with fillings of cabbage, mushrooms and meat, or fish, were common

for those that could afford it. *Khren* (horseradish sauce) was often the only addition to the natural juices that the dish was cooked in. *Kholodets* (aspic) is another favourite method of preparing meat and fish.

Welcome treats

Possibly the greatest sign of respect that can be shown to a guest is the giving of *karavai*, an intricately decorated bread shaped like a cake, which is presented normally at the border of a village or as the guest enters the house, and is accompanied by a small pot of salt. This ritual symbolises the wealth of the village or host. One is expected to break off a corner, dip it in the salt and taste it before advancing.

As bread was eaten with every meal and was what people survived on during the harder times, it was seen as dear to life and therefore a sign of readiness to welcome newcomers. It is a tradition often observed at weddings, when the two newly related mothers prepare the *karavai* for the newlyweds' return.

The *gribok* (mushroom) is at the heart of a national pastime: whole families spend their weekends together in the country, gathering mushrooms to preserve for the rest of the year in various concoctions of vinegar, spices and herbs. The culture of mushroom-gathering is one instilled from an early age and most Russians will be able to recite a lengthy list of edible and deadly sorts. The marinading of *griby* and *ogurtsi* (mushrooms and cucumbers) is another passion of the Russians, and one of the few occasions when Russian men will glady role up their sleeves and help out in the kitchen.

A real treat when visiting Russia is tasting the *ikra* (caviar) which comes in *chornaya* and *krasnaya* (black and red) and is sold by the kilo to the rich and in little tins to the tourists. Be sure to check the date stamped on the packaging before making your purchase. Red caviar is best eaten on white bread spread with a generous layer of butter, and black from little egg-baskets (made from the white of hard-boiled eggs, carefully cut into a basket form). Despite being significantly cheaper than at home, black caviar in a restaurant can still push up your bill dramatically. ❑

LEFT: vodka is available in both plain and flavoured varieties, including lemon and pepper.
RIGHT: selling fruit from the garden.

A TREASURE TROVE OF RUSSIAN CULTURE

St Petersburg is the cultural capital of Russia, reflected in its wealth of architecture, art, music and literature

When foreigners are asked, "What impressed you most in St Petersburg?", about 90 percent give the same reply: "The architecture and the cultural wealth." This is not surprising since it is indisputable that the city played a unique role in the history of Russian culture, a role that still fertilises today's cultural scene. It was here that Alexander Pushkin wrote his greatest poems, that Mikhail Glinka composed his masterpieces, that Ilya Repin painted his best pictures and that Andrei Voronikhin designed his neoclassical structures. These are only a handful of the many geniuses of Russian culture who lived, and whose art prospered, in this city.

Geniuses of architecture

Genuine art is timeless – a truth confirmed by countless palaces, parks, bridges and embankments throughout St Petersburg. Many Russian and foreign architects came, over a period of over 200 years, to work in the "Northern Palmyra", as the city came to be called. The architectural ensembles that sprang from their ingenuity are still cause for wonder.

In spite of Peter the Great and Lenin, it is the architects of the 18th and 19th centuries who brought worldwide fame to St Petersburg, and not the statesmen. They came from France, Italy, Switzerland, England and Germany, as well as from Russia, to design some of the finest baroque and neoclassical structures of their age.

It all started with Domenico Trezzini (1670–1734), a Swiss by birth who came when the city was founded and worked there from 1703 until his death. In and around St Petersburg he built the earliest churches, government offices, palaces and country villas; on Peter the Great's instructions he even designed a series of

standard houses for the different strata of society (houses for the nobility, for well-to-do families and for people of low birth).

Trezzini's structures are typical of early Russian baroque. Their distinctive features are

streamlined silhouettes with modest interiors, and a combination of austere and baroque elements. Trezzini designed Peter's Summer Palace (1710–14), and the Cathedral of St Peter and Paul (1712–33), one of St Petersburg's most magnificent structures. Towering over the cathedral is a belfry with a spire that was to be the tallest structure in the city and the symbol of the Russian Empire's new capital.

Artists and laymen unanimously regard the Italian Bartolomeo Rastrelli (1700–71), who worked in St Petersburg in the mid-18th century, as the greatest master of Russian rococo. His finest masterpieces are the Great Palace at Peterhof (Petrodvorets), the Smolny Convent

---

PRECEDING PAGES: the St Petersburg ballet school.
LEFT: *Anna Akhamatova* by Natan Altmann, 1914.
RIGHT: statues from Peterhof's Golden Hill cascade.

(1748–59), the Vorontsov Palace (1749–57) in Sadovaya Street and the Stroganov Palace (1752–54) at the corner of Nevsky prospekt and the Moika Embankment.

These architectural ensembles, magnificent and impressive in their design and solemnity, were built, according to Rastrelli himself, for "the glory of Russia". Rastrelli's structures are distinguished by clear-cut architectural forms, complicated patterns of colonnades, and spaciousness combined with inimitable plasticity.

RESTORING THE CITY

St Petersburg's architectural legacy was under threat for most of the 1990s. Today hundreds of millions of dollars are being spent to renovate and restore the city centre as part of its tricentenary.

lucidity of their plans and the monumental plasticity of forms achieved with the help of grand colonnades, which stand out against a background of smooth surfaced walls. The main building of the Academy of Sciences (1783–89), the former Assignation Bank (now home to the Financial-Economic Institute) in Sadovaya Street (1783–90), the Hermitage Theatre with the arch over the Winter Ditch (1783–87), and the Smolny Institute (1806–09) were built to his designs. Russian neoclassi-

The founders of neoclassicism in Russian architecture are Vassili Bazhenov (1737–99) who designed the Mikhailovsky Castle (1799–1800), together with Vincenzo Brenna (1745–1800) and Ivan Starov (1745–1808) who built the Tauride Palace (1783–89) and the Holy Trinity Cathedral of the Alexander Nevsky Monastery (1778–90). Bazhenov was the chief architect of Emperor Paul I. His masterpiece, the Mikhailovsky Castle, became the last residence of the ill-fated tsar who was strangled there on the night of 12 March 1801.

The buildings designed by Giacomo Quarenghi (1744–1817), another great Italian who worked in Russia, are distinguished by the

cism reached its peak in the early 19th century when Andrei Voronikhin (1759–1814), born a serf, built such masterpieces as the Cathedral of the Kazan Icon of the Mother of God (1801–11) on Nevsky prospekt, and the Mining Institute (1806–11) on the Neva Embankment.

When architect Andreyan Zakharov (1761–1811) rebuilt the Admiralty he created a jewel of Russian and world architecture. Thomas de Thomon (1760–1813) designed the majestic building of the Stock Exchange (1804–10), which now houses the Central Naval Museum, and the two landmark rostral columns (1806) on the Spit (Birzhevaya

Strelka, now Pushkin Square) on Vasilievsky Island. Of great significance for St Petersburg were the ensembles and individual buildings designed between 1818 and 1834 by Carlo Rossi (1775–1849), especially the Arts Square ensemble (1819–25) where the Russian Museum is located, and the building of the General Staff Headquarters (1819–29), with its monumental arch over Bolshaya Morskaya Street.

The latter building rounds out the Palace Square ensemble. Frenchman Auguste Montferrand (1786–1858) created the inimitable St Isaac Cathedral (1818–58) and the Alexander Column (1830–34), remarkable

Literary capital

There is scarcely a single Russian writer who, no matter where he was born or where he lived, has not cherished St Petersburg, who has not written poems or prose about it and who has not rejoiced when thinking of the city on the Neva. In this sense St Petersburg is probably the most "literary" city in the world.

The heart and soul of Russian literature, Alexander Pushkin (1799–1837), spent most of his time writing in St Petersburg. Except for a few influential years spent in exile and on trips to Boldino and Moscow, he was a true product of the atmosphere that prevailed in St Peters-

for its massive monolithic proportions as well as for its austere beauty.

St Petersburg's residents deeply cherish the memory of their great architects. One would probably not be able to find in any other Soviet town so many streets and squares named after their city's architectural planners as there are in St Petersburg. This is not accidental, because architecture is not only St Petersburg's "calling card", it is its essence. After years of neglect efforts are being made to restore the city centre.

LEFT: the stunning Chesma Church, built by Felten in 1777–80.
ABOVE: windows at the Nevsky Monastery.

burg. Like nobody else, Pushkin loved "Peter's creation", and he himself created an impressive poetic image of the great city. Whole chapters of *Eugene Onegin* (1823–31), in which Pushkin described St Petersburg's high society and theatrical life, with its spectators and actors, were inspired by the city. His unfinished novel, *Peter the Great's Negro* (1827), depicts the city at the time of Peter the Great.

In Pushkin's mind St Petersburg symbolised a new, "unshakeable" and powerful Russia. After the failure of the Decembrists' uprising in 1825, however, he thought of the city as a place of "ennui, cold and granite". After being mortally wounded in a duel with George d'Anthes,

Pushkin died at No. 12, Moika Embankment.

The work of Nikolai Gogol (1809–52) is also associated with St Petersburg, where he lived from 1829 to 1836 before going abroad; here he wrote his best works, including *The Government Inspector*, *Marriage* and *The Greatcoat*.

"You can see the influence of St Petersburg," wrote Vissarion Belinsky, a prominent Russian critic, "on the greater part of Gogol's works, not in the sense that he owed St Petersburg his manner of writing, of course, but

mon." St Petersburg's "dream" and "ideal" did not seem lofty for Dostoevsky; he did not feel "a common unifying thought in the crowd, all were by themselves." For Dostoevsky, St Petersburg was "the most abstract and imaginary city." A similar vision was later reflected in the works of the Russian symbolists.

At various times Leo Tolstoy (1828–1910), who contributed his first works to the journal *Sovremennik* (Contemporary), the playwright Alexander Ostrovsky (1823–86), who also con-

in the sense that he owed St Petersburg many of the characters he created." Gogol created an image of St Petersburg as a "smart European", a "dandy". But it was against the background of all this that "unusually strange happenings" took place, "everything breathed deception" and acquired a "fantastic tenor". Thus was Gogol's St Petersburg.

Fyodor Dostoevsky (1821–81), born in Moscow, wrote almost all of his novels in St Petersburg. With his brother he edited the magazines *Vremya* (Time) and *Epokha* (Epoch) here. In St Petersburg he saw "a mixture of something purely fantastic and perfectly ideal, and at the same time insipidly prosaic and com-

tributed to St Petersburg's literary journals, and Anton Chekhov (1860–1904), who had his plays staged at the Alexandrinsky Theatre, came to St Petersburg on short visits.

St Petersburg also figured prominently in the works of the great Russian poet Alexander Blok (1880–1921) who spent almost his whole life there. In the poem *Retribution* (1910–21), Blok wrote about the St Petersburg of the late 19th century as a city in which irresistible anti-autocratic forces were in the making:

In those dead and gloomy years
Somehow it seemed that Petersburg
Was still the heart and soul of Russia,
But doom was knocking at the doors.

No matter what Blok wrote about St Petersburg, he did so with a deep love. Anna Akhmatova (1889–1966), Osip Mandelshtam (1891–1938) and many other poets and writers also wrote affectionately about the city which, in opening out its heart and soul to them, itself became the heart and soul of Russian literature.

Russian music

Russian classical music is bound up with St Petersburg because it was here that the composers whose works constitute the musical treasure-trove of Russia created their masterpieces. Mikhail Glinka (1804–57), who is the unchal-

and a new period in history has started, a period of Russian music." In hindsight these now seem prophetic words. It should also be mentioned that a series of romances that Glinka composed, in 1840, as a setting for Nestor Kukolnik's lyrics were dedicated to his favourite St Petersburg. The series was called *Farewell to St Petersburg*.

An extremely creative group of composers lived in St Petersburg in the 1860s. Three of them reached world fame: Modest Mussorgsky (1839–81) was author of many vocal pieces and the deeply emotional operas *Boris Godunov* and *The Khovansky Affairs*; Alexander Borodin

lenged founder of Russian classical music, the author of the brilliant operas *Ivan Susanin* and *Ruslan and Lyudmila*, and no less brilliant symphonic pieces and romances, wrote almost all of his works in St Petersburg. It should be remembered that after the premiere of *Ivan Susanin* in 1836 Vladimir Odoyevsky, the musical critic and poet, wrote: "What has long been sought after and not found in Europe has come with Glinka's opera – a new wave in art

LEFT: Gogol reading to a group of friends from his work *The Government Inspector*.
ABOVE: Mikhail Glinka, the founder of Russian classical music.

(1833–87), author of such epic works as the opera *Prince Igor* and the *Second Symphony in B Minor* was also a master of chamber music; and Nikolai Rimsky-Korsakov (1844–1908) – who wrote many operas based on history, like *The Tsar's Bride*, on fairytales, like *The Snow Maiden*, on epics, like *Sadko,* and on satires, like *The Golden Cockerel* – was at the same time a brilliant conductor whose music had a subtle lyrical character.

The Russian Musical Society, which introduced regular concerts, was established in 1859 in St Petersburg on the initiative of the composer and pianist Anton Rubinstein (1829–94). In the same year the Society started its first musical classes, on the basis of which Rubinstein organised Russia's first conservatoire in 1862. Among the first graduates of the conservatoire was Peter Tchaikovsky (1840–93), the greatest of Russia's symphony and opera composers, author of such masterpieces as the operas *Eugene Onegin* and *The Queen of Spades*, the ballets *Swan Lake* and *The Sleeping Beauty*, and suites like *The Nutcracker*, not to forget his *Sixth (Pathétique) Symphony*. "Like Pushkin, he has become integrated into the very foundations of the Russian national conscience", wrote Dmitri Shostakovich (1906–75), the pre-eminent Russian composer of the 20th

century and another graduate of the St Petersburg (Leningrad) Conservatoire.

Shostakovich lived in the city until 1942. Many of his best works were written and performed here for the first time, in particular the opera *Lady Macbeth of Mtsensk* and the ballet *The Age of Gold*. He lived in Leningrad for the first months of the 900-day siege, during which he wrote his famous *Seventh (Leningrad) Symphony* which was performed in the besieged city by the Leningrad Radio Orchestra in 1942.

Igor Stravinsky (1882–1971), the outstanding Russian composer and conductor, who lived in the US after 1910, also began his musical career in St Petersburg, as did another classic composer of the 20th century, Sergei Prokofiev (1891–1953). Although Prokofiev lived in Moscow for most of his life, he often returned to St Petersburg for premieres of his works.

Choreographers and dancers

St Petersburg produced not only great composers, but also splendid opera singers and brilliant pianists and conductors. The "Northern Palmyra" is, however, probably most famous for its ballet. As early as the beginning of the 19th century, ballets produced by the famous choreographer Charles-Louis Didelot (1767–1837) were performed at St Petersburg's Bolshoi Theatre.

Alexander Pushkin, who often went to the theatre, highly appreciated Didelot's ballets and saw in them "a lively imagination of extraordinary charm". In the early 20th century, Anna Pavlova (1881–1931), Waslaw Nijinsky (1889–1950) and Michel Fokine (1880–1942) danced with enormous success on the stage of the Mariinsky Theatre.

But the best years of those inimitable dancers were spent abroad, where they performed in the ballet troupe called the Russian Seasons, which was formed in 1907 by the prominent Russian choreographer Sergei Diaghilev (1872–1929). The Soviet ballerinas Galina Ulanova and Maya Plisetskaya started their careers in Leningrad, and it was also here that Rudolf Nureyev, Natalia Makarova and Mikhail Baryshnikov, whose art is now known all over the world, won their fame.

The city's ballet continues to thrive today, often touring abroad and meeting with rave reviews in London, Milan, New York, and Germany. Among the great dancers today are Svetlana Zakharov, Yuliana Lopatkina, and Diana Vishnyeva.

Though the great names of St Petersburg culture are names from the past, especially from the city's heyday in the 19th century, a golden age for Russia generally, it does not mean that the city today is devoid of great talents. There is spirit of renaissance in the air and the people of St Petersburg try hard to keep alive the essence of its splendid past. ❑

LEFT: portrait of Leo Tolstoy.
RIGHT: Alexander Pushkin, the beloved master of Russian literature.

THEATRE AND CINEMA

St Petersburg's theatrical reputation rests on its brilliant actors and directors while its filmmakers have brought the city to life

Since the mid 1990s, the theatre in St Petersburg has produced some of the country's finest drama, taking home many awards at the country's most prominent theatre ceremonies, the Golden Mask, held each spring. Yet, as odd as it may sound, at the same time the city's theatre scene is in crisis.

The explanation to this strange contradiction is that there are a small number of stage directors producing great work, but the general level of theatre deserves little applause. Unlike many theatres in America and Britain, Russian theatres work with a repertoire of say 20 to 30 plays that appear regularly throughout the year.

For almost three decades, the best theatre in St Petersburg was the Bolshoi Drama Theatre (BTD) headed by Georgy Tovstonogov (on the Fontanka). After the death of its director, as well as leading performers, the 1990s found both the BTD, as the theatre is called, in a crisis. But now there are signs that it is enjoying a renaissance as new, young talent flocks to this venerable theatre.

Theatrical life

The city's theatre life is based not around a number of theatres, but more around certain individuals – actors and directors. Take Lev Dodin's Maly Drama Theatre, the city's most acclaimed theatre, which rose to prominence during perestroika when his works were both risqué and daring for the time. His recent critically acclaimed plays are *Chavengur* (with the accent on the last syllable), a play about the origins of Soviet power in the 1920s, and *Chaika*.

Other great Maly Drama productions include plays based on Fyodor Abramov's novels *The House* and *Brothers and Sisters*, as well as contemporary works, such as *Pilgrims on the Run*, a merciless exposé of Russia today.

Yet Dodin is one of few outstanding directors in the city. Another interesting director is Gregori Dityakovsky whose production of *Lost*

LEFT: a portrait of Fiodor Shaliapin as Boris Gudunov.
RIGHT: inside the Mariinsky Theatre.

in the Stars won a Golden Mask award. It is performed at the Theatre on the Liteyny, under a different director.

There are many theatres in St Petersburg but, frankly, few of them deserve to be called theatres at all. For many years now the Aleksandrinsky Theatre has been experiencing financial

problems, despite its status as the main "academy" of theatrical art in St Petersburg.

"There are no great movements being made in theatre in St Peterburg, especially in comparison to Moscow which has always had a more vibrant theatre scene," said local theatre critic Aleksandr Ures. "In St Peterburg, there are no interesting theatres per se, but rather interesting stage directors, actors and individual plays."

There are some bright young directors, but they prefer to be independent, outside of the formal theatre system that has existed up till now. One of the favourite venues of independent directors is the Mironov Russian Enterprise Theatre, named in honour of the famous

Russian actor, Andrei Mironov, and another is the Baltiisky Dom theatre. Both are on the Petrograd Side.

Most theatres are state-financed, but in the past 10 years a number of privately financed, independent theatres have sprung up. One of the most interesting is the Farces Theatre, run by stage director Viktor Kramer. He is also unhappy with the Soviet-era theatre system, which he thinks is moribund and failing. While many theatres are now in financial crisis, determined individuals such as Kramer have been able to secure financing, mostly from friends and contacts in the business

EXPERIMENTAL THEATRE

One of the most interesting and original theatre venues is the Alternative Stage Station, where a number of experimental theatre groups regularly perform. Among them are dance companies Iguana Dance and Canon Dance, as well as the comic theatrical group Comic Trust. The latter's performances have almost no spoken words, but rather gestures, grunts, and various other sounds, so the non-Russian-speaking spectator can enjoy the shows, which are among the most acclaimed comedy acts in the city. The Alternative Stage Station is located in the Five-Year House of Culture, behind the Mariinsky Theatre, on Ulitsa Dekabristov. Tel. 328-1619/114-2027.

world. Though the theatre system seems to be breaking down there is no lack of creative ideas in Russia theatre, which is powered by strong and outstanding individuals who are dedicated to what they do.

There is no doubt that the city's most famous theatre is the Mariinsky Theatre (which, for some unfathomable reason, was renamed the Kirov Theatre of Opera and Ballet after the revolution; Sergei Kirov was a revolutionary and had nothing whatsoever to do with ballet). This is true both for opera and for the ballet, which is headed by the famed Valeri Gergiev.

Gergiev is considered to be a genius and one of the most formidable cultural figures not only in St Peterburg but the world. Even those who criticise him for being despotic are awed by his mind, talent, and energy. He has single-handedly raised the Mariinsky's opera from near obscurity in the mid-1990s to international acclaim, successfully staging about 15 premieres a season. Among his most prominent recent works are stagings of Wagner's *Der Ring des Nibelungen*, and Tchaikovsky's *War and Peace*, in collaboration with Russian-American film director Andrei Konchalovsky.

The imposing building of the Mariinsky is an entire palace; once inside, one remembers Meyerkhold's famous words, "How good it is for the soul to sit in this temple." Opposite the Mariinsky is the St Petersburg Conservatoire, where the best performers from all over the world come to play. Meanwhile, Yury Temirkanov, who worked at the Mariinsky for many years, now heads the famous orchestra of the St Petersburg Philharmonic, which was created by the great maestro Yevgeny Mravinsky. Even though the orchestra spends a good deal of its time playing abroad, it also remembers its loyal audience and plays frequently in St Petersburg.

Theatre life is a unique thing. Changes occur every hour. Who knows, maybe a masterpiece is being born at this very moment in one of the city's 50 or so theatres? There's good reason to hope for this – the city certainly has enough talented directors and actors. Come to meet them in the Actor's House on Nevsky prospekt, whether just to talk or see them in action.

The cinema scene

St Petersburg moviemakers are totally unlike their Moscow colleagues: in St Petersburg, they are impeccable, elegant, restrained. They are more European than the simple souls of Moscow. They are aristocrats in their souls regardless of social roots or the fact that they live in a city called "the cradle of the revolution" since October 1917 – the event which temporarily gave the "Palmyra of the North" (Leningrad) the name of the Bolshevik leader.

The great moviemakers, who made St Petersburg famous, were all of that type. This is true of Grigory Kozintsev (1905–73), the man who founded the world-famous FECS (*Factory of the Eccentric Actor*) in the 1920s, created the three-part sequence about Maxim in the 1930s, which the public loved, and turned to Shakespeare in

Nevsky prospekt) are ceremonious, strikingly similar to the style of reception that was in vogue during the days of the empire. It is a miracle how the city and its intellectuals have managed to retain their image in spite of all the suffering and hardships. The influence of arrow-straight avenues, thin spires and the glitter of grandiose palaces is clearly felt here.

As for the woes of St Petersburg, they have been legion. They, too, have been recorded by the masters of the screen in both documentaries and fiction. The terrible documentary chronicles of the 20th century will forever preserve the images of the blockade of 1941–43: the city cov-

the 1960s and the 1970s (his *Hamlet* and *King Lear* have justly made it into the gold collection of world cinema).

This is also true of Ilya Averbakh, Kozintsev's pupil, who passed away long before his time (1934–86), the director of such psychological films as *The Monologue*, *Declaration of Love*, and *Voice*. Finally, this applies to the young generation of Lenfilm moviemakers as well. Evenings and gala nights in the St Petersburg Cinema House (Karavannaya Street near

ered by huge mounds of snow; women standing in line near a hole drilled in the ice-covered canal (there was no running water); a woman, unsteady on her feet from fatigue and pain, dragging a sled bearing the corpse of her child.

A great event takes place in the Philharmonic: for the first time ever, the orchestra plays the Seventh (Leningrad) Symphony by Dmitry Shostakovich. Filming was shot with constantly freezing equipment by people who shared the hunger and constant danger of artillery fire with the rest of the city. The film is a heroic deed itself.

St Petersburg moviemakers are proud of their studio. Lenfilm has an interesting history, which starts with a small atelier in Aquarium

LEFT: a contemporary advertisement for the chronicle of 1911.
ABOVE: the Avror cinema on Nevsky prospekt.

Summer Garden. Over the years, the studio became the second largest movie company in the USSR (after Mosfilm). The golden era of the studio fell in the period between the two world wars: great films of that era included *Chapayev* by Georgy and Sergei Vasiliev (1934), the *Maxim* sequence (1935–39), the *Deputy of the Baltic* (1937) and the *Member of Government* (1940) by Alexander Zarkhi and Iosif Heifits.

It is curious how, in St Petersburg, people had little interest in the monumental epics that they loved so much in

FILM FESTIVAL

Each June, St Petersburg first hosts the International Festival of Documentary Films, followed by the Festival of Festivals, which shows over 100 world films, as well as holding symposia dedicated to cinematography.

Moscow – films showing battles, the taking of the Winter Palace and other tsarist strongholds in their city. The movies about Lenin were mainly made in Moscow.

In St Petersburg, the camera looked at the ordinary people, the rank-and-file participants in historic events. Chapayev, a partisan and Red Army officer in the Civil War; the St Petersburg professor of biology from the Baltic who was elected people's deputy; the Russian peasant woman who made it into the Supreme Soviet – these characters, played by such Russian stars as Boris Babochkin, Nikolai Cherkasov and Vera Maretskaya, are part of the classic collection of the images of Russian

moviemaking. St Petersburg films have a soft and humane intonation, a certain modesty and a preference for realism and psychology over formal experiments.

Modern film

The tradition lives on in the work of the younger generation at Lenfilm, and its best representatives are director Alexei Balabanov, whose *Brat* (Brother, 1996) and *Brat II* (2000) films are among the biggest box office hits in Russia in the past ten years. Both films are about the violent world of Russia's post-Soviet youth and their greed for money and power.

Alexander Rogushkin has produced a number of films that are already classics of the national culture. His most famous work is *The Peculiarities of the National Hunt* (1995), which tells the story of Russian men who go on a hunt but only spend their time drinking vodka. That film was followed by a sequel, *Peculiarities of National Fishing*.

A fresh look and profound analysis mark the films of Aleksei German: *Highway Inspection*, *Twenty Days Without War* (1977), *My Friend Ivan Lapshin* (1984), and his 1998 critically acclaimed film about Stalin's death, *Khrustelyev, Bring the Car*. German is a remarkable director whose work suffered in the era of stagnation: *Highway Inspection* was kept from the public for 15 years, and was salvaged only in 1988 by the "conflict committee", which released over 200 films made in the period 1960 to 1980 that had not been previously shown in the USSR.

The fate of that film was shared by other St Petersburg productions – for example, *The Second Attempt of Viktor Krokhin* by Viktor Sheshukov (about a boxer spoiled by the lies and falsity of professional sport). Aleksei German and his younger supporters ushered in a new era, the era of *The Burglar*, *Gunpowder*, *Forgive Me* and *Freeze-Die-Arise* (the producer of the latter, Vitaly Kanevsky, made his debut in motion pictures by winning the Golden Camera Award at the 1990 Cannes Festival). ❑

LEFT: a plaque outside the Lenfilm Studios.
RIGHT: a poster advertising one of the many theatre performances in St Petersburg.

THE CITY ON THE NEVA

The academician Dmitry Likhachev writes about the
eternal appeal of the city's architecture

The key feature of St Petersburg's architecture is the predominance of horizontal over vertical lines – a fact explained by the existence of numerous water surfaces in the city: those of the Greater Neva and Little Neva, the Greater Nevka and Little Nevka, the Fontanka, the Moika, the Griboedova Canal and the

reproduced exquisitely by Dostoyevsky in his *Adolescent*: "Amidst this fog I was a hundred times beset by a strange but persistent dream: what if this mist disperses, goes up and away; will not all of this rotten, slimy city rise together with it and disperse like smoke, leaving behind only the original Finnish swamp?"

Kryukova Canal, for example. The point of contact between water and land creates an ideal horizontal line. St Petersburg's water seems to fill the city right to the brim. This invariably surprises those visitors more accustomed to cities that stand on tidal rivers or those with fluctuating levels.

Running above the two horizontals formed by water and embankment is a thinner, less definite line formed by the rooftops which never, in keeping with the often-repeated order, rose higher than the Winter Palace.

The shimmering line of rooftops seen against the background of the sky makes the buildings seem illusory or ephemeral. This impression is

Perpendicular structures

Other characteristic elements of the city are the three spires, those of the Peter and Paul Fortress, the Admiralty and the Mikhailovsky Castle. They are viewed as perpendiculars to the horizontal lines, which favourably contrast and emphasise the latter. The spires are accompanied by tall belfries, such as that of the Chevakinsky on the Kryukova Canal (and once of the bell tower of the church at Sennaya Square, which, sadly, has now been pulled down). The enormous bulk of St Isaac's Cathedral with its gilt dome was meant to form the focus of St Petersburg's second centre, fulfiling a town-planning function similar to that of St Peter's Cathedral in Rome. Other church domes are evenly distributed all over the city and their spherical, non-rectilinear shapes sit like decorative flourishes, feminine in character, above the city's masculine lines. The city's main squares, Palace Square and the Field of Mars, stand near the Neva but are fenced off from it by a row of houses. The only square facing directly onto the Neva – Decembrist's Square with the *Bronze Horseman* – exposes Peter the Great and his steed to a broad stretch of water.

COLOUR

The colour of houses in St Petersburg plays so important a role that it would be hard to think of a major European city worthy of comparison with it.

built in an incoherent and unimaginative style like a box.

Another major infringement of the city's image is the Sovietskaya Hotel in the old Kolomna District. Its isolated buildings of varying heights break St Petersburg's typically coherent skyline and produce an impression of uninspired and gloomy confusion.

The colour spectrum

Of the other characteristics of St Petersburg, I consider most important the following two:

In front of the Finland Station, on the other side of the Neva and somewhat higher up the river, stands Lenin on top of an armoured car. The majestic gesture of the *Bronze Horseman* is a contrast to Lenin's oratorical gesture. The square is quite satisfactory in respect to town-planning terms, except for the unwieldy office building which ploughs the statue into one corner.

Modern violations

The dominance of horizontal lines in the city is badly distorted by the St Petersburg Hotel,

the city's colour spectrum and its harmonious combination of major architectural styles. St Petersburg needs more colour than any other city because it is deprived of it by mist and rain. That is why brick masonry was not left unplastered, and plaster required painting. Soft watercolour tones prevail in the gamut of the city's colours.

The city's historical past, which is comparatively short (only three centuries long), may be viewed as a completed stage production, since it is quite obvious that the city's historical drama has been played out, no matter what its future significance for the country may prove to be. ❏

LEFT: atlantes carry a heavy load at the Hermitage.
ABOVE: a boat on the Moika.

PLACES

A detailed guide to the entire city, with principal sites
clearly cross-referenced by number to the maps

While St Petersburg was built on a shifting swamp in the Neva delta, the Enlightenment ideas of rationality and reason provide the durable foundation of the city's urban planning and architecture. Most streets and prospects were designed and built in straight lines, unlike medieval Moscow's multitude of crooked and winding side streets. Navigating St Petersburg is not a difficult task for most visitors.

Though St Petersburg is Europe's youngest city – it turns 300 in 2003 – it has one of the largest and finest collections of 18th-and 19th-century architecture on the continent. Despite the tumult of the past 100 years – three revolutions, two world wars, and the repression of the Soviet era – St Petersburg has managed to preserve its appearance much the way it was in 1917.

The subsequent move of the capital to Moscow in 1918 was a blessing in disguise, and even after the destruction of World War II, nearly all buildings were rebuilt in their original appearance. Even today city fathers guard their architectural heritage jealously, forbidding any innovation in the city centre that might alter or spoil its grandeur.

Fighting this battle has not been easy, and much work was done in the 1990s to maintain and reclaim the city centre's past. Soviet-era street names were changed back to their tsarist era names, for instance. Some Soviet monuments were removed, and now more and more monuments are being erected to leading forgotten personalities of the tsarist era.

Still, that doesn't mean the city has erased its Soviet legacy. There are still dozens of statues to Lenin in public places, as well as other Soviet insignia in public places.

Architectural variety

In terms of architecture and epochs, St Petersburg has something for everyone – there is the grandeur of the baroque, the dignity of neoclassicism, the power and authority of the French Empire style, the historical ecleticism and art nouveau styles of the turn of the 20th century, as well as the constructivism of the 1920s and early 1930s.

St Petersburg is not only Russia's most European city, it is perhaps the most European of all Europe's cities. From 1703 until 1917, architects from all over Europe – Italian, Swiss, Dutch, British, German, and French – were handsomely paid to build a great capital for the tsars.

European architects, engineers, gardeners and other craftsman were given opportunities unheard of in the ancient and crowded

PRECEDING PAGES: the Throne Room of the Great Palace at Peterhof; baroque gilded room at the Grand Palace at Peterhof; the fountain and Kazan Cathedral at night.
LEFT: gilded atlantes at the Catherine Palace, Pushkin.

cities of Europe. Among them in the 18th and 19th century were Italians Francesco Bartolomeo, Antonio Rinaldi, Carlo Rossi, and Giacomo Quarenghi; Swiss architect Domenico Trezzini, Frenchmen Auguste Montferrand and Thomas de Thomon; as well as Britons Charles Baird and William Hastie. By the late 19th and early 20th century, Scandinavian architects became more prominent, such as the great Swedish art nouveau designer, Fyodor Lidval.

In St Petersburg, they had a vast amount of space and a licence to systematically create grand buildings where previously there were none. Russian architects also made significant contributions, such as Vasily Bazhenov's Engineering Castle, Andrei Zakharov's Admiralty, and the Kazan Cathedral, built by the freed serf, Andrei Voronikhin.

As the years went on and European fashions changed, so did Russian imperial preferences. During Peter's time, as well as during the reign of his daughter, Elizabeth, the baroque flourished. Structures such as the 12 Collegia and the Catherine Palace (named in honour of Peter's wife) in Pushkin are among the most notable.

Catherine's legacy

Catherine the Great, a German princess, loathed what she thought were the extravagances of the baroque style and instead preferred the strict facades of Classicism, which were considered to be more in line with Enlightenment ideas on reason. The most prominent buildings of her day include the Tauride Palace, the Marble Palace, and the Russian State Bank (now the Financial and Economics Academy on Griboedova Canal).

Napoleon's defeat at the hands of the alliance led by England and Russia greatly altered St Petersburg's urban landscape, which came to be dominated by triumphal arches, squares for military parades and ceremonial columns.

Among these are Palace Square in front of the Hermitage with its arch of the General Staff Building and the Alexander Column, as well as the Moscow Triumphal Arch on Moskovsky prospekt, as well as Senate and Mikhailovsky Squares.

By the early 19th century, the city became famous in Europe for its harmony in style and architecture, earning it the nickname, Palmyra of the North, after the great city in antiquity.

Besides the historic centre, there are a half dozen palace residences in the suburbs that deserve your attention. But don't be overwhelmed by the wealth of places to see and visit. Better to take your time, enjoy each sight, and appreciate its beauty and soul. And if you don't see something, then you have an excuse to come back. ❏

RIGHT: details of a street painting of St Petersburg.

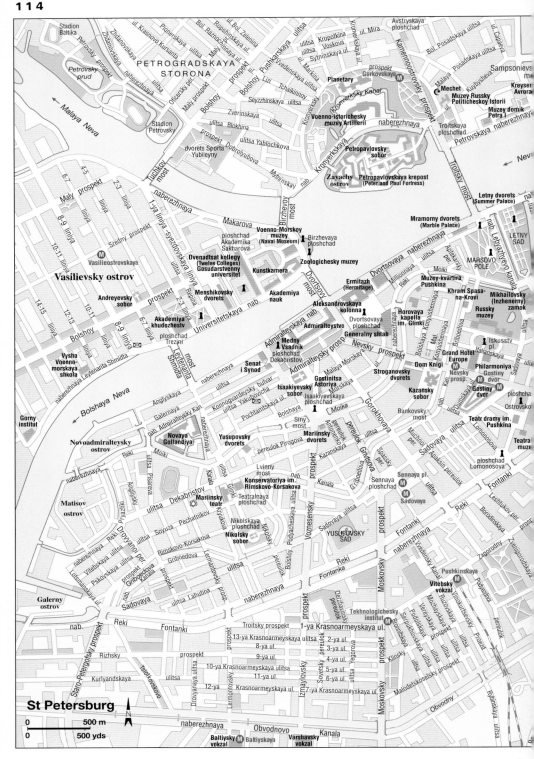

St Petersburg

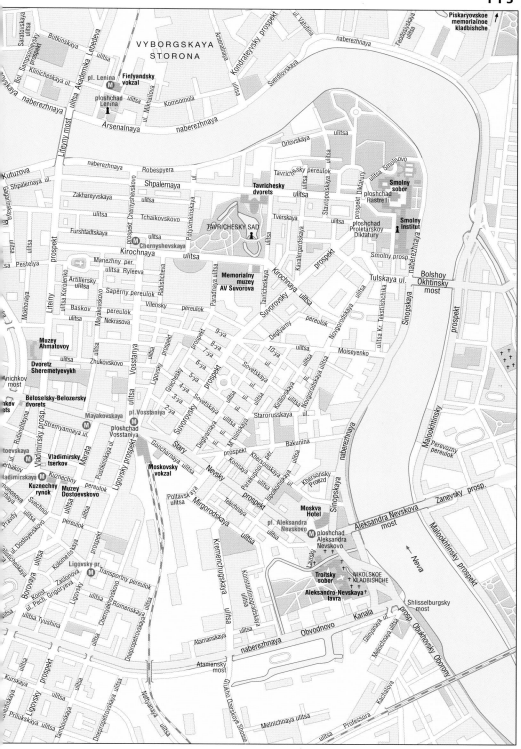

Piskaryovskoe
memorialnoe
kladbishche

VYBORGSKAYA
STORONA

Saratovskaya ulitsa
Botkinskaya
Bol. Sampsonievsky prospekt
Kutuzova
Klinicheskaya ul.
pl. Lenina
Finlyandsky
vokzal
ploshchad
Lenina
Arsenalnaya
naberezhnaya
Akademika Lebedeva ulitsa
ul. Mikhailova
Komsomola
Liteiny most
naberezhnaya
Kondrateyevsky prospekt
ul. Vatulina
naberezhnaya
Sverdlovskaya

Shpalernaya ulitsa
Gagarinskaya
Shpalernaya ul.
Zakharevskaya ulitsa
Chernyshevskovo prospekt
Tchaikovskovo ulitsa
Robespyera
Polyomkinskaya
Orlovskaya ulitsa
Tavrichesky pereulok
Stavropolskaya ulitsa
ulitsa Smolnovo
Smolny
sobor
ploshchad
Rastrelli

Furshtadtskaya ulitsa
Tavrichesky
dvorets
Tverskaya
Kavalergardskaya
ploshchad
Proletarskoy
Diktatury
Smolny
Institut

Kirochnaya ulitsa
Chernyshevskaya
TAVRICHESKY SAD
Tavricheskaya
Smolny prosp.

Manezhny per.
ulitsa Ryleeva
Radishcheva
Paradnaya
Memorialny
muzey
AV Suvorova
Kirochnaya ulitsa
Tulskaya ul.
Bolshoy
Okhtinsky
most

Pestelya
Artillersky
ulitsa
Saperny pereulok
Vilensky pereulok
Suvorovsky prospekt
Novgorodskaya ulitsa
ulitsa Kr. Tekstilshchika
Sinopskaya
prospekt

Mokhovaya
Liteiny prospekt
ulitsa Korolenko
Mayakovskovo
Baskov pereulok
Nekrasova ulitsa
Deghtyarny pereulok
Moiseyenko
9-ya
8-ya
7-ya
6-ya
5-ya
4-ya
3-ya
2-ya
10-ya
ulitsa
Sovetskaya
ul.

Muzey
Ahmatovoy
Zhukovskovo ulitsa
Vosstanya ulitsa
Grechesky prospekt
Sovetskaya ul.
Kirillovskaya
Novgorodskaya ulitsa
Moiseyenko

Dvorets
Sheremetyevykh
Anichkov
most
Beloselsky-Belozersky
dvorets
Mayakovskaya
pl. Vosstaniya
Suvorovsky prospekt
Degtyarnaya ul.
M. Tynskaya ul.
Staroruss kaya
Bakunina

Rubinshteyna
Stremyannaya
ploshchad
Vosstaniya
Goncharnaya
Khersonskaya
Khersonsky
Poezd
naberezhnaya
Sinopskaya
Zanevsky prosp.

Vladimirsky
tserkov
Vladimirsky prosp.
Marata
Pushkinskaya ul.
Ligovsky prospekt
Stary Nevsky
Konnaya ul.
Perekupnoy
Ispokomskaya ul.
Malookhtinsky prospekt

toevskaya
Vladimirskaya
Kuznechny
rynok
Muzey
Dostoevskovo
Kuznechny pereulok
Strechnoi pereulok
Moskovsky
vokzal
Nevsky prospekt
Mirgorodskaya ulitsa
Poltavskaya ulitsa
Telezhnaya ul.
Moskva
Hotel
pl. Aleksandra
Nevskovo
ploshchad
Aleksandra
Nevskovo
Aleksandra Nevskova most
Lavrsky
Neva

Pravdy
Dostoyevskovo
ul. Dostoyevskovo
Kolmenskaya
Kremenchugskaya ulitsa
Konstantinogradskaya ulitsa
Troitsky
sobor
NIKOLSKOE
KLADBISHCHE
Aleksandro-Nevskaya
lavra
Shlisselburgsky
most
prosp. Obukhovskoy Oborony
Kachalova

Borovaya ulitsa
Ligovsky pr.
Transportny pereulok
Zaslonova ulitsa
Ligovsky pr.
Konst. Pech. Grigoryeva
Chernyakhovskovo ulitsa
Romenskaya ulitsa
Dnepropetrovskaya ulitsa
Ligovsky prospekt
Glinyanaya ul.
Melnichnaya ulitsa
Obvodnovo Kanala

Kurskaya
ulitsa Tyushina
Atamanskaya
Atamansky
most
naberezhnaya
Netlyanaya ulitsa
GluKho Darskoye Shosse
Melnichnaya ulitsa
Professora

FINDING YOUR WAY

*From the Admiralty, St Petersburg's main streets radiate like the spokes
of a wheel; the canals and other streets cross these spokes
running parallel to the main channel of the Neva*

Map
on pages
114–115

None of the great 19th-century imperial powers could boast that its capital stood on 42 islands and isles – that is, except for St Petersburg, the capital of the Russian Empire. As the years went by, St Petersburg first surrendered its status as a capital to Moscow, then it even lost its name.

But it has never lost its fame as the Venice of the North and with good reason: Nevsky prospekt, the city's main avenue, passes over as many as four islands. Walking along Nevsky it is difficult to realise this fact – somehow, the Moika, the Fontanka and the Griboedova canals, all of which are crossed by Nevsky, do not look as if they separate one island from another.

A city of islands

The place where the island nature of the city does dawn on you is on the tip of Vasilievsky Island. If you stand on the Spit, between the two huge red Rostral Columns, with your back to the Stock Exchange (today, the Naval Museum), you have the feeling that the city is built right into the water. The islands on which downtown St Petersburg stands are united into a series of large groups by the capricious bends of the Neva.

The central group, which is also the largest, with Nevsky and nearly all of the main highlights of the town, is to your right, across the Neva. It consists of Admiralteysky (Admiralty) Island, where the Winter Palace ensemble, the Admiralty itself and St Isaac's, are situated, and the adjacent Novoadmiralteysky (New Admiralty) Island. Novaya Gollandiya (New Holland), Kolomensky, Matisov, Kazansky, Pokrovsky and Spassky islands, all lie to the west, where they are embraced by St Petersburg's largest island, called Bezymianny (Nameless). This downtown group also includes the isles on which the Summer Garden, the Field of Mars and the Alexander Nevsky Monastery, at the eastern end of Nevsky prospekt, are built.

The second group of islands, to your left, is called the Petrograd Side. The eye is immediately caught by Zayachy (Hare) Island, where the majestic Peter and Paul Fortress stands. The other islands on that side are Petrovsky, Krestovsky, Aptekarsky, Yelaginsky and Kamenny. Kirov Park stands on Yelagin Island. Kamenny (Stone) Island, formerly known as Worker's Island, is where the elite of St Petersburg built their dachas.

Standing at the Spit, you are on Vasilievsky Island. This is part of the Baltic shoreline. You'll find the Sea Terminal and one of the town's best hotels, the Pribaltiskaya at the Gavan (Harbour).

LEFT: the golden spires of the city.
RIGHT: a view across the Neva towards Vasilievsky Island.

Getting around

Since the upper layers of the city are unstable (Peter built St Petersburg on bogs and marshlands), it was decided that a deep Metro would be both cheaper and easier to build than a more shallow one. Construction started in 1940, but the war froze the project, and the first line did not come into operation until 1955. Today, four lines cover some 150 km (90 miles). On the map each subway line seems to cross the Neva but, in fact, the river passes quite a way above.

Besides going under the river, you can, naturally, also go on the river – there is certainly water enough. Summertime traffic on the water is heavy. Unfortunately, most of the city's rivers and canals are too narrow for river-going passenger transport, but they are just right for small launches, which will take you on an exciting water-tour of this Northern Venice. You only have to strike a bargain with one of the numerous boatman along the quay in front of the Winter Palace.

Official routes run along the Neva, the Bolshaya (Greater), Malaya (Little) and Srednyaya (Middle) Nevka to Krestovsky Island and into the centre of St Petersburg's archipelago. Should you want to go on a longer trip, you can take the hydrofoil to Peterhof (Petrodvoretz).

In addition, St Petersburg has buses and trams, but they are often slow and unreliable. Minibus taxis with fixed routes take 10 passengers and offer better service than the city bus lines. Then there are taxis, with or without meters. The latter, most of whom are regular drivers trying to earn some extra cash to make ends meet, are more numerous and cheaper than official licensed taxis but it is wise to have some idea of the correct fare before you start your journey. Suburban trains, often dirty and overcrowded, can take you to any of St Petersburg's satellite towns.

The main streets

Nevsky prospekt is the main artery or, rather, the backbone of downtown St

BELOW: aristocratic mansions on the Fontanka.

Map
on pages
114–115

Petersburg. It starts at Dvortsovy (Palace) Bridge, which links Vasilievsky and Admiralteysky Islands, runs across ploshchad Vosstaniya or Uprising Square, and ends in Alexander Nevsky Square. To one side of the square is the entrance to the Alexander Nevsky Monastery; the Moskva Hotel occupies the other side. The section of Nevsky between Dvortsovaya and Ploshchad Vosstaniya forms a perfectly straight line.

The largest avenues act as the city's "ribs" to Nevsky's "spine". Running at right angles to Dvortsovy Bridge and Nevsky are two embankments, Dvortsovaya naberezhnaya and Angliyskaya naberezhnaya (English Embankment). In the place where Nevsky crosses Sadovaya Street (Garden Street), you will find, in a large rectangular two-storey building, the Gostiny dvor department store.

Further on, Liteyny (Foundry) and Vladimirsky Avenues, Marata Street and Mayakovskovo Street branch off to the left and right from Nevsky. After that,

Nevsky continues and crosses the Ligovsky prospekt intersection. From Alexander Nevsky Square, two streets start out in opposite directions along the Neva embankment - Sinopskyaya Embankment and prospekt Obukhovskoy Oborony. On the far side of the Neva, Zanevsky prospekt continues where Nevsky leaves off; the street that crosses it at right angles and runs along the bank is called Malookhotinsky prospekt.

Further to the south, Komsomolskaya Square is the starting point for two other thoroughfares - Marshal Zhukov prospekt, which leads to the Tallinn Highway, and Krasnoputilovskaya Street, which leads to the Moscow Highway via Victory Square (Ploshchad Pobedy). Prospekt Stachek itself leads to the Peterhof Highway.

From the Petrograd and Vyborg sides several important roads stretch out to the north. Near the Field of Mars, Troitsky Bridge (Trinity Bridge) links Dvortsovaya Embankment to the starting point of Kamennoostrovsky prospekt, the main

BELOW:
mansions on
the Moika.

artery of the Petrograd Side. Bolshoy Sampsonievsky prospekt (formerly Marx prospekt), which starts at Lenin Square, close to the Finland Station on Vyborg side, continues as Engels prospekt and brings you to the Vyborg Highway, which leads to the city of Vyborg and eventually to Finland.

From the city centre the avenue can also be reached via Liteyny prospekt over Liteyny Bridge crossing the Vyborg Embankment. Suzdalsky prospekt and Rustaveli Street form a semi-circle to the northeast of the city.

The original layout

St Petersburg grew up around the Peter and Paul Fortress on Zayachy Island. The first houses were built near the fortress, on the Neva shoreline, of what was later named the Petrograd Side. Admiralty House was then built on the left bank of the Neva. In the early 18th century, three avenues fanned out from that spot - Nevsky prospekt, Voznesensky prospekt, and Gorokhovaya Street. The architects of the first master layout of 1737, Pyotr Yeropkin, Mikhail Zemtsov and Ivan Korobov, figured that the trident formed by these three avenues would be the backbone of future construction. Their plan was to build separate areas for the "noble" and the "base" classes. The plan also envisaged further construction of administrative buildings on Vasilievsky Island.

The next master plan was prepared by a group of architects led by Alexei Kvasov (1763–69). This time, emphasis was laid on regulated patterns. The plan was approved and became the basic grid for further construction.

Architectural wonders

If urban development can be compared to the stages of human life, then the time of youth and bloom for St Petersburg was the second half of the 18th and the first half of the 19th century. It was then that the city's main architectural wonders were built – Dvortsovaya Square with the Alexander

BELOW: the former Stock Exchange on the Spit.

Map on pages 114–115

Column and the Winter Palace, the Kazan Cathedral, the square known today as Ostrovskovo Square, the Alexander Nevsky Monastery and the Smolny ensemble.

The middle of the 19th century is associated by local people with three major projects: Blagoveschensky Bridge, St Isaac's Cathedral and the Petersburg Railway. All three, St Isaac's in particular, took decades to complete. Sceptics called the bridge project a swindle and prophesied that it would collapse immediately after its opening.

Public opinion on the subject was reflected by the wits of the day, who said, "We'll see the bridge over the Neva, but our children won't. The railroad, our children will see, but we won't. And neither we nor our children will see St Isaac's completed." The second half of the 19th century brought an incredible boom in speculative housing and amusement establishments, along with numerous banks and industrial enterprises.

Returning to our human-life analogy, the city of the late 19th century was the young and energetic bon vivant, who had just developed a taste for entrepreneurial activity and had suddenly started earning good money.

The builders of today's (still growing) St Petersburg continue their predecessors' task. Day by day they spin the web of streets, tie the knots of squares, thread the beads of buildings. All this, however, takes place in the suburbs – though a small number of elite apartment buildings are going up in the centre these days to cater to the new aristocracy. But there is even more restoration work in the central part of town as the city fathers spruce the city up for 2003.

In the late 1980s, St Petersburg had over 1,800 avenues, boulevards, streets, side streets and quays with a nett length of over 2,000 km (1,200 miles). The longest streets in the city are the Obukhovskoy Oborony prospekt and the Moscow and Leninsky prospekts, each of which is roughly 10 km (6 miles) long.

In Peter's time, over 40 large and small rivers threaded the city, serving as thoroughfares. But even such an impressive

number of waterways could not satisfy all the city's transport needs. Hence the 20-odd man-made canals and ditches, regarded today as souvenirs of the past epoch.

A city of bridges

Peter prohibited the construction of bridges for fear of hampering navigation on the Neva. In 1727 the Tsar died, and the first bridge across the Neva was built. It stood on floats and could be moved to make way for shipping.

By the time it finally became clear that the first solid bridge, the Blagoveschensky most (bridge), would not collapse after all, the floating bridge lost its importance. It was still used until 1916, when it burned to the ground (or, rather, to the water) after a stray spark flew out of the funnel of a passing tug.

Today, the number of bridges in St Petersburg – over 100 – far exceeds the number of rivers and canals. The bridges on the Neva can be raised to let larger vessels through.   ❑

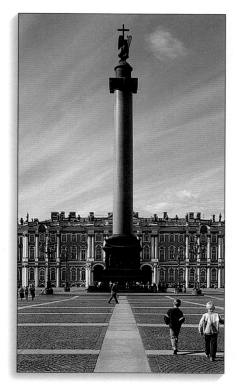

RIGHT: the Alexander Column and the Winter Palace.

Map on pages 126–127

ALONG THE EMBANKMENT

Some of St Petersburg's most spectacular sights are to be found in this once most fashionable part of the city along the banks of the Neva

St Petersburg's imperial heritage is best seen along the quays of the Neva's left bank. It is customary to start a visit to the city with the **Medny Vsadnik ❶** (the *Bronze Horseman* – an equestrian statue of Peter the Great) on ploshchad Dekabristov (Decembrists' Square) – it was, after all, Peter who founded the city.

The *Bronze Horseman*, the square's visual centre, looked down on the events of 14 December 1825, the date of the Decembrists' abortive Revolution. In the Soviet era, most of the old names gave way to new ones that were, directly or indirectly, connected with the Revolution and the post-revolutionary era.

It would only be just to say that even the conservative tsarist system had trouble finding an appropriate name for the square. Its original name was Senatskaya (the Senate was the highest state body in tsarist Russia).

Next to the Senate, there was the Synod – the highest authority in the Russian Orthodox Church, established by Peter the Great to replace the office of the Patriarch, and which existed up to the 1917 Revolution. When the monument to Peter was opened in 1782, the square was renamed Petrovskaya. But, somehow, the name did not stick, and in 1825 it was once more called Senatskaya. Today, however, city fathers have refrained from returning to that name, and it retains the Soviet-era name, Decembrists' Square.

The Decembrists

On 19 November 1825, Emperor Alexander I died suddenly. By 14 December, a group of progressively minded officers of the Imperial Guard decided to take power. The rebels assembled the troops under their command in Senate Square, and deployed them in square formation around the statue of the *Bronze Horseman*. Then the unexpected happened. The senators, who had been warned about the coming rebellion, hurriedly swore allegiance to the new emperor, Nicholas I, and left the building. The initiative had been taken from the rebels. Nicholas ordered the troops loyal to him to attack. By six o'clock that evening, the insurrection was over. The surviving rebels filled the dungeons of the Peter and Paul Fortress that night. Five of them were later sentenced to death and more than 500 to hard labour. The Decembrists, as the rebels came to be known, were later seen as early revolutionaries, hence the eventual renaming of the square after them.

But let us return to the monument. Sculptor Etienne Falconet started work-

ing on it in 1768. In compliance with the desire of Empress Catherine II (who is mentioned in the inscription in Russian and Latin, Petro Primo Catherina Secunda, on two sides of the pedestal), he aimed to personify enlightened absolutism in his statue of the monarch leading the country along the road of progress. Catherine, as historians will confirm, aspired to this image herself, and corresponded with progressive French writers, such as Voltaire.

Falconet became totally absorbed in his task. To give him an insight into the dynamics of movement, accomplished horseman reared their mounts, the prize stallions of the royal stables, Diamond and Caprice, in full gallop.

When Falconet drew his sketches, he made the grooms hold the horses motionless on a specially made platform. An illustrious cavalry general, who resembled Peter in body and build, endlessly posed for Falconet until the sculptor finally decided how to cast his statue.

Decembrists' Square

To the right of the monument stands the yellow edifice that was once the home of the Senate and the Synod, the **Rossiisky Gosudarstvenny Istorichesky Arkhiv ❷** (Central State Historical Buildings). In 1829–34, Carlo Rossi redesigned the entire complex, his last large project. Architect Staubert managed the actual construction. The new project reflected the tastes of the tsar and the Synod. The buildings were united by a baroque, statue-decorated arch. Colonnades were erected, and statues of Justice, Piety and other allegorical figures appeared on the facade as symbols of the united might of secular and clerical power.

In 1955 the buildings got their "historical content" back. They were turned over to the Central State Historical Archive of the USSR (now of Russia), which is responsible for millions of documents pertaining to the activities of central state authorities since the early 18th century. Deeper into the square, two columns mark

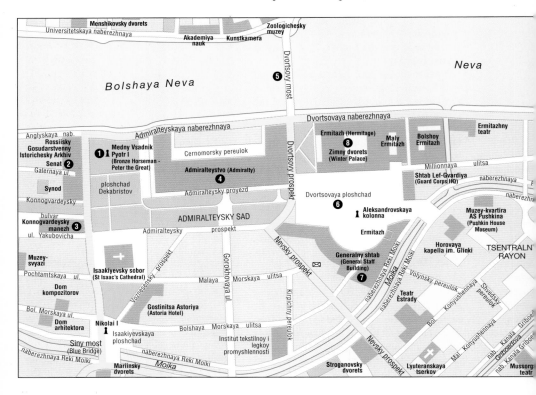

Map on pages 126–127

the beginning of what was once a canal. Later it was filled in and is now called Konnogvardeysky bulvar after the building with the eight-column portico on the corner that used to be the riding school of the Cavalry Guard, and which is now the **Konnogvardeysky manezh** ❸ (Horseguards' Manége; open Fri–Wed 11am–7pm; entrance fee).

The Admiralty

Returning to Decembrists' Square, we continue our walk along the Palace Quay. The **Admiralteystvo** ❹ (Admiralty), on the other side of Decembrists' square, is now a naval academy. It is a tremendous building that stretches along Admiraltesyskaya naberezhnaya (Admiralty Embankment) for 407 metres (1,300 ft); each of its two wings is 163 metres (535 ft) long. The Admiralty's form resembles a backwards letter E, though don't mistake the separate apartment buildings, built along the embankment in the late 19th century, to be part of it. Considered a

major architectural accomplishment at the time it was built, the international community shares this opinion today: the Admiralty is now on the UNESCO list of masterpieces of world architecture.

The history of the Admiralty dates to the early days of the city, when Peter ordered the construction of a fortress on the side of the former Admiralty yard in 1707. In 1738, it was redesigned under the guidance of Ivan Korobov, who preserved the layout but reinforced the structures of the building and made the spire taller. The significance and central situation of the Admiralty cried out for a more formidable structure, so Andrean Zakharov prepared a reconstruction plan in 1801. The architect struck the best possible proportions in order to play down the monotony of the facade and make it attractive to the eye.

The new Admiralty was to symbolise the maritime might of the Russian empire, as the numerous sculptures on the facade show. The arch is crowned by the statue of Victory with flags. Somewhat higher, in the centre of the bas-relief entitled Virgin of the Russian Fleet, Peter the Great accepts Neptune's trident as a symbol of supremacy on the high seas. The corners of the cube-shaped tower carry sculptures of the great military leaders of antiquity – Achilles, Ajax, Pyrrhus and Alexander the Great. In all, there are 56 large sculptures and 11 bas-reliefs. The Admiralty is still connected with the navy. The Dzerzhinsky Higher Naval School has owned the building since 1925.

Pointed like a needle, the Admiralty's spire is crowned by a frigate-shaped weathervane. This frigate has now become the city's emblem. There is one drawback to the Admiralty building: there is no spot left today from which the entire building can be observed in its full splendour. According to the rules of fortification (the Admiralty was originally planned as part of the city's defences), it was prohibited to build houses in the immediate vicinity so as to make it impossible for an enemy to approach the fortress under cover. The rules were observed but the open space around the building gradually filled with trees; these now make up the

Along the Embankment

0   300 m

0   300 yds

Troitsky most

Neva

❶❶

Dvortsovaya naberezhnaya

❶❶ Mramorny dvorets (Marble Palace)

nnichesky institut

Millionnaya ul.

Aptekarsky pereulok

Institut Kultury im. Krupskoy

naberezhnaya Kutuzova

Letny dvorets-muzey Petra I (Summer Palace) ❶❹

A.V. Suvorov

MARSOVO POLE ❾

naberezhnaya Lebyazhyevo Kanala

Lebyazyy Kanal

I.A. Krylov

Borcam revolyucii

LETNY SAD ❶❸

(SUMMER GARDEN)

Fontanka

Reki Fontanki

Moika

(FIELD OF MARS)

naberezhnaya Reki Moiki

Moika

naberezhnaya

Oruzheynike Fedorova ul.

Gangutskaya ul.

Solyanoy pereulok

Khram Spasa-na-Krovi (Church on the Spiled Blood)

MIKHAYLOVSKY SAD

Pestelya ul.

Panteleymonskaya tserkov

Muzey Gangutsky

Russky muzey (Russian Museum)

Sadovaya ul.

Mikhailovsky zamok - Inzhenerny zamok (Engineers' Castle) ❶❷

Pestelya ul.

Admiralty Park and effectively block the view of the Admiralty from Dvortsovaya Square. The view from the opposite bank of the Neva was spoiled in the late 19th century by the Minister of the Navy who sold it into private hands, "with criminal unconcern", as the papers complained at the time, the land between the wings of the Admiralty. The empty space quickly filled with apartment buildings.

Along Palace Quay

Moving from Decembrists' Square along Admiralty Embankment, we soon reach **Dvortsovy most** ❺ (Palace Bridge). Beyond the bridge lies the building that was once the sanctuary of supreme power and the coordinating centre of the vast Russian Empire for two centuries. There, stretched out along Dvortsovaya (Palace) Embankment, is the luxurious residence of the tsars – the Winter Palace.

If we leave the quay, we can walk along the street between the wing of the Admiralty and the side facade of the Winter Palace. Up ahead, we shall see **Dvortsovaya ploshchad** ❻ (Palace Square) with the Alexander Column against the background of the gigantic inverted half-circle of the General Staff Building.

The huge Palace Square – which became the arena for the events of 25 October 1917 (7 November according to the new calendar), events which influenced the destinies of both Russia and the world at large – has an area of 59,964 sq. metres (645,447 sq. ft).

On the night of 25 October the cruiser Aurora fired a signal charge, the cue for troops loyal to the Military-Revolutionary Committee of Petrograd to cross the square and arrest the provisional government inside the Winter Palace. Previously the provisional government had ignored the Committee's ultimatum to surrender its authority. The operation was nearly bloodless (6 killed, 50 wounded). The Government was arrested and the Bolsheviks seized power in a coup d'etat. A new epoch had begun in the land of Russia.

BELOW: facade detail of the General Staff Building.

Map on pages 126–127

One account says that when the main forces of the operation stormed the palace they found a unit of revolutionary seamen already there; the sailors had infiltrated the building through the sewer system. Some witty people use this story to claim that "the Revolution was ushered in through a sewer".

The Alexander Column

But let us now leap back another century in the square's history, to 1812. Russian troops drove Napoleon's army from their native country all the way back to Paris. Something grandiose had to be erected to commemorate their historic victory. In September 1812, it was decided to set up a triumphal column in the middle of the square. Ironically, the design that won the contest belonged to French architect Auguste Montferrand.

Work on the **Aleksandrovskaya kolonna** (Alexander Column) started only in 1830 and took four years. It took three years to cut the granite monolith, weigh-ing some 700 tons, out of a rock face on the Karelian Peninsula, and then eventu-ally transport it to Palace Square. In 1832, under the guidance of the craftsmen who had also installed the columns of St Isaac's, over 2,000 volunteers (partici-pants in the war against Napoleon) and 400 builders raised the column on the pedestal with the help of an intricate sys-tem of ropes and pulleys. The installation took all of 100 minutes, even though preparations had taken much longer. The column is not attached to the pedestal; to this day, it stands in place under its own weight, which was reduced to 650 tons after smoothing and polishing.

The column rises 47.5 metres (156 ft) above the ground, outscoring its rivals in other capitals, including the 44.5-metre (146-ft) Trajan Column in Rome and the 46-metre (151-ft) Vendome Column in Paris. The figure of an angel was mounted on top of the column. The statue was cre-ated by Boris Orlovsky to symbolise the peace that had come to Europe after the

BELOW: raising the Alexander Column in 1832.

victory over Napoleon's armies. In 1834 work was completed and the inauguration ceremony was finally held.

The base is decorated with bas-reliefs by P. Svintsov and I. Leppe (they used drawings by Giovanni Scotti). The bas-reliefs depict the rivers that the Russian troops had to cross in pursuit of Napoleon, and allegories of Wisdom, Plenty, Victory, Peace and Justice. The column is the knot that holds together the architectural ensemble of the square. The square means a lot to the people of St Petersburg and is much favoured by tourists. People come here to celebrate – or to protest.

In the tragic days of December 1989, when the country lost human rights activist, Andrei Sakharov, hundreds of people came here to mourn him. In the evening, in accordance with Christian tradition, scores of candles were lit around the column.

And in August 1991, when hard-line communists attempted a putsch against Mikhail Gorbachev, over 100,000 people flooded into the square to protest this attempt to crush Russia's nascent democracy and turn back the clock.

Around the column

The impetuosity of line and the imposing dimensions of the **Generalny shtab** ❼ (General Staff Building), which formed the background for the Alexander Column when we looked at it from the Winter Palace and the Admiralty, fills one with a sense of the spirit of the empire. Once again, that spirit found expression in stone under the hands of a famous Italian.

In 1819, Carlo Rossi set out to transform the Dvortsovaya Square ensemble into a showcase for the monarch to rest his eye upon if he chanced to look out of a window in the Winter Palace. Ever the master of extra-large architecture, Rossi got down to his task. He redesigned the facades, whose overall length totalled 2 km (1¼ miles). The inverted half-circle was 580 metres (1,900 ft) long.

He designed a triumphal arch in honour of the victory over Napoleon, which blended both buildings into a single whole. They were supposed to house the Ministries of Foreign Affairs and Finance, and the General Staff.

An impressive 10-metre (33-ft) tall sculpture, the chariot of winged Glory drawn by six horses, was installed on top of the arch. Stepan Pimenov and Vasily Demut-Malinovsky created the sculptures.

The sceptical and the envious said that the arch would collapse under the weight of the bronze statues on top. But Rossi, who had no reason to doubt the accuracy of his calculations, assured Emperor Nicholas I that if the arch went he would go with it. They say that on the day the arch finally stood without supports, the architect climbed to the top of the structure to show everyone its sturdiness. Note that the arch is actually made up of two arches, which run at an angle to each other – yet the structure does not appear incongruous.

The Hermitage museum recently acquired the eastern wing of the General Staff Building, totalling 40,000 sq metres (47,800 sq yds), and is now restoring it at

LEFT: the archway of the General Staff Building.

Map on pages 126–127

a cost of about $150 million. Some rooms are already open to the public. The renovation project is in cooperation with New York's Guggenheim Museum of modern art, which in 2000 signed a five-year strategic alliance with the Hermitage to develop joint projects at sites around the world, including common exhibition space in Las Vegas. The General Staff Building will house the Hermitage's decorative arts collection, as well as its Impressionist and Post-Impressionist collection, while some rooms will be dedicated to contemporary art – a departure for the usually traditional Hermitage.

Before we turn our gaze towards the Winter Palace, let us examine another building, the one between the Hermitage and the General Staff Building on the other side of the square. The building is the **Shtab Lef-Gvardiya** (Headquarters of the Guard Corps), built in 1837–43 by Alexander Bryullov. Its greatest merit is its modesty and total harmony with the rest of the ensemble.

BELOW: corner of the General Staff Building on Palace Square.

The Winter Palace

Construction of the **Zimny dvorets** ❽ (Winter Palace; open Mon–Wed, Fri, Sat 10.30am–6pm; Thurs noon–8pm; closed Mon; entrance fee) was started in 1754 during the reign of Peter's daughter, Elizabeth, who wanted the residence to demonstrate Russia's growing might. It was completed in 1762, in the reign of Catherine the Great, who ascended the throne after the death of her husband, Peter III, himself assassinated (with the blessing of his tender and loving wife) after 12 months in power.

The famous Italian architect Bartholomeo Rastrelli built the Winter Palace, considered a yardstick of the Russian baroque. He made a point of writing later that the palace "had been built exclusively to the greater glory of Russia." The telltale signs of the Russian baroque include the alternately projecting and sunken elements of the facade, curves, abundant sculpture and decoration and the invariable two-colour painting pattern. In

1838–39 the palace was restored by architects Vasily Stasov and Alexander Bryullov after the 1837 fire.

In order to give off a sense of power, a building must be large. And large it appears today, even in the age of skyscrapers and concrete high-rises. This is what the figures say: length – roughly 200 metres (656 ft); width – 160 metres (525 ft); length of the perimeter cornice – 2 km (1¼ miles); height – 22 metres (72 ft). The palace has 1,057 rooms with a net area of 46,516 sq. metres (500,000 sq. ft), 117 staircases, 1,786 doorways and 1,945 windows. The interior is decorated with polished marble, lapis lazuli, malachite, porphyry, jasper and other semi-precious stones. Other materials used in the interior decoration include bronze, crystal, gilt, rare woods and tapestries.

Catherine, as well as all of her successors, preferred the Winter Palace as her residence. Pavel I was the only exception: haunted by fears of assassination, he moved from the Winter Palace to the Mikhailovsky Castle (which he had built as a safer place) – and was killed there.

In the last quarter of the 19th century, when the revolutionary movement was dominated by terrorist acts, the tsar almost met his end in the Winter Palace. Stepan Khalturin, a young carpenter on the palace staff, smuggled small amounts of dynamite into the palace on orders from the terrorist Norodnaya Volya (People's Will) group until eventually enough was accumulated for his purpose.

The bomb went off under the tsar's dining room, and the only thing that saved Alexander II's life was that the usually punctual tsar was a few minutes late for lunch. The terrorists finally killed him in 1881, however. Ignaty Grinetsky threw a bomb at him as he stepped out of his carriage, mortally wounding the tsar and killing himself in the process.

The Hermitage

After 1917, the Winter Palace was looted and interiors defaced and neglected, in

BELOW: the Winter Palace.

Map on pages 126–127

line with the Bolshevik policy and attitudes toward anything connected to the old regime. The grand palace was turned into a movie theatre, a House of Culture and Recreation for the workers, and even for some time housed a museum to the poet Alexander Pushkin. The long restoration of its lost beauty began when the building was turned over to the **Muzey Ermitazh** (Hermitage Museum; open Mon–Wed, Fri, Sat 10.30am–6pm; Thurs noon–8pm; closed Mon; entrance fee) after the Second World War.

Today, the museum (*see pages 149– 154*) also occupies several other buildings which face Millionnaya ulitsa (Millionaire's Street) and Dvortsovaya naberezhnaya: the **Ermitazhny teatr** (Hermitage Theatre, built in 1787, by Giacomo Quarenghi), formerly Catherine's personal theatre and now the museum's lecture hall; the Stary Ermitazh (Old Hermitage, built in 1775–84 by Yury Felten) and the Novy Ermitazh (New Hermitage, built 1839–1952, built by Nikolai Yefimof and Vasily Stasov in accordance with Leo von Klenze's designs).

The New Hermitage was built as Russia's first public art gallery. The museum dates to 1764, when special rooms in the Winter Palace were assigned for works of art that were purchased abroad. As far as public access of the collection was concerned, Catherine declared that only she and the palace mice could admire the pictures freely. Later the collection was made accessible to the cream of the nobility who were presented with special tickets that allowed them to come and go whenever they chose to do so.

Today, the Hermitage is one of the world's largest and richest museums. Its collection includes pieces from many historical periods, and to visit every one of its rooms would involve an excursion of nearly 20 km (13 miles).

The **Oriental Wing** displays works of art from ancient Egypt, India, Arab countries, China and the Caucasus. A separate exhibit displays the material culture of the

BELOW: a gallery in the Hermitage.

ancient Slavs – archaeological finds from Kiev, Novgorod and Pskov. The **Western Wing** has hundreds of masterpieces, including works by Leonardo, Titian, Rubens, Raphael, Van Dyck, Poussin, Rembrandt, Murillo, Watteau, Picasso, Matisse, Modigliani, Michelangelo, Canova, Falconet and Rodin.

The **Golden Treasures** is exhibited in a special section of the Hermitage; in fact an entire vault which is carefully guarded and shuts tight every night. Admittance to the vault is limited and only by guided tour which start from the main lobby of the Winter Palace at 12.15pm and 2.15pm daily. On display are 4th century BC Scythian gold figures, some of the finest ancient Greek gold jewellery in the world, and Indian and Chinese gold and gem-studded objects.

Many fine ancient Greek artefacts came to the Hermitage from the Crimea region, which Russia conquered in the late 18th century. The Crimea, as well as most of the Black Sea coast, was controlled by ancient Greek city-states, and included large cities, such as Pantikapae (now Kerch in Ukraine), which was the fourth largest ancient Greek city. British armies and archeologists pillaged Pantikapae during the Crimea War (1853–56), and many artefacts are now in the British Museum.

The Field of Mars

A 15-minute walk along the quay separates the Hermitage and the place whose name asserts that it belongs to Mars, the Roman god of war. When the city was founded, this marshy piece of land located between the source of the Moika and the Neva was ignored by the builders. Then, in 1710, when the Summer Garden was founded, the marshes were drained, yielding a flat field where nothing ever seemed to grow. It was, in fact, so out of favour with vegetation that it was dubbed the Sahara of St Petersburg.

As we look at the prolific hedges and manicured lawns of the **Marsovo Pole** ❾ (Field of Mars) today, it isn't easy to

BELOW: the Eternal Flame at the Field of Mars.

Map on pages 126–127

imagine what the place used to look like. The war god's name was given to the area at the end of the 18th century, when Pavel I started to use it as a drilling ground for his troops, as the ancient Romans did on their Field of Mars.

On 23 March 1917 (4 April by the modern calendar), a crowd set out for the Field of Mars to mourn those who had fallen in skirmishes with troops loyal to the deposed tsar. To the accompaniment of a burial march and 180 rifle salvos, the remains of 180 revolutionaries were buried there. The next day, the first stone was laid in the foundation of the future memorial. Architect Lev Rudnev completed it in the summer of 1920. In 1957, a memorial (eternal) flame was lit in the centre of the monument in honour of the Revolution's 40th anniversary. Today, however, Russians have mixed feeling toward this place. Some newly-weds do come to pay homage on the day of their wedding, but by night boisterous, irreverent youth usually gather round the flame to keep warm, to drink and play music.

The Marble Palace

On Millionaire's Street, we find the **Mramorny dvorets** ❿ (Marble Palace; closed Tues; entrance fee) built in 1768–85 by Antonio Rinaldi.

The palace was intended for the illustrious aristocrat and statesman of the 19th century, one of Catherine the Great's favourites, Grigory Orlov. In terms of architectural style, the palace is a mixture of classicist and baroque. The materials used more than make up for the relative modesty of its facade and consist of natural marble and granite (unlike most of the other buildings in the city).

In the early 1930s one of the party chieftains must have asked why such a splendid building as this was totally left out of the campaign to promote the ideas of the Revolution.

The situation was soon remedied, and a branch of the Central Lenin Museum (in Moscow) was opened here after several changes in the interior layout. Now, the Marble Palace, part of the Russian Museum, exhibits both 18th-century Russian art, as well as temporary exhibits of modern Russian and international art.

At the beginning of **Troitsky most** ⓫ (formerly Kirovsky Bridge) stands the 8-metre (26-ft) tall statue of Alexander Suvorov, the famous 18th-century general. The granite pedestal, created by Andrei Voronikhin, bears, under the figures of Glory and Peace, the inscription Prince of Italy, Count Suvorov-Rymniksky, 1801. The sculptor who worked on the statue, Mikhail Kozlovsky, didn't pay much attention to likeness in his desire to show Suvorov as the ideal warrior.

Mikhailovsky Castle

Close to the spot where the Moika joins Lebyazhy (Swan) Canal, we see, behind the trees, the building which to this day retains a patina of dread and mystery: **Mikhailovsky zamok** ⓬ (Mikhailovsky Castle; currently closed tel: 319 94 18 for information), the place where Pavel I was assassinated. Pavel hated his mother Catherine so much that when he suc-

RIGHT: the Mikhailovsky Palace.

ceeded her to the throne, he embarked on a policy that was in every way opposite to the one his mother had pursued. He liberated those Catherine had imprisoned and filled his suite with those who had been out of royal favour in the preceding reign. In doing so, he displeased too many, for Catherine had many more admirers and supporters than she did enemies. In fact, even those whom Pavel thought were close to him believed his policies erroneous and felt no gratitude to him at all. The officers of the guard, too, were angered over the Prussian-style discipline that Pavel set out to enforce in the army.

The tsar sensed that conspiracy was afoot, and feared for his life. He was afraid of the Winter Palace with its endless rooms, any of which was ideal for regicide; in addition, the palace reminded him of Catherine.

In 1797, Pavel ordered the Mikhailovsky Castle to be built on the southeast edge of the Field of Mars. The project was drafted by the great Russian architect of the

period, Vasily Bazhenov, while Italian Vincenzo Brenna supervised the work.

The castle was planned as an impenetrable fortress whose water-filled moats, dirt walls, drawbridges and secret passageway out of the castle could protect him from the conspirators. Since the castle had the protection of a natural waterway only on the north side (the Moika) and the east side (the Fontanka), canals were dug along its south and west facades. Later in the 19th century they were filled up, but city fathers have now approved plans to re-excavate them in time for 2003.

Early in 1801 the castle was ready. Pavel immediately moved in and recovered from his previous paranoia, apparently thinking that he was safe at last. But, as fate would have it, he was destined to live in the castle for a mere 40 days. On 11 March he was strangled in his bedchamber by soldiers of his own household guard, and Alexander I became tsar.

In the ensuing years, none of the Russian emperors desired to set up residence in Mikhailovsky Castle. A charity home for widows opened in the castle after the tsar's death. Soon after that it was turned over to the Military Engineers' College. The preparations for this takeover lasted for several years and when they were completed the building received the name by which it is known today, **Inzenerny zamok** (Engineers' Castle).

In the 1830s, 16-year-old Fyodor Dostoyevsky, was a cadet at the college. But the Engineer's College did not only train masters of the classic novel; many famous engineers graduated from its walls, among them Pavel Yablochkov, the inventor of the arc lamp.

The castle is now part of the Russian Museum, but is closed, under reconstruction. When it reopens it will provide additional exhibition space for Russian art, as well as show rooms dedicated to the era of Pavel I.

The Summer Garden

One can enter the **Letny Sad** ⑬ (Summer Garden; open daily 10am–8pm; closed April; entrance fee) from either the

LEFT:
a statue protected from the rain in the Summer Garden.

Map on pages 126–127

banks of the Neva river which is bordered by a famous ornamental grille, or from the side of the Inzenerny zamok (castle), from where we shall enter. This entrance has a charm of its own. For instance, there is the nearly 5-metre (16-ft) tall porphyry vase, the work of Aldvalen masters, which was presented to Nicholas I by Karl Johann, the king of Sweden, and installed in the garden in 1839. The Summer Garden is well advanced in years. Besides being the oldest part of the city it is also one of those places where the city originated and, as such, shows some of the creative drive of Peter the Great's efforts. The garden is only a year younger than the city of St Petersburg itself.

The garden was planned for the summer residence of the royal family, and Peter took a most active part in its construction. The trees and hedges were kept trimmed. The park abounded in sculptures, summer houses, fountains and pavilions. The pond at the south end had symmetrical outlines. Symmetry and geo-

metric forms were a bold innovation in 18th-century park construction.

The people who created the Summer Garden were not afraid of new fashions. By the middle of the 18th century the Summer Garden was no longer considered fit for the residence of the tsars. It became a resting place for aristocrats, and immediately started to change. Symmetry and geometry gave way to naturalistic landscapes.

In the middle of the 19th century, Nicholas I issued a special decree that regulated admission to the Summer Garden. The tsar allowed all army officers and decently dressed people to walk there. The lower classes were not permitted to go in. But if the lower classes dressed in the proper way, that rule could be bent. In the middle of the 19th century, for instance, Taras Shevchenko, the Ukrainian poet and artist who was born into a family of serfs, often came here to work. The garden was generally favoured by writers and artists. Its shady paths

BELOW: relaxing in the Summer Garden.

attracted and inspired writers like Alexander Pushkin, Vasily Zhukovsky, Ivan Krylov, Nikolai Gogol, Alexander Blok, and the future Nobel Prize winner in literature Ivan Bunin, as well as the musicians Fyodor Shaliapin, Peter Tchaikovsky and Modest Mussorgsky. One of them, the fable-writer Krylov, was even honoured with a bronze monument. This creation by Pyotr Klodt was installed in the Summer Garden in 1855.

Among the sculptures of the garden, note the 17th-century group entitled Cupid and Psyche. The sculptor depicted Psyche at that moment when she is illuminating the face of her sleeping lover. There are also sculptures of the Roman emperor Claudius, his wife Agrippina and stepson Nero. Finally, we come to the ultimate human values, portrayed in material form: Beauty, Truth, Nobility, Glory and even Victory – the garden overflows with allegorical figures, reflecting fully the eclectic spirit and classical aspirations of the 18th century.

To the right of the central avenue, as you move towards the Neva, several buildings remain intact. The first is the Coffee House, built by Carlo Rossi in 1826 in place of the grotto that had existed in Peter's time but which was later destroyed by a flood. Rossi strove to recreate the outlines of the old grotto in his design. Next comes the Tea House (1827) by Louis Charlemagne.

The Summer Palace

The **Letny dvorets** ⓮ (Summer Palace; open daily 10am–6pm, closed April; entrance fee) stands behind the Tea House and is one of St Petersburg's first stone edifices. It was built by Domenico Trezzini in 1712. Peter moved in before the decorators had finished working on the place and spent all his summers there until the day of his death in 1725. Today the Summer Palace is a museum.

The palace has a simple layout. The rooms on both floors are positioned almost identically: each floor has six halls, a kitchen, a corridor and servants' quarters. The first floor of the palace was intended for Peter's wife, Catherine, who reigned as Catherine I for two years after his death.

From the palace, whose northern entranceway is decorated with an allegorical sculpture depicting Russia's victory in the Northern War, the road takes us to the ornamental grille that runs along Kutuzova Embankment. The grille was made in 1784 by Felten and Yegorov. The influence of its ornamental pattern is felt whenever one looks at other St Petersburg ironwork. Consider, for instance, the fence around the church in the Peter and Paul Fortress, or the one near the former Bank of Issue (Nos. 30–32 Griboedora Canal). The beautiful **Summer Garden** was very nearly destroyed in 1989 when archaeologists searching for the original 18th-century appearance of the park stumbled across some unexploded German artillery shells from the time of the Blockade. The garden contains a statue of Ivan Krylov, a writer of Russian fables. Animal characters from his tales are shown in bas-relief around his statue. ❑

Map on pages 126–127

LEFT: renovating a statue in the Summer Garden. **RIGHT:** making music at the entrance to the Hermitage.

Map on page 142

DOWNTOWN

The route of this chapter starts at St Isaac's Cathedral and takes in the Mariinsky and Yusupov palaces, the Mariinsky Theatre and the St Nicholas Cathedral

Giacomo Quarenghi constructed the **Konnogvardeysky manezh** (Horse guards' Manège) between 1804 and 1807. The architect skilfully tied the edifice into the general square ensemble. In 1817, the statues of Castor and Pollux (cast by Paulo Trickorni), were installed on the facade (they are miniature copies of the statues in front of the Quirinal Palace in Rome). They did not stay for long – naked young men of dubious pagan ancestry were not wanted as neighbours by St Isaac's Cathedral, and the Synod had them removed in 1840.

After 1917, the revolutionary authorities closed St Isaac's, but the moment of triumph for the mythological heroes came only in 1954, when they were reinstalled in their old places. In 1977 the building was handed over to the Artists' Union, which opened an exhibition centre there.

St Isaac's Cathedral

Isaakiyevsky sobor ❶ (St Isaac's Cathedral; open daily 11am–6pm, closed Wed; entrance fee plus photography fee) looms majestically over Isaakievsky ploshchad (St Isaac's Square). Shining with its golden dome (it took 100 kg/220 lbs of the precious metal to cover it), it is the fourth – and final – version of the Church of Isaac Dalmatiisky, Peter the Great's patron saint. St Isaac lived in the 4th century and was punished for his Christian faith by the Roman Emperor Valens but was later set free by Emperor Theodosius.

The construction of the cathedral was started in 1818 and completed 30 years later. The interior is decorated with malachite, lapis lazuli, porphyry and other costly materials. Its walls are in some places up to 5 metres (16 ft) thick. The building has a length of 111 metres (366 ft), a width of 98 metres (320 ft) and a height of 102 metres (333 ft). Its construction cost 10 times more than the

Winter Palace. Up to 14,000 visitors can be accommodated in the cathedral at the same time.

The high reliefs in the cathedral are of exceptional beauty. On the southern pediment we find *The Adoration of the Magi* by Ivan Vitali, where Mary and the child are surrounded by the kings of Mesopotamia and Ethiopia. The relief above the western portico, *The Meeting of St Isaac of Dalmatia with the Emperor Theodosius*, is by the same sculptor (Theodosius and his wife have the features of Alexander I and his spouse).

In the corner of the relief there is a semi-naked man with a model of the cathedral in his hands; it depicts Auguste Montferrand, the architect of the edifice.

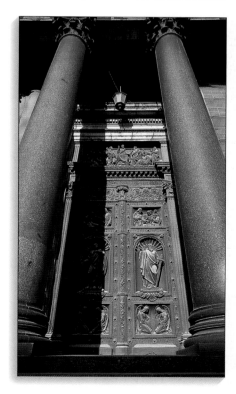

LEFT: St Isaac's Cathedral.
RIGHT: the West Door of St Isaac's.

The reliefs on the eastern and the northern pediments depict *The Meeting of St Isaac with the Emperor Valens* and *The Resurrection of Christ*, respectively.

The **kolonnada** (colonnade; entrance and photography fee) around the dome (the third largest cathedral dome in Europe) has some spectacular central views of the city.

In the centre of St Isaac's Square, in front of the cathedral, there is an equestrian **monument to Nikolai I** (1859, by Klodt and Montferrand). The wily Klodt paid lip-service to the wife and daughters of the late emperor who wanted to perpetuate an idealised image of Nicholas, though he actually created a mercilessly realistic portrait of the clever yet ruthless and cold man that the people called Nikolai Palkin ("Nicholas of the Stick").

The Nicholas I statue is perhaps the only one in Europe that stands on two points (the horse's two hind hooves); other great European equestrian statues usually stand on three (two hind hooves and the tail). Today, scholars do not understand how Klodt achieved such perfect balance, and so they fear touching and restoring it.

Around the Mariinsky Palace

Between the monument and the **Mariinsky dvorets** (Mariinsky Palace), built between 1839 and 44 by Andrei Stakenschneider for Nicholas I's daughter, Maria, and now occupied by the St Petersburg City Council, lies the **Siny most** (Blue Bridge). Unlike other bridges in the city, which are usually continuations of streets or roads, this bridge is a continuation of a square. Its width (100 metres/328 ft) makes it difficult to guess that you are standing on a bridge with the Moika flowing underneath. The bridge owes its name to the underside, which was painted blue. Siny Bridge is a place of sad fame: serfs were bought, sold and exchanged here from the 18th century until serfdom was abolished in 1861.

To the left of the cathedral, on the other

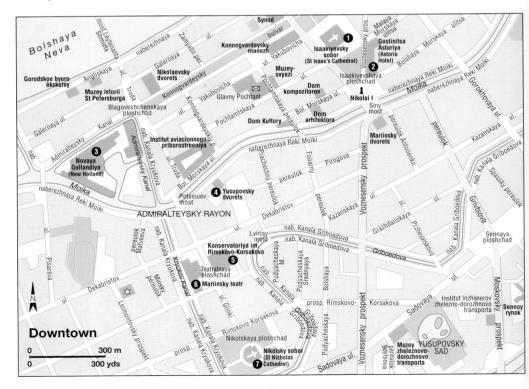

Map on page 142

side of Voznesensky prospekt, stands the **Gostinitsa Astoriya ❷** (Astoria Hotel) (1910–12). The Astoria was the best hotel in town before 1917. It was patronised by army top brass. After the Revolution, it was the turn of the party top brass. Lenin and the delegates of the Second Communist International stayed here, as did the writer H. G. Wells in 1934. Another fashionable old hotel, the Angleterre, is now a part of the Astoria. More accurately, that is where it once stood: the Angleterre was razed to the ground in 1988 following an irresponsible ruling by the Leningrad Executive Council. Even round-the-clock pickets organised by people who wanted to save the Angleterre proved futile. The hotel was demolished and rebuilt from scratch by foreign companies. It was in one of the Angleterre's rooms that the famous Russian poet, Sergei Yesenin, was found dead on 27 December 1925. The Soviet government said he committed suicide, but now scholars believe he was murdered, or at least forced into suicide.

Ploshchad Blagoveshenskaya faces the quay of the canal that separates Admiralty Island from New Holland Island. **Novaya Gollandiya ❸** (New Holland) was an ideal place for storing flammable shipbuilding materials (rope, wood, etc.) – it was close to the Admiralty and safely surrounded by water. Savva Chevakinsky, the architect who presided over the construction on the island, stacked the timber vertically rather than horizontally. The length of the timbers used by the shipbuilders varied, so he built several warehouses of several different heights.

The Yusupov Palace

Truda Street leads to Potseluev most. Nearby, on the bank of the Moika, is the yellow **Yusupovsky dvorets ❹** (Yusupov Palace; Moika Canal Embankment 94; open daily 11am–6pm; entrance fee), which was built in the 1760s by Vallin de la Mothe and Andrei Mikhailov Junior. Before the Revolution, the palace was owned by one of the wealthiest families

BELOW: the Blue Bridge on the Moika Canal.

in Russia, the Yusupovs, said to be as rich as the tsars themselves; indeed they were the imperial court's closest allies, and rewarded accordingly. That wealth was spent on building a number of Yusupov palaces throughout the city. After the Winter Palace, the palace has probably the finest interiors in the city. There is also a small theatre, where concerts are held regularly. The Yusupov palace on the Moika witnessed one of the most ghastly episodes of the tsarist era.

Grigory Rasputin

In 1907, the Rector of the St Petersburg Spiritual Academy introduced Grigory Rasputin to the court. Under the guise of a starets (holy man), who posed as a faith healer, Rasputin was the ultimate conman, devoid of any trace of decency. Some contemporaries said that he had almost hypnotic power that put the royal family under his power.

He established a particularly strong hold over the Empress, who blindly

believed that only the prayers of the "holy man" could save the life of her haemophiliac son, Prince Alexei, and help her husband with affairs of state.

The uneducated Rasputin was soon enmeshed in the dirty dealings of the various political forces around the throne, and he served to destabilise further the already rocky boat of Russian politics. For a fee Rasputin could get rid of ministers, including cabinet members, organise deals and distribute state orders. Rasputin's wild orgies were even talked about abroad. His imagination knew no bounds where sex was concerned. The least of his "innocent pranks" was to arrange several naked girls on the floor in the form of a cross.

In an attempt to save the crumbling monarchy and lead the country away from disaster, several influential people, including Felix Yusupov, State Duma Deputy Vladimir Purishkevich and the Tsar's relative, Grand Prince Dmitry Pavlovich, decided to rid the nation of Rasputin.

In the small hours of 17 December 1916, the holy man was lured to Yusupov's palace and given cakes laced with cyanide. Some time passed, but the Siberian demon exhibited no inclination to leave this world. Shaken, the conspirators must have explained this as the intervention of the Devil himself, for they could not have known then that the sugar contained in the cakes weakened or neutralised the poison's toxic effects.

They were, nevertheless, sober-minded people, and they decided to shoot Rasputin. He was aware, by this time, that something was afoot and tried to get away from the palace. They shot him several times, tied the body with a rope, and dropped the bundle into the waters of the Moika. When the body was found later, it was learned even that had not been enough for Rasputin – dropped into the icy water, he had nearly managed to extricate himself from the knots that held him. Yusupov had to flee the country after the plot was uncovered.

The palace now houses an exhibition dedicated to Rasputin and the grisly events which took place here that fateful day in December 1916.

LEFT: Grigory Rasputin.

Map on page 142

Theatre Square

From New Holland and the Yusupov Palace, our route leads over Potseluev most into Teatralnaya ploshchad (Theatre Square). The square derives its name from the artistic establishments that are situated there – the Mariinsky Theatre and the Rimsky-Korsakov Conservatoire.

The square's theatrical history dates to the middle of the 18th century. In 1782, a stone structure was built in place of the old wooden theatre. In 1783, Catherine the Great said that the theatre was "intended not only for comedy and tragedy, but for opera as well", and it was named the Bloshoy Theatre.

In 1803, the opera and ballet troupes were separated off from the drama group. For nearly a third of a century after that the Italian conductor and composer, Caterino Cavos, headed the opera troupe. The ballet troupe was managed until 1829 by the French ballet master, Charles Didelot. The ballet stars of the early 19th century were Yevgenia Kolosova, an accomplished performer of folk dances, and Avdotia Istomina, to whom Pushkin dedicated a few lines of poetry and who performed ballets written in accordance with plots the poet supplied. In 1836, when Mikhail Glinka's *Ivan Susanin* (*Life for the Tsar*) was produced on the Bloshoy's stage, the theatre ushered in the new age of Russian classical opera.

The **Konservatoriya imeni Rimskovo-Korsakova** ❺ (Rimsky-Korsakov Conservatoire; open for performances only) was founded in 1862 by the composer Anton Rubinstein and renamed after Rimsky-Korsakov in 1944. It became the first establishment for higher musical education in Russia. The list of the school's graduates is adorned with the names of Tchaikovsky and Shostakovich, among other famed composers.

Mariinsky Theatre

Meanwhile, an enormous new theatre was built in Moscow in 1825, also called the Bloshoy. The Moscow Bloshoy produced

BELOW: statue of Rimsky-Korsakov.

Map on page 142

operas and ballets by Russian and foreign authors and featured renowned masters of the stage, but St Petersburg was not about to be outdone.

It needed a new opera, and one that could rival Moscow's Bolshoy. The right building was found in front of the Conservatoire. Albert Cavos helped restore the burned-down building in 1859, redecorated it, and the **Mariinsky teatr** ❻ (Mariinsky Theatre, also known as the Kirov; open for performances only), named in honour of Alexander II's wife Maria, was born the following year.

The theatre proved a formidable rival for the Bloshoy. At the end of the 19th and the beginning of the 20th century, its stage saw performances by the Russian ballet stars Anna Pavlova, Matilda Kseshinskaya, Vatslav Nijinsky and Tamara Karsavina, the sister of Lev Karsavin, the religious philosopher. Tamara Karsavina was vice-president of the Royal Dance Academy in London between 1930 and 1955. Fyodor Shaliapin and Leonid Sobinov performed on the Mariinsky stage. Marius Petipas and Lev Ivanov were directors here and the Konstantin Korovin/Alexander Golovin team painted the sets.

After the Revolution the theatre went through hard times, since many members of the troupe emigrated. Then things took a turn for the better. In the Soviet era it gained new popularity thanks to composers Prokofiev and Khachaturian, the ballet stars Galina Ulanova and Vakhtang Chabukiani and the conductors Yevgeny Mravinsky and Vladimir Dranishnikov. During this period the theatre achieved world renown as the Kirov.

Today, the theatre is thriving once again under the leadership of Valeri Gergiev, who has built up the opera repertoire with many new productions, especially works by Verdi and Wagner. Every June, for the entire month, Gergiev presides over the White Nights Festival which brings the world's top opera and ballet performers to the banks of the Neva. The theatre is now in the midst of a $150 million expansion and modernisation programme, that includes taking over neighbouring buildings, such as the Pyatiletka House of Culture, and even New Holland, where maestro Gergiev, who is a friend of President Putin, plans to build a world class performing arts centre.

Cathedral of St Nicholas

Beside Kryukov Canal in Nikolskaya ploshchad (St Nicholas Square), is the blue and gold **Nikolsky Morskoy sobor** ❼ (Cathedral of St Nicholas; open daily for services) otherwise known as the "Saolor's Church" (the Sailor's Church), built between 1753 and 1762 by Savva Chevakinsky.

This working cathedral is often compared with Rastrelli's Smolny Cathedral and is considered to be one of the finest examples of Russian baroque. The cathedral is split into two churches on upper and lower floors. The low, vaulted exterior is beautifully decorated with icons by Fedot and Menas Kolokolnikov. In the ground of the cathedral is the bell tower, crowned by a spire. ❑

LEFT: St Nicholas Cathedral. **RIGHT:** ironwork detail at the Mariinsky Theatre.

THE HERMITAGE

*The Hermitage is one of the world's most richly endowed museums
and contains magnificent art treasures – yet only one-twentieth
of its collection can be put on display at any one time*

There are only a few museums of this class in the world – perhaps the Louvre in Paris, the British Museum in London and the Metropolitan Museum of Art in New York. The Hermitage *(see page 132)* is not only one of the great repositories of world art but, unlike the other three great museums of the world, it was both an imperial residence and a family home. Indeed, parts of the museum, especially in those rooms where the imperial family lived, have a warmth which is not found in the large halls of the Louvre or the Met.

The facts and figures about the Hermitage are astounding: it has nearly 400 exhibition halls and is annually attended by more than 2 million visitors, who would have to walk over 20 km (13 miles) to view the displays in all the halls. It is impossible to list all the treasures kept in the Hermitage, which total about 3 million items. In fact, only 5 percent of the collection is on display. About 1 million items are coins and medals – one of the largest numismatic collections in the world – but of most interest to visitors are the 15,000 paintings, 12,000 sculptures, 600,000 works of graphic art, and 224,000 works of applied art. The Hermitage library, one of the world's largest depositories of books on art, runs into no less than half a million volumes.

While quantity in art means little, the Hermitage collections include top-class masterpieces. Judge for yourself. Among them are the Madonnas by Raphael and Leonardo da Vinci, Giorgione's *Judith*, Titian's *St Sebastian*, a sculpture by Michelangelo, and 24 paintings by Rembrandt, including such all-time stars as *The Return of the Prodigal Son* and *Flora*.

The Hermitage contains one of the world's finest collections of the French impressionists and post-impressionists. Classical sculptures, Egyptian mummies that lay buried underground for several millennia and superb pieces of Scythian gold are also to be seen here. In short, the Hermitage has unique exhibits dating from every period between the late Stone Age and our own day.

Fine architecture

Now add to this the interior decoration of the Hermitage with its magnificent marble stairways and columns, parquet floors of rare beauty, ceilings ornamented with fancy gilt stucco moulding and period furniture. Vases, standard lamps and tables made of ornamental stones – true *chefs-d'oeuvre* executed by Russian and European masters – alone number upwards of 400. The halls, the most famous among

them being the Malachite Hall, are also decorated with coloured stone. The architectural appearance of the complex of buildings housing the Hermitage today is majestic. They were constructed in two stages, in the second half of the 18th century and in the mid-19th century. They reflect the changes in artistic taste and architectural style that took place with the transition from baroque to neoclassicism.

The embankment of the Neva offers a magnificent view of the grandiose Winter Palace, the small pavilion of the Lesser Hermitage standing nearby and the so-called Old Hermitage. The arch over the Winter Canal, well-known to lovers of the opera and traditionally associated with the scenery for Peter Tchaikovsky's opera *The Queen of Spades*, serves as a passage leading to the Hermitage Theatre. This splendid and world-famous ensemble was created by four outstanding 18th-century architects – Bartolomeo Rastrelli, Yuri Velten, Jean-Baptiste Vallin de la Mothe, and Giacomo Quarenghi.

A private collection

The Hermitage was initially set up as the private museum of Empress Catherine the Great. In the 18th century, the setting up of royal picture galleries was regarded as an affair of national importance in the countries of Europe. Catherine the Great started her gallery a year after her ascension to the throne in 1762. Though she began to collect art later than the other European monarchs, no expense was spared for the purpose.

Undoubtedly, not the least part in this was played by political considerations. The empress needed to enhance the prestige of the Russian court. After the acquisition of the first lot of canvases by Dutch and Flemish painters in Berlin, systematic purchases of works of art at auctions in Paris and The Netherlands began. This task was given to Russian ambassadors to European courts.

Not just individual paintings, but also famous European collections were purchased, thus ensuring the high artistic

BELOW: the lavish interior of the Hermitage.

level of the imperial collection. Great Britain was aghast when the tsarina's agents came to purchase the famous Walpole collection. Parliament debated whether or not to permit the sale, which eventually went ahead.

Soon Catherine the Great's gallery came to occupy one of the leading places in Europe. Sculptures, works of graphic art and carved gems were also bought for the Hermitage. In the course of time, several other beautiful buildings – that came to be known as the Lesser Hermitage, the Old Hermitage and the Hermitage Theatre – were built next to the Winter Palace, the royal residence in St Petersburg. They were needed to accommodate the growing collection. Catherine wrote in one of her letters: "Although I am all alone, I have a whole labyrinth of rooms… and all of them are filled with luxuries…" She added ironically: "Only mice and myself feast our eyes on it."

The history of the Hermitage has some exciting and, sometimes, dramatic pages.

It was here in the hall where paintings of the Italian and Spanish schools hang, converted into an interrogation room, that the arrested participants in the suppressed Decembrist uprising (14 December 1825) were questioned. Tsar Nicholas I himself stayed in a neighbouring hall amid pictures by Rubens and Van Dyck during the investigation.

It was also here in Voltaire's library, purchased by Catherine the Great in her day and kept at the museum, that the great Russian poet Alexander Pushkin worked on some of his books. Incidentally, he made a drawing of the statue of the celebrated philosopher in his notebook.

In December 1837 a great fire, which raged for more than a whole day, destroyed the Winter Palace. The inner passages linking the palace with the museum were dismantled and the museum's windows facing the palace were bricked up, and thus the Hermitage was saved. Fortunately, the palace was completely restored to its former grandeur

BELOW: the
Raphael room.

twelve months later. It was in the Winter Palace that the Provisional Government (which came to power after the overthrow of the autocracy in February 1917 – and whose sittings were held in the Malachite Hall) was arrested on 25 October 1917.

At first, the Bolshevik confiscations of aristocratic estates brought more art into Hermitage vaults but by the mid-1920s and into the 1930s, in order to finance their dream of world revolution, the communists started selling valuable works at bargain prices to Western collectors.

Restoration after the war

The 900-day siege of Leningrad from autumn 1941 to early 1944 was a bitter trial for the Hermitage, just as it was for the city itself. The museum's treasures were evacuated and, fortunately, saved. True, a large canvas by Van Dyck was lost. The buildings suffered heavy damage. Nonetheless, within a few years of the war's end they were completely restored. Not long ago, in 1985, a mod-

ern vandal damaged Rembrandt's *Danae*. One of the visitors to the Hermitage, later deemed insane, splashed the painting by the great Dutch master with sulphuric acid. It took St Petersburg restorers ten years to bring Rembrandt's masterpiece back to life in what is considered to be one the greatest art restoration jobs in recent decades.

As for the restoration of the whole of the Hermitage, which began in 1990, it will probably take well past 2010 to finish it, and hopefully be completed in time for the museum's 250th anniversary in 2014. The biggest problem is finance, but restoration work is in progress. A number of Russian and international corporate giants, such as IBM, Japan Tobacco and Interros Holding have made large contributions to the museum. There is also an international network of Friends of the Hermitage in the Netherlands, USA and Canada, which raises money for projects.

But the Hermitage cannot wait. Its buildings were not well maintained in Soviet times and its display area is far from sufficient. Despite the fact that the former Menshikov Palace has been turned over to the collection and now houses a display devoted to the early 18th-century period of Russian culture, the Hermitage's exhibition halls can accommodate only a small fraction of what is kept in the rich depositories of the Hermitage. The museum recently acquired a new building, the General Staff Building on Palace Square, now under restoration to a cost of $150 million but which will add about 40,000 sq metres (47,840 sq yards) of display space.

They say that a person would have to spend about 70 years, working at it eight hours a day, in order to just glance at each Hermitage exhibit. Until such time as human beings extend their longevity, we must restrict ourselves to picking out just a few of its masterpieces.

The best bits

A substantial share of the Hermitage collection is devoted to the history of Western European art. Paintings, sculptures, drawings and works of applied art dating

BELOW:
Renoir's portrait of the actress Jeann actress Jeanne Samary at the Hermitage.

from the 11th to the 20th century occupy 120 halls. Works of all the masters of the Renaissance, such as Leonardo da Vinci, Raphael, Michelangelo and Titian, are to be seen here. It should be mentioned that Leonardo's famous *Madonna Litta* was bought by Stepan Gedeonov, the first permanently appointed director of the Hermitage, in Milan in 1864 from the family of the Counts Litta, related to the Russian imperial house. Later on, he bought Raphael's *Madonna Conestabile*, which arrived at the museum in 1881. Thus, it is Gedeonov whom the Hermitage has to thank for these two gems in its collection.

The Spanish collection of the Hermitage is regarded as one of the world's best. Its gems include *Boy with a Dog* by Bartolome Esteban Murillo and also the *Portrait of the Actress Antonia Zarate* by Francisco Goya, presented to the Hermitage by the late US industrialist Armand Hammer. The Hermitage had no paintings by Goya before then. The museum does, however, have a fine col-

BELOW: the Poussin Room.

lection of drawings by the great Spaniard.

The art of Flanders, Britain and Germany is represented in the Hermitage by first-rate works, with large numbers of paintings by Rubens and Van Dyck. The Hermitage collection of works by French artists is the largest outside France itself. The paintings in this collection – ranging from Jean-Antoine Watteau and Jean Honoré Fragonard to Pierre Auguste Renoir, Claude Monet, and Henri Matisse – are on display in more than 40 halls.

The Hermitage has one of the finest collections of Impressionist and post-Impressionist art thanks the fine tastes of turn of the 20th century industrialists and art collectors, Sergei Shchukin and Ivan Morozov, who recognised great art in works by Matisse, Cezanne and Picasso but which French critics panned.

Today, the Hermitage has the largest Matisse collection in the world, as well as one of the largest Picasso collections. Monuments of the classic world – ancient Greek and Roman sculptural portraits and

vases – occupy more than 20 rooms on the ground floor in the building of the New Hermitage.

The Oriental collection

The collection of the Oriental section, comprising 160,000 exhibits, is the largest in the country. They include ancient Egyptian papyruses, sculptural pieces and many other objects from Babylon, Assyria, India, China, Japan, Turkey, and other countries, embracing a period which began with the 4th millennium BC.

The Hermitage collection of monuments and artefacts from the countries of the Near and Middle East includes the world's largest collection of Persian silver and carved gems dating from the period of the Sassanids (3rd–4th centuries AD), a collection that is famous all over the world. By the way, when the Austrian writer Stefan Zweig came to the USSR in 1926, he visited the Hermitage. They say that he deliberately walked through 40 or 50 halls with his eyes closed so as not to

see anything before he could stop near the canvases by Rembrandt and the collection of works by Watteau and Fragonard. Staggered by what he saw, Zweig asked to be shown something absolutely unique which was not to be seen anywhere else. He was shown the Sassanids' silver and Scythian gold.

The Chinese collection

The section on the art of the countries of the Far East holds the country's largest collection of monuments of Chinese culture and art. Its oldest exhibits include inscriptions on fortune-telling dice (there are some 200 of them) dating from the period of the Shang Dynasty (14th–11th centuries BC) and unique silk fabrics and embroideries (1st century BC) found during excavations at Noin-Ul in Mongolia in the 1920s. They are characteristic of the culture of the period of the Han Dynasty.

Also to be seen at the Hermitage are sculptural pieces and samples of wall-painting taken from Qian Fo-dong (Monastery of the Cave of the Thousand Buddhas) near Tun Huang in Sinkiang in 1914–15. Chinese art, too, is widely represented at the museum by porcelain, lacquerware, enamels, and paintings.

The lingering presumption that the Russian tsars knew how to live in a grand way and were good judges of aesthetic beauty is quite justified. Indeed, it would not be an exaggeration to say that each of the almost 400 exhibition halls of the Hermitage is very nearly a unique work of art created by talented Russian architects and artists and by the restorers who recreated their splendour.

The main staircase of the Winter Palace, built in the baroque style, is where every visitor to the Hermitage begins his acquaintance with the museum. Here everything is harmonious and exquisite. The same can be said about the antechamber with its famous Malachite Temple – a rotunda made of ornamental stones from the Urals – and about all the other halls of the Hermitage including, for example, the austere and majestic Grand Hall or the splendid St George Hall.

LEFT: Leonardo da Vinci's *Madonna with a Flower*. **RIGHT:** the ❑ Hermitage.

Map on pages 160–161

NEVSKY PROSPEKT

All major activity in the city centres on Nevsky prospekt; every day people from the outlying residential districts converge on Nevsky to work, shop, or simply to see and be seen

Nevsky prospekt begins in the heart of the town, at **Dvortsovaya ploshchad** ❶ (Palace Square). The prospekt may appear to be grey and monotonous in bad weather owing to its ironed-out skyline, for which Nicholas I bears responsibility by issuing a decree forbidding the construction of houses taller than the Winter Palace.

Nevsky, as St Petersburgers call the prospekt, can only be understood by walking its entire length. If you are not in the mood to cover the 4.5 km (2¾ miles) to the Alexander Nevsky Monastery, try at least to walk at least the 2 km (1¼ miles) to Anichkov Bridge over the Fontanka. Then take a bus to Ploshchad Vosstaniya or Uprising Square, named in honour of the liberal February 1917 Revolution and not the Bolshevik seizure of power, and walk around it before moving on to visit the Alexander Nevsky Monastery.

The Great Perspective Road

To answer the question how Nevsky came to be where it is now, we must go back several hundred years to when the marshy territories of the Neva estuary, the cradle of the future city, were part of lands controlled by the city-state of Novgorod. To the east of the estuary there was a road, the Novgorod Road, which ran along today's Ligovsky Prospekt, leading to the city of Novgorod. When the Admiralty Yard was built it needed wood, metal, fabrics and other materials. Yet there were no good routes linking the Yard to the Novgorod "highway".

In 1709–10, the Great Perspective Road was built through the forests, running from the Novgorod Road to the Admiralty. In 1738 it was renamed Nevskaya Road, since the Admiralty was situated on the bank of the Neva. In fact, all roads in St Petersburg lead to the Neva. In 1783 the road became an avenue.

Before the revolution, Nevsky prospekt and the neighbouring streets were called the City of St Petersburg. Between the Admiralty and Anichkov Bridge, 28 of Russia's largest banks and insurance companies had their offices. No. 9 was a bank, too; now it is an airline ticket office and the shuttle bus to Pulkovo Airport leaves from nearby. The architect Marian Peretiatkovich, who built the bank in 1911–12, fashioned it after the Palace of the Doges in Venice. It is this similarity that makes the house unlike any other structure in town.

The first street that crosses Nevsky is **Malaya Morskaya**. Here at No. 17, Nikolai Gogol, the prominent writer, lived between 1833 and 1836 in a modest

PRECEDING PAGES: Beloselsky Palace. **LEFT:** taking a rest outside of Kazan Cathedral. **RIGHT:** World War II sign warning pedestrians on Nevsky prospekt of shells.

three-room apartment. In this house he wrote his play, *The Government Inspector*, his famous novel about the Cossacks, *Taras Bulba*, and the early chapters of the prose-poem, *Dead Souls*.

The Stroganov Palace

The sign near No. 14, which reads "This side most dangerous during shelling", is not there to scare pedestrians. It is a reminder of World War II. When reconnaissance reported that the heavy German artillery that shelled Leningrad during the blockade was deployed in a forest to the southeast of the city, such signs were put up on northwest sides of all streets to prevent further casualties.

The short section of Bolshaya Morskaya Street, to the left of Nevsky's No 16, was planned by Carlo Rossi to run exactly along the Pulkovo Meridian. On a sunny day, you know when it is noon: the houses have no shadows. No. 15, on the opposite side, is known as the "house with columns". It was built in 1760 for the St Petersburg Chief of Police. In 1858 it was purchased by the wealthy Yeliseev family, who redecorated it and slightly altered the initial harmony of its facade in the process. Today it houses the **Kino Teatr Barrikada** (Barrikada Cinema). No. 17 and was built by Bartholomeo Rastrelli. The famous Italian also built in 1753–54, on the corner of Nevsky prospekt and the Moika Canal, house No. 19, the **Stroganovsky dvorets** ❷ (Stroganov Palace; open Wed–Sun 10am–6pm; waxwork display open Mon–Fri 11am–7pm, Sat and Sun noon–8pm; entrance fee), for Count Stroganov, whose coat of arms is still visible over the gates. This building now belongs to the Russian Museum, and is under restoration. Temporary exhibitions are held in the completed rooms and there is also a modest wax work display.

Unorthodox churches

There were many Christians in St Petersburg who did not belong to the Orthodox church. They too required churches, and

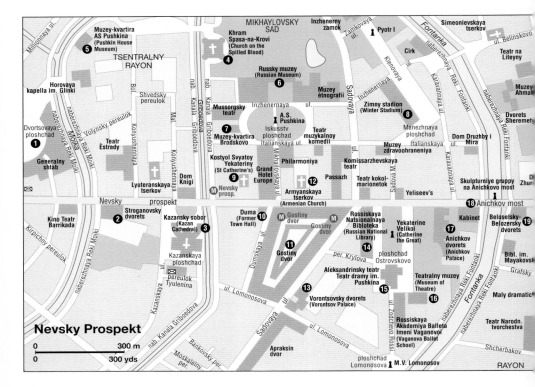

Nevsky Prospekt

0   300 m
0   300 yds

Map on pages 160–161

so the 18th and the early 19th century was marked by the construction of so-called heterodox, i.e. non-Orthodox Christian churches: Number 20 used to house a Dutch church (1837, by Paul Jaquot); today it is home to the district's public library, named after Alexander Blok. Nearby (Nos 22 and 24), is the **Lutheran church** (open Mon–Fri 10am–6pm; 1832–38, architect Alexander Bryullov). The church was converted into a swimming pool during Soviet times but the Lutheran congregation has restored it to a place of worship.

The Kazan Cathedral

Let us cross the street to get a better view of one of St Petersburg's architectural masterpieces – the **Kazansky sobor ❸** (Kazan Cathedral; closed Wed), built in 1801–11 by Andrei Voronikhin. A total of 96 columns, 13 metres (42 ft) high, make up the frontal Corinthian colonnade and produce one of the best sights in the city. Huge, 15-metre (49-ft) long bas-reliefs at both ends of the building depict biblical themes, sculpted by Ivan Martos and Ivan Prokofiev. The statues of generals on each side of the portico were installed to commemorate the 25th anniversary of the victory over Napoleon. One depicts Field Marshal Kutuzov, his sword pointing towards the imaginary enemy, and the other pensive figure is Barclay-de-Tolley (sculptor Boris Orlovsky). Kutuzov, the commander of the Russian forces that opposed Napoleon, is buried here in a vault in the northern chapel. The Kazan Cathedral (which currently houses a museum) presents its side wall to Nevsky, rather than its facade, because the altar in Orthodox churches is positioned near the eastern wall – and Nevsky runs along the northern side of the cathedral.

Another victim of the collapse of Communism, following an intense campaign by the city's Orthodox community, has been the Museum of the History of Religion and Atheism, which occupied the cathedral for decades. The museum, though conceived as a clever exercise in state propaganda, is now world recognised as one of the largest collections of religious art. It has approximately 150,000 items from ancient Egyptian mummies to paintings of modern art.

The museum, now located on Pochtamskaya Street but closed to the public as repairs on the new building have not yet been completed, also has a large collection of religious art taken from Germany during World War II, but which still remains hidden in storage. Scholars are only now studying and cataloguing these items.

On the other side of the street, the house with a globe on the corner tower was once the Russian headquarters of the Singer sewing machine company. Now it is the largest bookstore in St Petersburg, the **Dom Knigi** (House of Books). Here you can find books in various languages in fiction and non-fiction. Several local publishing houses have their offices here.

Church on the Spilled Blood

On the left-hand side of Griboedova Canal is the **Khram Spasa-na-Krovi ❹** (Church on the Spilled Blood; closed

Wed; entrance fee) which is also known as the Church of the Redeemer. Designed by Mkarow and Parland the church was built between 1883 and 1907. The reference to blood is a reminder that members of the revolutionary Narodnaya Volya group murdered Alexander II on that spot in a terrorist attack on 1 March 1881.

The architecture of the church contains elements of the Russian Revival style and is reminiscent of Moscow's St Basil's Cathedral. The exterior is embellished by nearly 7,000 sq metres (75,300 sq ft) of mosaic portraits of the saints while the central tympanum mosaic depicts scenes from the Old Testament. Adding to the colourful exterior are 20 granite plaques recording the historic events of the reign of Alexander II, and five domes covered with jewellers' enamel. The interior of the church, reopened in 1998 after 20 years of restoration, is entirely covered by mosaics based on paintings by famous Russian and religious artists and made from over 20 types of minerals.

Not far from the Church on the Spilled Blood, if you walk west following the course of the Moika at naberezhnaya Reki Moiki is the **Muzey-kvartira AS Pushkina** ❺ (Pushkin House Museum; open Mon–Wed 11am–5pm; entrance fee). It was here that Pushkin wrote his novel *The Captain's Daughter* and the poem *The Bronze Horseman*. The poet spent his last days here after being mortally wounded in a duel. Pushkin died on 29 January 1837 and every year on the anniversary of his death devotees of Russia's greatest poet come to the house to pay tribute.

Square of the Arts

Walking south along Griboedova Canal, turn down the first turning left on to Inzhenernaya Street which leads to **ploshchad Iskusstv**, called the Square of the Arts during Soviet times. The centre of this architectural ensemble is the yellow Mikhail Palace, now home to the **Russky muzey** ❻ (Russian Museum; open daily 10am–5pm, except Tues; entrance fee), which was built by Rossi for Nicholas I's brother, Mikhail, in 1819–25. At the end of the 19th century, the palace was rebuilt and redecorated. Fortunately the entrance stairway and the white column hall managed to escape this sad fate. In 1898, under Nicholas II, the palace was opened to the public as the Imperial Russian Museum; today the museum houses one of the world's greatest collections of Russian art *(see pages 173–177)*.

In 1910–12, two huge edifices were built alongside the palace. The right wing is part of the Russian Museum, and the left acted originally as the ethnography section. In 1934 this section gained independence and became the Museum of Ethnography of the Peoples of the USSR, now known simply as the **Muzey ètnografii** (Museum of Ethnography; open daily 10am–5pm, closed Mon and the last Fri of every month; entrance fee). The museum has over 450,000 pieces in its collection, which pertain to the customs, rituals, languages and religion of practically every nation in the former Soviet Union. The collection includes

LEFT: the Singer symbol above Dom Knigi.

Map on pages 160–161

Ukrainian and Byelorussian embroideries, Turkmenian carpets, amber from the Baltic republics, Vologda lace and many, many more items.

Directly in front of the museum is Mikhail Anikushin's **Monument to Alexander Pushkin** (1957). The house where the Assembly of the Gentry used to meet is now home to the Philarmoniya. Nearby are the Teatr muzykalnoy komedii and the Komissarzhevskaya Drama Theatre. Also on the square is the small **Muzey-kvartira Iosefa I. Brodskovo** ❼ (Brodsky House Museum; open daily 10am–5pm, closed Mon; entrance fee). Once home to the famous painter, today the museum contains a small collection of works by Russian artists.

The **Zimny stadion** ❽ (Winter stadium; entrance fee for events and exhibitions), to the east of the Museum of Ethnography, was built in the 1820s by Rossi as an imperial riding school and converted into a sport's stadium in 1948.

Returning to Nevsky, the house at No.

30 is another of Rastrelli's great creations. The building, one of the oldest in town, is also owned by the Philharmonic, and houses a small recital hall, as well as offices for private businesses.

St Catherine's Church

The next building is **Kostyol Svyatoy Yekateriny** ❾ (St Catherine's Catholic church; open for services) built by Jean Baptiste Vallin de la Mothe in 1763–83. The last king of Poland, Stanislaw August Poniatowski, who lived out his days in St Petersburg, is buried here. To the right of the entrance is the tomb of Marshal Maureau, who emigrated from France after Napoleon seized power. Maureau fought in the Russian army against Napoleon. He lost a leg in the Battle of Dresden in August 1813 and died the next day. His ashes were then buried, with honours, in the grounds of St Catherine's Church.

Beyond the Catholic church is the **Grand Hotel Europe**, the city's top and most expensive hotel. Across the street

BELOW: the Church on the Spilled Blood.

from it is the "building of the silver rows" and the former **Duma** ❿ (Former Town Hall and municipal council, 1799–1804), crowned with a pentagonal turret. In its day the turret was used as a fire-tower, from where firemen sounded the alarm in the event of fire or to warn of flood or a particularly vicious frost. Ironically, the tower itself caught fire in 2000, and is now under repair.

Around Gostiny dvor

In former times, travelling merchants stayed at special hotels, where they were given room, board and an opportunity to ply their trade. Such a hotel was called a **Gostiny dvor** ⓫ (merchants' yard), deriving from the Old Russian word for merchant, *gost*. Vallin de la Mothe in 1761–85 built the new Gostiny Dvor in the capital of the Russian Empire. The length of its facades totals nearly 1,000 metres (3,300 ft). The rectangular neoclassical building had such a felicitous design that it was copied when similar

establishments were built in other cities. The place retains its trading function to this day – it is now one of the city's largest department stores, along with the more upmarket Passazh, at 48 Nevsky prospekt.

On the opposite side of the road to Gostiny dvor between houses 40 and 42 (set back from the road) is the light blue neoclassical building of the **Armyan-skaya tserkov** ⓬ (Armenian Church; open daily). Designed by Yuriy Velten, the Armenian church was opened in 1780, only to be closed in 1930s and used as a workshop until it was reopened as a church in 1993. The **Vorontsovsky dvorets** ⓭ (Vovontsov Palace; closed to the public) on the south east side of Gostiny dvor was designed by Bartolomeo Rastrelli. The building is now occupied by a military academy.

The Russian National Library

Gostiny Dvor faces the Temple of Minerva – the **Rossiskaya Natsionalnaya Bibloteka** ⓮ (Russian National Library;

LEFT: a café outside of Gostiny dvor.
BELOW: the Armenian Church.

Map on pages 160–161

open July and Aug, Mon and Wed, 1–9pm, Tues, Thurs–Sun 9am–5pm; Sept–June daily 9am–9pm), whose main facade looks over the nearby ploshchad Ostrovskovo (1828–32, by Carlo Rossi). This library, the second largest in the country after Moscow's Russian State Library, was opened in 1814. It served as a place to work for St Petersburg writers, scientists, composers, architects and revolutionaries, Vladimir Lenin among them.

Among its treasured possessions is the oldest surviving handwritten book in Russian, the 11th-century Ostromirov Gospel, Voltaire's library (6,814 volumes), and the world's smallest printed volume, the size of a postage stamp, containing Krylov's fables. The print on the pages of the book is so clear that it can be read with the naked eye. The oldest manuscripts in the library's possession date to the 3rd century BC.

Since the Soviet Union collapsed, the Russian National Library has been targeted many times by thieves, with the most spectacular heist taking place in December 1994 when a group of thieves tried to steal 47 medieval European and 45 ancient Chinese, Mongolian, Tibetan, and Hebrew manuscripts, worth about $300 million, and sell them to a collector in Israeli. A joint operation by Russian and Israeli police rounded up the culprits, and the scrolls were recovered.

In the centre of ploshchad Ostrovskovo stands the **Pamyatnik Yekaterine Velikoi** (Monument to Catherine the Great, 1873). The great Empress is surrounded by her faithful supporters and favourites – Prince Potyomkin-Tavrichesky, with a Turkish turban underfoot; Generalissimo Alexander Suvorov; Field Marshal Pyotr Rumiantsev; Princess Catherina Dashkova; the President of the Russian Academy of Sciences, book in hand; the poet and statesman Gavriil Derzhavin; Admiral Chichagov and other policymakers of 18th-century Russia.

Opposite the monument on Nevsky prospekt is **Yeliseev's,** a fine example of

BELOW: the National Library.

Style Moderne and housing Yeliseev's delicatessen on the ground floor. Behind the Catherine monument, if we look from Nevsky, is the **Aleksandrinsky teatr**  (also known as the Teatr dramy im. Pushkina or the Pushkin Drama Theatre; tel: 315 44 64) built in 1823 by Carlo Rossi. On the other side of the theatre is ulitsa Rossi. The first of its buildings is the Vaganova Ballet School, which was founded in 1738.

Its neighbour is the **Teatralny muzey** (Museum of Theatre, open daily 10.30am–6pm, Wed 10.30am–1pm; closed Thurs; entrance fee), which has 400,000 items including photographs, sketches of scenery, sheet music and original items belonging to the stars of the Russian stage.

Ulitsa Rossi leads into **ploshchad Lomonosova** (Lomonosov Square), another of Rossi's creations. In the centre of the square is a monument to Lomonosovo. Here the facade of the Bolshoi Drama Theatre stretches to the Fontanka Embankment. The building was built in

1831–3 by Bryullo; the facade is Rossi's design. Further along the right-hand side of Nevsky, deep in the overflowing greenery of the square, stands **Anichkov dvorets** (Anichkov Palace; open for special events). Its construction was started in 1741 for Count Razumovsky. After the Revolution, it was turned into the Palace of Youth Creativity; today it hosts concerts and special events.

Over the Anichkov Bridge

Nevsky crosses the Fontanka through **Anichkov most** (bridge). Both the bridge and the palace are named after Anichkov, the engineer who supervised the construction of the first wooden bridge over the Fontanka in 1715. Today's stone bridge is 54.6 metres (179 ft) long and 37 metres (121 ft) wide. It was built by Alexander Bryullov and engineer Andrei Gotman in 1839–41.

The Anichkov bridge is best known for its sculptures. When Pyotr Klodt first cast the statues, Emperor Nicholas I impulsively gave them to the Prussian king. In Prussia, the statues were installed near the Great Palace in Berlin and Klodt was made honourary member first of the Berlin, and then of the Rome and Paris Academies of the Arts. Meanwhile, plastercast statues were installed on Anichkov Bridge. Klodt replaced them with bronze ones, but not for long: Nicholas once more decided to give them as a present, this time to the King of Naples.

Klodt was told to make bronze copies from the old moulds, but he thought that the central bridge of the capital deserved better. In 1850, a new set of statues was installed on the bridge, and remained there until World War II. During the blockade, Klodt's horse statues were buried in the garden near Anichkov Palace, in order to protect them from the shells. In 2000, the statues got their first cleaning since being cast in the mid 19th century, and can now be seen their original grandeur.

On the south bank of the river is the beautiful red facade of the **Beloselsky-Belozersky dvorets** (open daily; entrance fee; guided tours available). Designed by Andrey Stakenschneider in

LEFT: Rossi Street and the Aleksandrinsky Theatre.

Map on pages 160–161

the mid-19th century, the rococo exterior of the building is decorated with Corinthian pilasters and bearded atlantes supporting elaborate balconies. On the first floor is an exhibition of wax figures of famous Russians from the 7th century to the present day.

Around Vladimir Church

Further along Nevsky prospekt, the road crosses Liteyny prospekt (leading off north to the Neva) and the Vladimirsky prospekt (to the south). The latter comes to an end in front of the **Vladimirskaya tserkov** ⑳ (Vladimir Church; open 9am–8pm), a functioning Russian Orthodox church on Vladimirskaya ploshchad. A magnificent monument to 18th-century Russian architecture, the church has an impressive bell tower and five domes.

Nearby, in Kuznechny pereulok, is the **Kuznechny rynok** ㉑ (Kuznechny Market; open Mon–Sat 11am–8pm), a fruit and vegetable market. The prices in the market are quite high but it sells a variety of produce from all over the country and makes a good photo opportunity.

Just beyond the market at 5 Kuznechny pereulok is the basement entrance of the **Muzey Dostoevskovo** ㉒ (Dostoevsky Museum; open Tues–Sun 11am–6pm, closed the last Wed of the month; entrance fee). Dostoevsky lived in this small apartment overlooking the Griboedova Canal from 1878 until his death on 28 January 1881. After his death, his wife Anna Grigorievna had his study photographed which was later used when the house was restored. There are many of the novelist's personal belongings on display, including his hat. Dostoevsky wrote *The Brothers Karamazov* here. On Sunday afternoons, film adaptations of his novels are shown downstairs.

The **Muzey Arktiki i Antarktiki** ㉓ (Museum of the Arctic and Antarctic; open Wed–Sun 10am–5pm, closed last Sat of the month; entrance fee) is housed in the church of St Nicholas on ulitsa Marata. The museum is popular with

BELOW: Vladimir Church.
RIGHT: one of Klodt's horses on the Anichkov Bridge.

children who enjoy the taxidermy exhibition and displays documenting various Russian expeditions to the polar regions.

Moscow Station

A short walk from here takes us to ploshchad Vosstaniya, where the eye is drawn towards **Moskovsky vokzal** ㉔ (Moscow Station). Nearly 100 daily long-distance trains connect the city with the rest of the country. The station was built in 1851 when the first trains ran from St Petersburg to Moscow but was then rebuilt 100 years later, preserving the outside appearance.

The station has recently been painted what locals call a "tea with milk" colour, something resembling a pale yellow. It was previously light green, but when scholars recently discovered documents in the archives saying it was originally painted the pale yellow, in typical conservative St Petersburg fashion city fathers decided that architectural orthodoxy must prevail. There is a small garden in the centre of the square, where stands an Egyptian-like obelisk to the "Hero City of Leningrad," which was erected in 1985 on the 40th anniversary of the victory over Nazi Germany. From this point, one has a splendid view along the lower part of Nevsky all the way to the Admiralty.

Alexander Nevsky Monastery

Our trip along Nevsky prospekt ends at the **Aleksandro-Nevskaya lavra** ㉕ (Alexander Nevsky Monastery). *Lavras* were the highest-ranking monasteries. Before the revolution, though Russia had many monasteries, there were only four lavras: Kievo-Pecherskaya, Sergeyev Posad (north of Moscow), Pochayevskaya and the Alexander Nevsky.

The monastery ensemble includes the **Troitsky sobor** Ⓐ (Trinity Cathedral) built in 1778–90 by Ivan Starov in neo-classical style. The interior of the cathedral is worth exploring for its iconostasis. The two-storey house to the left of the entrance (by Starov and Trezzini) houses

BELOW: inside Alexander Nevsky Monastery.

Map
on pages
160&169

two chapels – the Alexander Nevsky Chapel above and the **Khram Uspeniyo Bogoroditsy** ⓑ (Church of the Annunciation). Walking though the park near the monastery, you will see a large yellow building behind a fence.

This is the St Petersburg Orthodox Theological Academy and Seminary, where both clergymen and regents of the church choir (excellent specialists in religious music) are trained. The necropolis of the monastery includes those graves that lie inside the churches as well as several large cemeteries – Tikhvinskoe, Lazarevskoe, Nikolskoe (outside the monastery's limits) and the small cemetery near the Troitsky Cathedral.

The **Lazarevskoe kladbishche** ⓒ (Lazarus cemetery) is the oldest in town. It was "founded" in 1716, when Peter the Great buried his sister, Natalia Alekseevna here. Here, also, are the graves of Mikhail Lomonosov, the architects Andrei Voronikhin, Andreyan Zakharov, Carlo Rossi and Giacomo Quarenghi and the

builder of the *lavra*, Ivan Starov. In front of the cemetery is the **Tikhvinskoe kladbishche** ⓓ (Tikhvin cemetery) where the remains of several artistic geniuses lie: the composers Peter Tchaikovsky, Modest Mussorgsky and Nikolai Rimsky-Korsakov, the actress Vera Komissarzhevskaya, the writers Fyodor Dostoevsky and Ivan Krylov, and the sculptor Pyotr Klodt.

Today, the cemeteries are part of the **Muzey gorodskoy skulptury** (Museum of City Sculpture; open daily 9.30am–6pm; closed Thurs; entrance fee).

To the southwest of the monastery at No. 30 Rastannaya Street is another necropolis – the **Literatorskiye Mostki** (open daily 9.30am–6pm, closed Thurs). This is the last resting place of the writers and literary critics Ivan Turgenev, Mikhail Saltykov-Schedrin and Vissarion Belinsky, the chemist Dmitry Mendeleev (the father of the Periodic Table), the physiologist Ivan Pavlov, the "Father of Russian Marxism" Plekhanov and some members of Lenin's family, including his mother.

BELOW: a symbol of the Orthodox church.

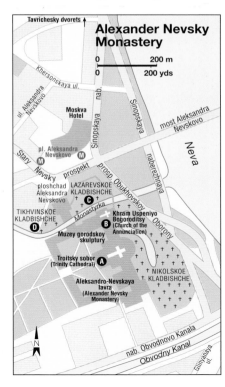

Potyomkin's villages

The **Tavrichesky dvorets**  ㉖ (Tauride Palace; not open to the public) was built by Catherine II for her favourite, Count Grigory Potyomkin. Potyomkin was a man of formidable talent. He commanded military expeditions into the Crimea, and finally annexed the peninsula to Russia (winning the title Tavrichesky in the process). His greatest talent, however, was in his ability to pull the wool over the eyes of his beloved mistress – and get away with it. When Catherine set out to inspect the Crimea – the newly added pearl in Russia's crown – the clever count decided that the unpleasantness of everyday existence which Catherine was certain to encounter on the road would disappoint Her Majesty.

So Potyomkin thought and thought and finally found an answer. He arranged for the old huts to be substituted with freshly whitewashed cottage facades along the entire route of the imperial journey (most of which lay through his vast estates).

Peasants were dressed up in pretty clothes and ordered to smile, sing songs and generally act in the pastoral manner as soon as they saw Catherine's carriage. Meanwhile, 10 steps away from the road, their dirty shacks remained as before. Catherine was pleased, and Potyomkin rejoiced.

After Catherine died, Pavel I, seeking revenge against the late favourite of his late mother, ordered stables to be set up in the grand halls of the Tauride palace. When Pavel died, the stables were removed.

The palace was redecorated, and once again became fit to be the residence of the royal family. Alexander I lived here for a time in the first third of the 19th century, and he was followed by the heir to the Persian throne. The palace then stood empty until 1906, when the State Duma (Russian Parliament) took it over. Today, it belongs to the Inter-Parliamentary Assembly of the Commonwealth of Independent States, and is closed to the public.

In the south end of the Tavrichesky sad

BELOW: the Smolny Cathedral.

Map on pages 160–161

(Tauride Garden), which is now a park, where Kirochnaya Street crosses Tavricheskaya Street, is the **Memorialny muzey A.V. Suvorova** (Suvorov Memorial Museum; open 10am–5.15pm, closed Wed, Thurs and last Mon of each month; entrance fee). Suvorov (1729–1800) was one of Russia's greatest military leaders, best known for beating the Turks and suppressing rebellion throughout the empire. But when he went up against French armies in 1798–99, he was forced to retreat across the Alps, which Russians nevertheless consider a great feat.

The highly nationalistic museum will acquaint you with his life and achievements, presented in a way with which some scholars might well take issue.

The Smolny

One of St Petersburg's most interesting historical ensembles is found not too far away on Rastrelli Square. It is simply called **Smolny** ㉗, a name that derives from the fact that the site was once occupied by the Smolyanoi (Tar) Yard, where tar was prepared for the shipyards. The yard was later moved to another location, and Peter's daughter Elizabeth decided to found a monastery on the spot.

The first buildings were built in the baroque style by Rastrelli in 1764, and are among the finest baroque structures in the city. The central part of the light-blue coloured cathedral is the **Khram Voskresenya Gospoda** (Resurrection Cathedral; closed Thurs; entrance fee), which rises to almost 100 meters (328 ft), and has five onion domes and a central cupola. Rastrelli's design was never fully realised, however; among them was a 150-metre (492-ft) bell tower that should have stood in front of the cathedral.

In the 1780s, Catherine II ordered the facilities of the monastery to be turned over to Russia's first educational establishment for women – the Institute of Noble Maids. But the Noble Maids found the monastic cells too small, and in 1806–08 a separate building was erected in the monastery grounds, designed by Giacomo Quarenghi; it took the form of a classical palace.

The Smolny Cathedral holds services over the weekend and occasional musical concerts during the summer months.

The **Smolny institut** existed until August 1917, when the Noble Maids were forced to give way to the Bolsheviks. Smolny then became the headquarters of the Military-Revolutionary Committee, the conspiratorial centre where the Bolshevik putsch was prepared and carried out in October 1917.

Today, the governor of St Petersburg and his administration occupy the former Smolny Institute. Several rooms have been made into a public museum, but tours must be reserved ahead of time. (tel: 276 1461; open weekdays 11am–4pm)

Two symmetrical pavilions serve as the entrance to the park in front of the Institute. One of them bears an inscription from the Communist Manifesto: "Workers of the world, unite!"

In the park there are bronze busts of Karl Marx and Friedrich Engels, and a 6-metre (20-ft) high statue of Lenin. ❑

RIGHT: the Smolny from the Neva.

THE RUSSIAN MUSEUM

The Russian Museum houses the largest collection of Russian art in the world ranging from folk art and medieval icons to conceptual works of the present day

In a way, it is thanks to the Tretiakov Gallery that the Russian Museum exists today. This is how the story goes: in 1893, Emperor Alexander III (himself an avid collector of Russian painting) deigned to bestow his royal attention on the Tretiakov Gallery. Having examined the collection, Alexander exclaimed, "How fortunate Moscow is! We have nothing of the kind down in St Petersburg!" Soon afterwards, the decision was taken to open a museum of Russian art in the Russian capital.

And open it did – in 1898. The museum occupied one of St Petersburg's architectural marvels – the Mikhailovsky Palace. Built by Carlo Rossi for Alexander I's younger brother, Grand Prince Mikhail, in the first quarter of the 19th century, it became part of what we now know as the Square of Arts.

Before inspecting the collection itself, have a look at the palace. The main facade, with its majestic Corinthian colonnade, is set back deep into the front garden. Rossi decorated the ground floor of the facade with symbols of martial glory – armour, helmets, shields and swords. Mighty lions stand on guard at the main entrance.

The grounds are separated from the square outside by a wrought-iron grille. Laconic yet solemn, it is certainly one of the most beautiful in St Petersburg with its rows of gold-pointed spears. Especially eye-catching is the combination of black iron and glittering precious metal. Rows of spears are interspaced with iron columns adorned with military trophies.

The opposite facade (looking out into the Mikhailovsky Garden) is altogether different: soft and mellow, it gives the impression of poetic harmony with the outlying scenery. Its serene beauty reflects the quiet, cosy thoughtfulness of the garden, which is enclosed on the side by the Cathedral On the Spilled Blood with a magnificent wrought-iron grille. Come autumn, the leaves of old St Petersburg maples, which are of the same delicate yellow hue as the palace walls, gently fall on the steps of the garden entrance.

The collection

It started with works of Russian art assembled from country residences of the tsars, the Hermitage, the Academy of Arts and, of course, from private collections. There were about 2,500 of them – mostly paintings, sculptures and drawings.

Today the Russian Museum, with almost 400,000 items, is the world's largest repository of Russian art. No other museum comes near to its collection of

LEFT: the Crowning of Mikhail Romanov. **RIGHT:** bust of Peter I.

graphic and sculptural works. You will also find period furniture, samovars, carved stones, china and Russian gems.

The section on Old Russian art displays icons, frescoes and mosaics. It would not be an exaggeration to call the Russian Museum a veritable encyclopedia of national art from its origins in the 10th century to the experimental works of the present day.

Portraits galore

The Tretiakov Gallery and the Russian Museum so readily typify their home cities, and complement each other. Where Moscow (the Tretiakov) has more works by the democratically minded "unofficial" painters of the second half of the 19th century, as well as unofficial art of the Soviet period, St Petersburg (the Russian Museum) is ahead with classical 18th-century works (mainly portraits) and early 19th-century painting.

This can be explained by the fact that the Imperial Court resided in St Peters-burg at the time and vogue painters, in search of lucrative orders, flocked to the capital where most aristocrats lived. The Academy of Arts was here as well, serving as a magnet for academic, "official" painting.

The portrait genre came to dominate both painting and sculpture in the second half of the 18th century. The Russian Museum proudly displays the works of Fyodor Shubin (1740–1805), the greatest sculptor of the time, who created enough portraits of contemporaries to stock an entire gallery.

The most interesting paintings of the period are a suite of seven Smolny Girls by Dmitry Levitsky (1735–1822). Catherine the Great hired the artist to paint the seven top graduates of the Smolny Institute (a privileged school for daughters of the gentry). The girls are depicted showing off their talents and abilities. They act out a graciously pastoral scene from an amateur play, dance and play musical instruments.

BELOW: the Guard staircase.

Icons

As the years went by, the Russian Museum collections grew, especially after the 1917 Revolution when aristocratic collections and religious works belonging to the Orthodox Church were confiscated by the communists. A special place in the museum is occupied by northern icons, which are amply represented.

The main prize of the early icon collection is the small 12th-century work, *Angel Gold-Hair*. It was part of a triptych of Christ flanked by angels. The unknown painter was clearly a person of considerable talent and poetic vision. He saw the angel as the embodiment of humaneness, undying beauty, purity and youth. This message from the distant 12th century reminds us of the eternal nature of the virtues of compassion and sympathy.

Another of the museum's outstanding icons is entitled *Boris and Gleb*. This 14th-century work by an unknown artist is a pearl of Old Russian art. It shows two young, early-11th-century princes, Boris and Gleb, sons of Kiev's Prince Vladimir. Both were murdered in the course of a dynastic dispute with their elder brother, Svyatopolk (*circa* 980–1019), whom the people stigmatised as "the Damned" for this foul deed. The church canonised Boris and Gleb. Russia's first saints are considered the guardian spirits of the country.

At some point between 1360 and 1370, somewhere in Rus (the chronicles do not say where exactly) the greatest Russian painter of the Middle Ages was born. His name was Andrei Rublev. Only a few of his works survive. The Russian Museum has several Rublevs, including *Apostle Peter* and *Apostle Paul*. These huge icons (nearly double a man's height) were part of the grandiose iconostasis in the Assumption Cathedral in Vladimir, where Andrei Rublev and his friend Daniil Chyorny worked in 1408.

Prized pieces

Every museum has a *pièce de résistance*, an item prized above all other possessions.

BELOW: *The Almighty Saviour.*
RIGHT: *Descent into Limbo.*

Such items are usually extensively described in books, albums, postcards and booklets. The Russian Museum has several such masterpieces. One of them is *Pompeii's Last Day* by Karl Bryullov (1799–1852).

When it first appeared, the painting produced a bombshell effect in Russian society. Nikolai Gogol (then a young author) showered it with praise and called it "one of the most outstanding phenomena of the 19th century." One critic after viewing *Pompeii's Last Day* described the painting as "the first day of Russian art." Professors and students of the Academy of Arts gave solemn receptions and dedicated poems to the master painter.

Even Alexander Pushkin wrote several verses about the painting. Another great work, *Barge Haulers on the Volga* by Ilya Repin (1844–1930), was created 40 years later, but differs both in subject and plot, giving prominence to the brutal realities of Russian life as opposed to the idealised past of antiquity Repin's work *The Zaporozhie Cossacks Writing a Mocking Letter to the Turkish Sultan* is also in the Russian Museum. Vladimir Stasov, the prominent Russian art critic, had the following to say about it: "Repin is as much a realist as Gogol, and quite as national. It was with a courage unheard-of in our land that he plunged headlong into the depths of folk life, the interests and the pains of the life our people live… Repin is a mighty artist and a thinker." Ilya Repin lived up to these words, and left a legacy of true masterpieces, many of which can be seen on a tour of the Russian Museum.

Russian landscape painting would be nothing without Isaac Levitan (1860–1900). Anton Chekhov, the writer and Levitan's close friend, called him "the best Russian scenic painter." One of Levitan's paintings – *The Lake* (1900) – has for almost a century now been an irresistible attraction.

Amongst the other great paintings are the works of Mikhail Vrubel (1856–1910), the creator of the famed *Demons*, and, of

BELOW:
Knight at the Crossroads by Victor Vasnetsor.

course, the paintings of Nicholas Roerikh (1877–1947), one of those artists whose vision, as Alexander Blok put it, "reaches beyond the foreground of the world to that which is hidden from view."

The Russian Museum also houses the works of one of the 19th century's outstanding sculptors, Piotr Klodt (1805–67). Visitors to the city usually see his sculptures before they come to the Russian Museum – on the city's main street, Nevsky prospekt (or, more accurately, on Anichkov Bridge), where four of Klodt's creations stand. The monument to fable-writer Ivan Krylov, in the Summer Garden, is also his work.

Russian avant-garde

The museum also has the world's largest collection of Russian avant-garde painting, but not many are on display due to both a lack of space and a lack of interest among ordinary Russian visitors. The works of Natalia Goncharova (1881–1962), Mikhail Larionov (1881–1964) and Kasimir Malevich (1878–1935) show a clear connection with folk art as well as with medieval icons and frescoes. The Russian Museum has the world's largest collection of works by Kasimir Malevich – 136 paintings and drawings.

Other worthwhile works include Goncharova's *Sunflowers and Peasants*, or Vladimir Tatlin's (1885–1953) *The Sailor*. Avant-garde painters were not fully appreciated in their homeland during their lifetime, and still are not, so most of these works are often on tour abroad where they attract large crowds and earn the museum a sizeable sum.

Fate was not kind to some other representatives of the Russian avant-garde, including Vasily Kandinsky (1866–1944) and Alexander Rodchenko (1891–1956). As the Russian proverb says: "What we have, we don't cherish; once we lose it, we cry." Fortunately not all that many of their works were lost, thanks largely to the efforts of enthusiastic collectors. Now these riches are on display at the Russian Museum – the gloomy majesty of Kandinsky's fantasies and the strained compositions of Alexan-

der Rodchenko, along with the biological and physiological phenomena of creation by Pavel Filonov (1891–1941).

In recent years the opportunity has been provided to see other long-hidden masterpieces. In the past decade, the museum acquired three palaces in midtown – the Stroganoff Residence, the Inzhenerny Castle, and the Marble Palace – hoping in this way to cope with the catastrophic lack of space. St Petersburg remains a city of painting, sculpture and creativity. Timur Novikov's New Academy of Arts encourages a return to the values of pre-Revolutionary art, to beauty, to neoclassicism.

But these are of secondary importance. The main thing is visit the Russian Museum, which remains an encyclopedia of Russian life, Russian character, Russian soul. Come in and you'll see – besides the beauty of Russian nature, the charm of its women, the imaginativeness of its people – the spirit of the nation, which has, since time immemorial, found its reflection in genuine art. ❑

RIGHT: *Mother* by Kuzma Petror-Vodkin.

THE PETROGRAD SIDE

*The highlight of this route is the Peter and Paul Fortress with its
outstanding cathedral and historical buildings contrasting
with the relaxed beauty of the Kirov islands*

Map
on page
182

Looking at today's **Troitskaya ploshchad ❶** (Trinity Square) it is impossible to tell that it was here, under the protection of the Peter and Paul Fortress, that the capital's first houses appeared in the early 18th century. Along the northern side of the square stood the first Gostiny dvor (merchants' market), while along its eastern side was the Senate Building. In the centre, there was a church whose spire rivaled the masts of the ships in the port. The houses along the embankment belonged to powerful officials of the day – Gagarin, Zotov, Shafirov, Golovkin, Bruce (the scientist) and Siniavin, the director of the town chancellery.

Until 1728, before it moved to Vasilievsky Island, the Academy of Sciences had its headquarters in the houses of Shafirov and Golovkin. The palace, deep in the square, belonged to Peter's closest friend and *aide-de-camp*, Alexander Menshikov; he presided over magnificent diplomatic receptions, which is why it was known as Posolsky (Ambassador's) House.

All of that has disappeared, and today there is a park on the square, flanked on one side by Soviet-era housing and offices, and early 20th-century mansions on another. In the centre of the square stands one of the city's few memorials, a small stone plaque with a crown of thorns, to the millions who died during Stalin's reign of terror. Here, every 30 October, the Day of Victims of the Repression, thousands gather to remember those who were murdered.

Peter's cabin

In May 1703, not far from the future Trinity Square, local carpenters built the **Cabin of Peter the Great**, now the **Muzey domik Petra I ❷** (Museum of the Cabin of Peter I; open May–Oct 10am–6pm, Nov–Apr 10am–4pm Wed–Mon; entrance fee) in just three days. It

was here where the tsar, who supervised the construction of the Peter and Paul Fortress, spent the summer.

The palace is not large: 12 by 5.5 by 2.5 metres (39 by 18 by 8 ft). In Peter's time the rooms – study, dining room and bedroom – had had neither stoves nor fireplaces, nor even a stone foundation. The stone house was a much later project – built by architect Kuznetsov in 1846.

As soon as the palace in the Summer Garden was completed, Peter moved there, leaving the original house empty and neglected. Somehow it never disintegrated entirely and was fully restored to its original form in the 1920s and has been used as a museum since 1930. Not far from this house on the bank of the Neva

there are two curious sculptures of Shi Chze. These mythological creatures guarded the entrances to Buddhist temples and crypts in Mongolia, China, and Southeast Asia. Russian explorers brought these mythical animals all the way to the northern capital of Russia in 1907.

Revolutionary connections

On the spot where the Bolshaya (Greater) Nevka parts with the Neva, the **Kreyser Avrora** ❸ (Cruiser Aurora; Petrogradskaya Embankment; open 10am–4pm, closed Mon and Tues; entrance fee), cast anchor for the last time in 1948. One of the ship's legendary guns fired the historic shot (9.40pm on 25 October 1917) at the Winter Palace, giving the signal for the government headquarters to be stormed. (Some say that the ammunition used for the shot was a blank and others insist that it was a non-exploding shell.)

The cruiser's history began in 1903, when it had a baptism of fire in the Battle of Tsushima during the Russia-Japanese

war (1904–05). Its crew were the first in the Baltic Fleet to take the Bolsheviks' side. When the ministers of the Provisional Government were safely locked away in the Peter and Paul Fortress, the cruiser broadcast Lenin's address to the citizens of Russia proclaiming the victory of the proletarian revolution. The Aurora then became a training ship.

In the years of World War II the battleship's guns were deployed near the front line. In 1956 the ship was repaired and turned over to the Central Naval Museum (*see pages 202–203*).

On the corner of Kuybysheva Street and Kronverksky prospekt, at the northern end of the square, is the exquisite art nouveau **Osbnyak M Kshessinskoy** (Kshessinskaya Mansion). In Soviet times the masion housed the Museum of the October Revolution but it is now called the **Muzey Russky i Politicheskoy Istorii** ❹ (Museum of Russian Political History; open 10am–6pm; closed Thurs; entrance fee). The musuem provides a balanced

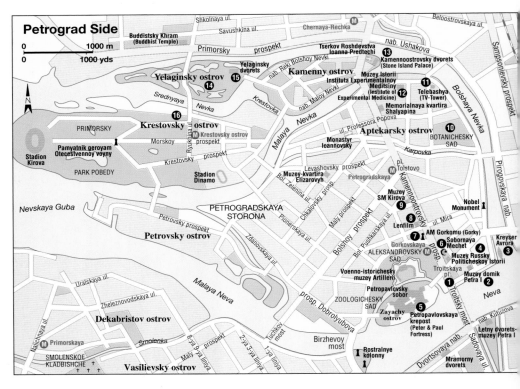

Map
on page
182

view of Russian history and chamber concerts are given in the mansion's main hall.

The mansion was orginally owned by Matilda Kshesinskaya, a prima ballerina favoured by Tsar Nicholas II. It is thought the mansion was a love token, and indeed, despite her successful career, Kshessinska could never have afforded to buy the house herself. As with most houses in St Petersburg, the mansion is also connected with the Lenin and the Revolution. From March to July 1917 it housed the Central and Petrograd City Committees of the Bolsheviks and as Lenin came here after his arrival at Finland Station on the night of 4 April. In the following weeks he visited the mansion almost daily to write articles and proclamations, address the crowd from the balcony and preside over meetings and party conferences.

The Peter and Paul Fortress

The **Petropavlovskaya krepost** ❺ (Peter and Paul Fortress; church and museums open 10.30am–5pm, closed Wed; grounds open to 10pm; single entrance fee) was founded in the summer of 1703. Though built with every innovation known to the fort engineers of the time, this powerful defensive stronghold was never once attacked by an enemy. The place cried out for a purpose until it finally became a political prison, a function it fulfilled for two centuries.

Peter had been in a hurry to build the fortress because the Northern War was in full swing and the danger of an enemy attack was real. Originally known as Fort St Petersburg, the fortress was built in record time and completed in the spring of 1704. It was originally built of wood and clay, materials which offended Peter's love of thoroughness.

Consequently Domenico Trezzini started to substitute wood with stone in 1706. Construction proceeded on a section-by-section basis in order not to weaken the military might of the stronghold. In 1740 the entire fortress was finally dressed in stone; it was then that

BELOW: the
cruiser *Aurora*.

it assumed its present complex geometrical form with forward-thrusting bastions that are named after the potentates who had personally managed their construction. Clockwise, from the main gates, they are the Gosudarev, Naryshkin, Trubetskoi, Zotov, Golovkin and Menshikov Bastions. The Ioannovsky and Alekseevsky Ravelins were added in 1730, and were then separated from the fortress with water-filled moats.

From Trinity Square, you can get to the fortress via **Ioannovsky most** Ⓐ (St John's Bridge) over the Kronverksky Strait, crossing from Zayachy to Petrograd Island. Ioannovsky most is the oldest bridge in the city, though the ironwork and lamps date to 1953.

The bridge leads to the main entrance – the **Ioannovsky vorota** Ⓑ (St John's Gate, 1740). Passing through, we find ourselves in front of the **Petrovskye vorota** Ⓒ (St Peter's Gate). Trezzini built the gate in 1718 in place of the old wooden one. Petrovskye vorota is the only triumphal structure of those times to survive in its original form. Conrad Osner's bas-relief, *Apostle Peter Overthrowing Simon the Magus*, is an allegory of Russia's victory in the Northern War. In 1722, the coat of arms of the Russian Empire was installed beneath the bas-relief.

Emblem of the third Rome

Russia's state emblem – the two-headed eagle and the horseman slaying the dragon – dates to the late 15th century. It emulated the emblem of the Roman Empire, where the eagle's two heads symbolised the empire's two capitals – Rome and Constantinople. When Constantinople fell to the Turks in 1453, Moscow became the "Third Rome", and this was expressed in the new emblem. Later, the two heads of the eagle were interpreted as the union between Christianity and monarchy – the foundation of the Russian Empire. Historical documents say that the horseman slaying the dragon was referred to as St George for the first time during the reign of Peter the Great's wife, Catherine I.

The gate is decorated with sculptures. In the right-hand niche is a statue of Bellona, the Roman goddess of war, and in the left stands Minerva, the goddess of wisdom, arts and crafts.

Peter and Paul Cathedral

The central passage leads from St Peter's Gate to the **Petropavlovsky sobor** Ⓓ (Peter and Paul Cathedral). The silhouette of the cathedral, just like the frigate on the Admiralty spire, is a symbol of the city.

The stone cathedral was founded in 1712 in place of the wooden Peter and Paul Church that was built in 1703. In the year the cathedral was founded, the capital of the empire was moved from Moscow to the new city, which was then less than a decade old.

Construction lasted until 1773 under Domenico Trezzini's supervision. Peter the Great wanted the cathedral to be built section by section. The first structure to be completed was the belfry and the rest of the cathedral followed (the belfry was

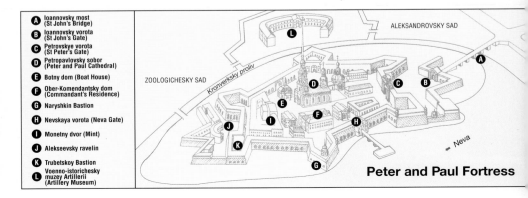

Ⓐ Ioannovsky most
(St John's Bridge)
Ⓑ Ioannovsky vorota
(St John's Gate)
Ⓒ Petrovskye vorota
(St Peter's Gate)
Ⓓ Petropavlovsky sobor
(Peter and Paul Cathedral)
Ⓔ Botny dom (Boat House)
Ⓕ Ober-Komendantsky dom
(Commandant's Residence)
Ⓖ Naryshkin Bastion
Ⓗ Nevskaya vorota (Neva Gate)
Ⓘ Monetny dvor (Mint)
Ⓙ Alekseevsky ravelin
Ⓚ Trubetskoy Bastion
Ⓛ Voenno-istorichesky
muzey Artillerii
(Artillery Museum)

ALEKSANDROVSKY SAD

ZOOLOGICHESKY SAD

Kronverksky proliv

Neva

Peter and Paul Fortress

Map on page 184

so heavy that if the entire church had been built at the same time, the added weight of the other structures would have caused the unstable ground to sink). The silhouette of the belfry bears a likeness to St Peter's in Riga and the Menshikov Tower in Moscow. Trezzini managed, however, to communicate a measure of originality to his creation by building in Petersburg-baroque style. The first wooden spire was crowned, just as the one you see today, with a statue of an angel carrying a cross.

In 1830 the spire was struck by lightning. The angel, whose wingspan totals 4 metres (13 ft), slumped to one side and threatened to fall. A roof-maker by the name of Pyotr Telushkin offered his services to set things right. Knowing nothing of climbing, he ascended the spire, secured a rope ladder to its summit, and used it several times before completing his mission. His daring and quick thinking earned Telushkin a great deal of money.

In 1858 the wooden spire was replaced with a metal one (under engineer Zhu-ravsky's guidance). With its height of 122.5 metres (402 ft), the Peter and Paul Cathedral remains St Petersburg's tallest building (excluding the TV tower).

Tombs of the Romanovs

The richly decorated main hall of the cathedral, which looks more like a gala ballroom, is dominated by its baroque iconostasis. The cathedral owes its fame to its tombs. All the Russian Emperors, from Peter the Great to Alexander III, lie here. Particular splendour distinguishes the tombstones over the remains of Alexander II, who was killed by terrorists, and his wife Maria. The tomb is made from 5 tons of Altai jasper and 6.5 tons of rodonite from the Urals. The stones took 16 years, from 1890 to 1906, to hand polish at the Peterhof Lapidary Works.

A special passage leads from the cathedral to the crypt of the Grand Princes, where close relatives of the tsars are buried. The crypt is now under restoration but is still open to the public. The fortress

BELOW: the Peter and Paul Fortress.

held its most recent csarist burial in July 1998 when the remains of Nicholas II, the Empress Alexandra, three of their daughters and two servants were buried in the Peter and Paul Cathedral. Russian President Boris Yeltsin, as well as the many Romanov descendants living abroad, flew in for the event that also attracted many other top names in Russian politics, business and culture. The remains of two of the children – the Crown Prince, Alexei, and Grand Duchess, Anastasia – have never been found, and stories persist about their supposed escape from execution at the hands of the Bolsheviks.

The Boat House to the Mint

On the eastern side of the cathedral is a cemetery where fortress commandants are buried. To the left of the main entrance is the elegant **Botny dom** ⓔ (Boat House), built by Vist between 1762–66, which was originally intended for the Grandfather of the Russian Fleet, Peter's first sailboat. Today, the orginal boat is in the Central

Naval Museum on Vasilievsky Island *(see pages 202–203)* and an exact replica can be seen here, in its place. In front of the Boat House, not far from the cathedral, in the former **Ober-Komendantsky dom** ⓕ (Commandant's Residence) there is a permanent exhibition entitled the "History of St Petersburg". Another exhibition, in the St John's Ravelin, explains (in Russian) the history of the Soviet space programme in the **Astronautics Museum**, to the right of the St John's Gate.

Behind the Commandant's Residence is the huge **Naryshkin Bastion** ⓖ, which points its two cannons at the Neva. According to the old Petersburg custom (which was reinstated in 1957), the guns are fired daily at noon. Walking back a little from the Naryshkin Bastion, along the wall towards Petrovskye Gate, is the **Nevskaya vorota** ⓗ (Neva Gate), which leads to the Komendantsky Moorage. Under the arch of the gate is a list of "catastrophic floods", the scourge of St Petersburg. It is difficult to solve the problem of floods even with today's technology since the reasons lie deep in the Baltic, into which huge quantities of water pour every spring and autumn.

Let us now return to the main entrance of the Peter and Paul Fortress. The building opposite the cathedral is one of the city's oldest enterprises – the **Monetny dvor** ⓘ (the Mint). Until Antonio Porto built an edifice specifically designed for the Mint (1798–1806), it was housed in the Naryshkin and Trubetskoy Bastions. Here, gold, silver and copper coins, along with orders and medals, were minted. Today it is the only mint in Russia producing metal coins, and large armoured trucks can be seen leaving the compound late at night.

Political prisoners

The dark pages of the fort's history are first and foremost connected with Trubetskoy Bastion and **Alekseevsky ravelin** ⓙ; the latter was constructed off the western wall in the reign of Empress Anna Ioannovna. The first political prisoner to be held in the **Trubetskoy Bastion** ⓚ (housing the Prison Museum)

LEFT: the beach at the Peter and Paul Fortress.

Map on page 184

was Crown Prince Aleksei, Peter the Great's son. He took part in a conspiracy by reactionary aristocrats against Peter's reforms. Disregarding the fact that he was his own son, Peter dealt with him as harshly as he did with all other conspirators. The statesman Artemy Volynsky was imprisoned in the 1730s for taking part in the conspiracy against Duke Biron, the all-powerful minister of Anna Ioannovna.

The cells also held Princess Tarakanova, the adventuress whose gamble to ascend the Russian throne backfired, as well as many courtiers who fell victim to palace intrigues. In 1790, the fortress also held Alexander Radischev, the author of *Voyage from St Petersburg to Moscow*, a critic of Russian absolutism.

The participants of the December 1825 rebellion were also incarcerated here. The most important prisoners were kept in a maximum security dungeon, the so-called "Secret House" of the Alekseevsky ravelin. Here, the defendants were condemned to hard labour and exile. The five leaders of the revolt were sentenced to death and hanged.

The prison was particularly "hospitable" to men of letters. In the middle of the 19th century, the fortress was "visited" by Fyodor Dostoevsky. It very nearly became the home of Vissarion Belinsky, the revolutionary democrat and literary critic. The commandant of the fortress used to approach Belinsky in the street and enquire "What's taking you so long? We've got a nice warm cell ready and waiting for you." But the humour was probably lost on Belinsky – only his early death in 1848 saved him from the dungeons of the Peter and Paul Fortress.

Another revolutionary democrat – critic, publicist and philosopher Nikolai Chernyshevsky – succeeded where Belinsky failed and managed to write a novel in his cell. The book, *What Is To Be Done?*, was even published in the 1860s through the negligence of some government official or another. In 1917, the fortress received the ministers of the deposed

BELOW: the wide square in front of the fortress.

Provisional Government, as well as some relatives of the tsar, who were later executed there. The Bolsheviks then transformed the prison into a museum. Other places, including the notorious Kresty Prison, were found for the enemies – real and imaginary – of the new regime.

In Stalin's day, when there were more political prisoners than ever there were in the times of all the Russian tsars put together, there were never enough jails. Hence a network of concentration camps, the brainchild of Leon Trotsky, was created throughout the country.

Around the fortress

To the north, the ensemble of the Peter and Paul Fortress adjoins a horseshoe-shaped building, which stands on Kronveksky (Kronwerk) Island. This is the **Voenno-istorichesky muzey Artillerii** ⓛ (Artillery Museum; open Wed–Sun 11am–5pm; entrance fee) which displays weapon systems, from ancient swords and muskets to the latest ballistic missiles.

Founded in 1703 as the **Arsenal**, it is now one of the world's largest military museums with 750,000 items. It was here that captured German rockets, created by the leading German rocket scientist, Werner von Braun, were brought and studied to aid the Soviet's effort to build ballistic missiles.

On the opposite shore of the Kronversky Strait, east of the Arsenal, is the **Decembrists' Monument**, an obelisk that marks the place were the leading Decembrists were executed. It bears a poem by Alexander Pushkin that he wrote to a friend who served a term of hard labour in Siberia:

Dear friend, have faith:
The wakeful skies presage a dawn
of wonder,
Russia shall from her age-old sleep
arise,
And despotism shall be crushed;
Upon its ruins our names incise.

If you want to relax after visiting the prison and the military museum, take a

BELOW: a rocket launcher in front of the Artillery Museum.

Map
on pages
182 & 184

walk through **Aleksandrovsky sad** (Alexander Park), which dates back to 1845. Alexander Park is semi-circled by Kronversky prospekt.

The revolutionary writer, Maxim Gorky, lived here in No. 23 between 1914 and 1921, before he left for Italy.

Rising over the treetops en route for Troitskaya ploshchad is the dome of St Petersburg's **Sobornaya Mechet** ❻ (Great Mosque) and two minarets decorated with blue majolica built by Vasiliev in 1914. The mosque resembles the 15th-century Tamerlain Mausoleum (Gur Emir) in Samarkand , and has one of the finest and most striking interiors in the city. Every Friday, the faithful gather here for prayer, and while there are no set opening hours, the mosque is usually open daily to visitors until early evening.

Kamennoostrovsky prospekt

We continue our tour along Kamennoostrovsky prospekt which leads through Petrograd to Aptekarsky Island, and which is the central avenue of the Petrograd Side. It took some time for it to gain its modern appearance. In accordance with the urban construction plan of 1831, several adjacent streets between Kronwerk and Kamenny Island were turned into an avenue.

After the completion of the **Troitsky most** (bridge) across the Neva in the early 20th century, there was a housing boom in this area because of both its central location and proximity to country dachas. Many of the apartment buildings are in the art nouveau style. Today, the area is popular with the intelligentsia and the new rich, many of whom have bought huge apartments in the district.

With the Revolution came the frenzy of renaming. In 1918, Kamennoostrovsky was changed to the Street of Red Dawns. The name survived until 1934 when Kirov, the Leningrad party secretary, was assassinated – after which the name was inevitably changed to Kirov prospekt. It was then, with the consent of Stalin (who

BELOW: Kamennoostrovsky prospekt in 1937.

was very pleased to see a dangerous competitor eliminated), that several places in Leningrad got Kirov's name – the above-mentioned avenue, a group of islands, a theatre, a stadium and many enterprises.

On the corner of Kamennoostrovsky and Kronversky avenues, near the apartment building with a semi-circular front, is the **Pamyatnik A.M. Gorkomu** ❼ (monument to Gorky) by Vera Isayeva, which was unveiled in 1968. The house on the opposite side (Nos 1–3), decorated with original animal sculptures, was built by Fyodor Lindval in 1902 in the northern version of the art nouveau style that flourished at the beginning of the century. When it was built, it was considered one of the most prestigious and luxurious houses in the city, and today many wealthy Russians here.

The Lenfilm Studios

In 1896, a cinema film was shown for the first time in Russia. Nos 10 and 12 are connected with the industry, having belonged to the **Lenfilm Studios** ❽ since 1924. This company developed the technology for recording sound on to camera film in the late 1920s, opening the era of soundtrack films in the former USSR. The studio produced such renowned movies as *Chapayev*, *Deputy of the Baltic* and *Peter the Great*.

The film studio's days are numbered, however. In 2001, President Vladimir Putin signed a decree to privatise the film studio, and most likely investors will purchase it, not to make films, which do not bring revenue because Russian audiences prefer American films, but for the valuable 4 hectares (10 acres) of city centre land which the studio occupies. Malaya Posadskaya joins Kamennoostrovsky prospekt. The composer Shostakovich lived at No. 14 Malaya Posadskaya and wrote several musical scores for films produced in the Lenfilm Studios. *(For more information on the film industry in St Petersburg see pages 97–101.)*

BELOW: a backyard facade on Kamennoostrovsky prospekt.

Map
on page
182

Russia's poets and thinkers

No. 21, hiding behind the trees, was originally designed for the Aleksandrovsky Orphanage. In 1844, the house was turned over to the **Tsarskoe Selo Lyceum** (whose graduates included Pushkin and his Decembrist friends, Ivan Puschin and Wilhelm Küchelbeker, and other famous figures of culture, science, diplomacy and politics). In the spring of 1844, the list of famous graduates expanded to include the satirical poet Saltykov-Schedrin.

The Lyceum building is the oldest on the avenue, and is now occupied by a high school. Sergei Kirov lived in apartment 20 of Nos 26–28 between 1926 and 1934. Indeed, it didn't take long for the Bolshevik revolutionaries to develop sophisticated tastes.

A Russian insurance company originally erected this building just before the outbreak of World War I with the most modern technology and comforts of the era. Even today, only the richest people in the city can afford to live in this building.

In 1938 Shostakovich took up residence in the apartment. In 1957 the **Muzey S.M. Kirova ⑨** (Kirov Memorial Museum; open daily 11am–6pm, closed Wed and the last Tues of the month; entrance fee) was moved to apartment 20 from the Kshesinskaya Mansion. The secretary lived in what was then considered a luxurious apartment, which included a dining room, a library (over 20,000 volumes), a study and a guest-room. The museum displays Kirov's personal effects, the telephone he used as a hotline connection to the Kremlin, documents and important historical photographs.

Kirov, whose popularity rivalled Stalin's, was a fine organiser and gifted orator. Sharing every delusion of his time, he remained a true-blue Bolshevik until his final breath, and had as much blood on his hands as the others. His speeches contained as many resolute demands to "make short work of the enemies" as Stalin's own. After Kirov was assassinated in 1934, Stalin and his henchmen were free to proceed with their campaign of mass terror against alleged enemies (who, it was claimed, had killed Kirov and were planning innumerable other atrocities), a campaign that rapidly grew into outright terror. Further up the Prospect is **ploshchad Tolstovo** (Tolstoy Square) which is dominated by the building known by locals as the "tower house" (1913–16, by Belogrud).

Leo Tolstoy Street, which starts at the "tower house", contains another research centre – the First Medical College. Bolshoy prospekt begins at this square which is now one of the city's most fashionable shopping areas, full of expensive clothing boutiques, as well as clubs and movie theatres.

Apothecary Island

Pioneer's Bridge, built in 1936, which spans the quiet and winding Karpovka River leads to **Aptekarsky ostrov** (island). The name Apothecary comes from the Apothecary's Kitchen Garden on the Karpovka, where medicinal herbs were grown from 1713. In 1823 the "kitchen garden" became the **Botanichesky sad ⑩** (Botan-

ical Gardens; open daily 11am–4pm, closed Fri). In 1931, the Komarov Botanical Institute was founded on the garden's premises. Today, the institute's garden has over 700 kinds of plants; there are an additional 3,500 in the hothouses, whose main pride has, for more than 100 years, been the Korolev Night Cactus, whose flowers open on warm summer nights and close at dawn.

The herbarium of the institute's botanical museum (same opening hours as the garden) has approximately 5 million samples of plants collected from all over the world. The museum is one of the largest in Europe. On display are medieval treatises on medicine and and exhibits explaining how to make potions from the medicine-man's handbook. A special exhibition is devoted to the extremely diverse flora of the former USSR and to environmental protection.

The **St Petersburgskaya Telebashya** ⓫ (St Petersburg TV Tower) is situated on the right-hand side of Kamennoostro-vsky Prospekt, on Chapygina Street. The TV tower was built between 1956 and 1962. In 1986 it was given a new antenna and, as a result, lost 6 metres (19½ ft) from its former 316 metres (1,036 ft). This, however, in no way affects the tower's status as the tallest structure in the city (it is 9 metres/29½ ft taller than the Eiffel Tower in Paris, which is, by the way, eight times heavier). On a windy day, the antenna's sway approaches 2 metres (6½ ft). The tower has an observation platform which at the time of writing was not open to the public.

Shaliapin's apartment

Beyond Chapygina Street, at No. 2b Graftio Street, lived the "great reformer of Russian opera", Shaliapin, between 1915 and 1922. To this day, lovers of chamber music are drawn to concerts performed in the hall of his house. The building also houses the **Memorialnaya kvartira F.I. Shalyapina** (Shaliapin Memorial Apartment open daily noon–

BELOW: a peaceful spot around the Kirov Isles.

Map on page 182

6pm, closed Mon and Tues and the last Fri of the month; entrance fee).

Not far from the end of the avenue, at the **Muzey Istorii Instituta Experimentalnoy Meditsiny** ⑫ (Museum of the Institute of Experimental Medicine; open daily Tues–Sun; entrance fee), Ivan Pavlov (1890–1936) worked for almost five decades.

After the revolution, his research – surprisingly – was not banned; Lenin considered his theory of reflexes and higher nervous activity an important contribution to materialist philosophy. The government turned a blind eye to Pavlov's religious activities as an elder of one of the city's Orthodox churches, which would ordinarily have branded him an ignorant and backward enemy of materialism (the official attitude to all believers). He was awarded the Nobel Prize for medicine in 1904 for his work and in 1935 Pavlov had a statue of a dog installed in the institute's forecourt as a symbol of human gratitude.

The Kirov Islands

Kamennoostrovsky prospekt ends at the wide Stone Bridge over the Malaya (Little) Nevka. Here, north of the Petrograd Side, lie the **Kirovske ostrova** (Kirov Islands, a picturesque archipelago with parks and old mansions. Originally, Peter the Great's comrade-in-arms, Chancellor Gavriil Golovkin, owned this piece of land lying between the Bolshaya Nevka and the Malaya Nevka. Ownership then passed to Chancellor Aleksei Bestuzhev-Riumin, who brought thousands of serfs over from his Ukrainian estates. Today the new residential areas built on the site of their settlements preserve the original names – Old Village and New Village.

Stone Island

In the 18th century, canals were dug to guard against "catastrophic floods". At the same time the construction of luxurious mansions and a park was started. The island was becoming the summer dacha area of the Petersburg nobility. Walking

BELOW: Kamennoostrovsky Palace.

along Kamenny ostrov's (Stone Island's) lime-tree alley to the eastern section we reach **Kamennoostrovsky dvorets**  (Stone Island Palace; not open to the public). The palace was built between 1776 and 1781 for the son of Catherine the Great, the future emperor Pavel. Today, a sanatorium occupies the Large Hall with caryatids and the Blue and Crimson Guest rooms.

The well-preserved **Tserkov Roshdestva Ioanna Predtechi** (Church of the Birth of John the Baptist) on Kamennoostrovsky prospekt was built by Velten between 1776–8. Its pointed tower and lancet windows lend the building a distinctly Gothic appearance.

The domed building on Malonevskaya Naberezhnaya Malaya (Nevka Embankment) No. 11 was built between 1831 and 1833 by Smaragd Shustov for the wealthy Dolgoruky family. Cast-iron sphinxes, made by sculptor Soloviev in 1824, sit on the granite mooring of the Malaya Nevka.

A memorial to the beginnings of the city is the oak tree that Peter I planted in 1714 on the Krestovka River. The oak has braved all the hardships of the Petersburg climate and has managed to survive to this day. The dacha where Pushkin spent the last summer of his life in 1836 has not survived. On its site the neoclassical out-of-town residence of Senator Polovtsev (1911–16, by Ivan Fomin) has been built. The Senator liked his rooms to be decorated with marble, Italian silks and gilt. From behind the stern classicism of the palace, the mellow traits of the Empire style, which was popular in the 1900s, shine through.

Yelagin Island

The island across the Srednyaya (Middle) Nevka belonged originally to Pyotr Shafirov, a diplomat from Peter's retinue. Then it came into the hands of the wealthy aristocrat Yelagin, who gave his name to the island. Yelagin's serfs irrigated the island and built a dam to guard against flood. Soon afterwards **Yelaginsky ostrov**  (open daily during the summer 10am–10pm; winter 10am–8pm) was made the summer residence of the tsars.

Alexander I commissioned Rossi to build a house there in 1818–22. The facades of the palace have different "tempers" – the one facing the river is somewhat sterner than the one overlooking the park. Both facades are decorated with white marble vases with tritons, which were sculpted according to designs drawn up by Rossi. Opposite the palace is the two-story semicircle of the kitchens. In order to save the inhabitants of the palace from kitchen odours, Rossi designed a windowless facade for the building. Those windows that it does have face the inner courtyard. Today **Yelaginsky dvorets**  (Yelagin Palace; open Wed–Sun 10am–6pm; entrance fee), also hosts temporary exhibitions.

Krestovsky Island

Before the Revolution the largest of the islands – **Krestovsky ostrov**  – was never as popular among the nobility as Kamenny and Yelagin islands. This is probably explained by the greater danger

LEFT: the Egyptian Styple statue (1842) at the Bolgorukov Mansion on Stone Island.

Map on page 182

of flooding (Krestovsky Island juts out further into the Baltic) and, of course, by the distasteful proximity of the worker's quarters on Petrograd and Petrovsky Islands. One of the few surviving 19th-century establishments on the island is the Yacht Club, founded in 1860.

On the western half of the island, sited on a man-made hill in the sea, is the **stadion Kirova**. It was built in 1950 and seats 100,000, which makes it the second largest stadium in Russia. The stadium is built on mud piped from the bottom of the Gulf of Finland, built up into a "volcano" with a very wide crater in which the stadium sits.

The avenue leading to the stadium is bisected by **Primorsky Park Pobedy** (Seaside Park of Victory; open daily) which covers 180 hectares (445 acres) of woodland. The park was planted on one Sunday in October 1945 when the citizens of St Petersburg answered an apeal to plant 45,000 trees in honour of the victims of the Blockade.

Across the Greater Neva to the Novaya Derevny (New Village District) are two other places of some interest: the **Buddistsky Khram** (Buddhist Temple; open daily noon–7pm) at No. 91 Primorsky (Maritime) prospekt, while several kilometers away, not far from the Chernaya Rechka metro station, there is monument on the site of Pushkin's fatal duel. Architect Gavriil Baranovsky, who was commissioned to build a Buddhist temple early in this century, consulted Lama Agvan-Khamba, who arrived from Lhasa just for this purpose.

The place of Pushkin's duel

The site of Pushkin's duel lies along the Chernaya Rechka (Black River). The prelude of Pushkin's duel with D'Anthes, the adopted son of Heeckeren, the Dutch ambassador, was quite ordinary for the life of high society in the beginning of the 19th century. Pushkin's young wife, Natalia, was beautiful, courteous and clever. Her popularity equalled that of her

BELOW: Yelagin Palace, Yelagin Island.

husband's. D'Anthes, the dashing officer and wit who was a sought-after guest in St Petersburg salons, fell in love with her. His insistent attentions placed Pushkin in a singularly uncomfortable position. As rumours were whispered from ear to ear, a hate letter was disseminated among the poet's circle of acquaintances, which pronounced Pushkin the historiographer of the Order of Horn-Bearers – a cuckold.

Yet Natalia remained faithful to her husband. She informed her husband about D'Anthes' attempts to seduce her, and about the dubious role of Heeckeren in the affair. Pushkin concluded that the hate letter was written by the old ambassador, who was quite capable of "helping" his adopted son with his love life.

On the other hand, the tongue-waggers spoke about the homosexual nature of D'Anthes' adoption by the old lecher – which made the young officer's chasing after women undesirable in Heeckeren's eyes. Meanwhile, D'Anthes grew more and more insistent. He never missed an opportunity to express his admiration to Natalia Pushkina. Finally, Pushkin could bear it no longer and, following the tradition of the times, challenged D'Anthes to a duel.

On this occasion the challenge was not taken up but trouble continued to simmer under the surface. The affair was finally settled with great difficulty. D'Anthes married Catherine, Natalia's sister.

Unfortunately, he persisted with his attentions towards Pushkin's wife, this time trying to achieve success as a "member of the family". Driven to breaking point by jealousy and suspicion, Pushkin mailed a letter full of insults to old Heeckeren. He wanted a duel and the insults were too serious to be avoided this time. D'Anthes challenged Pushkin.

Pushkin's death

The duel took place on 27 January 1837. Pushkin was mortally wounded on the bank of Chernaya Rechka, and D'Anthes received a bullet in his arm. Pushkin was brought to his apartment. His friends and the best doctors in town remained at his side. From time to time short bulletins about his condition were hung on the front door: crowds of people came to ask about the poet's health, since news of the outcome of the duel had spread through St Petersburg like wildfire. Vladimir Dal, the medic and philologist who was Pushkin's friend, remained with him to the last breath. This is what Vladimir Dal wrote: "He seemed to awake, suddenly, with a start. Eyes opened wide, face bright, he said, 'Life is over.' I did not hear, and asked, 'What is over?' 'Life is over!' he said distinctly and positively. 'Can't breathe, something's choking' were his last words… a ghost of a breath – and an impassable, immeasurable chasm separated the living from the dead!"

The pines which witnessed the duel have given way to willows and poplars. One hundred years after the event, in what was, for Russia, the far more tragic year of 1937, a 19-metre (62-ft) high stone of pink granite with a bas-relief was installed at the site of the duel where Russia's greatest poet met his untimely end. ❑

Map on page 182

LEFT: Natalia Pushkina. **RIGHT:** Church of the Birth of John the Baptist, Stone Island.

Map on page 202

VASILIEVSKY ISLAND

Vasilievsky Island, which once served as St Petersburg's port, has a rich naval history, but it is also the home of the city's intellectual elite and was settled by a rich merchant class

For a long time **Vasilievsky ostrov** (Vasilievsky island) had trouble finding a purpose, even though Peter was determined to create the administrative centre of the city there. Much effort went to make his vision come true, and Peter ordered all newcomers to the city to settle on Vasilievsky Island.

Plans were made to improve the transport system on the island with numerous canals that would have given the island an appearance similar to Venice. But Peter spent most of the national wealth on constant warfare with Sweden instead of building his capital, and after his death his successors abandoned his plans, in large part because the Vasilievsky Island was, and still is, the lowest point on the Neva estuary and most the readily flooded.

Later in the 18th century, the eastern spit of the island became an important economic and educational centre. Only towards the early 19th century did a significant residential neighbourhood appear when German emigrants, the most numerous nationality in St Petersburg after Russians, began to settle here.

Traces of their past presence can be seen in the Lutheran Church on Bolshoy prospekt, and at the German cemetery on the Smolenka river, next to the Smolenskoe kladbishche (the Russian Orthodox cemetery). Today, the island is once again in fashion among Russians with money. They are buying apartments in the new districts on the western end of the island which has a fantastic view to the Gulf of Finland.

The Twelve Colleges

In 1722, supervised by Domenico Trezzini, work began on the construction of the **Dvenadtsat kollegy** (Twelve Colleges) on the island. These "colleges" were the equivalents of today's ministries; united, they formed the highest government authority – the Senate. The Twelve Colleges still stand as a monument to Peter's intentions, along with the strict geometrical division of the island into 34 avenues. Roads, known as lines, also survive and these correspond to the banks of the filled-in canals, each forming a 90-degree angle to the three main avenues of Vasilievsky Island – Bolshoy, Sredny and Maly prospekts. All in all, there are 29 lines (each street comprises two lines), and the street that crosses Bolshoy prospekt at a sharp angle is known as the slanting line.

The Strelka

It is customary to start a visit to Vasilievsky Island on its Spit, also called the **Strelka ❶**, which divides the mighty

Neva in two. Of all of Peter's schemes, the Spit is the one that came closest to realisation. It became an important centre, though a commercial one rather than the political centre that Peter had in mind, and long retained that role.

In 1733, the seaport was relocated to the Spit, and remained there until 1855. Throughout this period, the area known today as **Birzhevaya ploshchad** (Stock Exchange Square) remained, as with any other port area in the world, the most lively and troublesome place in town. Bonded warehouses and the customs house were relocated near the port. At first these agencies found whatever shelter they could; later they built impressive headquarters. The square acquired its name from the Stock Exchange, a neoclassical building more akin to an ancient Greek temple.

The Naval Museum

The **Stock Exchange Building**, designed by Thomas de Thomon, was finished in 1810. The main interior feature is the exchange hall (900 sq metres/9,700 sq ft). The stairs leading to the building are so wide that they were used as a stage for 2,000 actors in the Soviet era, when mass performances were fashionable. On the main facade is the figure of Neptune gliding through the waves in his chariot in the company of two rivers – the Neva and the Volkhov. The other statues are of the goddess of Navigation and of Mercury, the god of trade. Inside, near the entrance, there are allegorical sculptures of Time, Plenty and Justice on one side and Commerce and Navigation on the other.

In 1940 the Exchange was turned over to the **Voenno-Morskoy muzey** ❷ (Naval Museum; open Wed–Sun 10am–5pm; entrance fee), which was founded in 1805. The collection of the museum includes more than 650,000 items. Among its better-known exhibits are model ships, Peter's boat, the personal effects of Admiral Pavel Nakhimov, weapons, flags and shipyard blueprints. There is

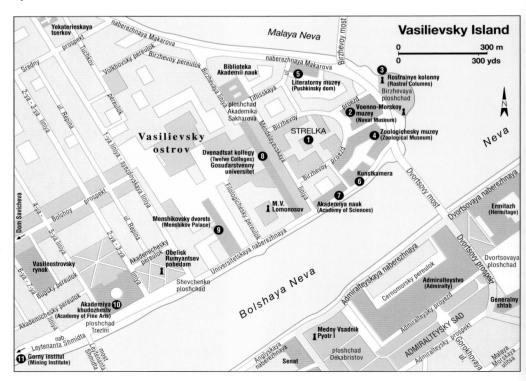

Map on page 202

also a salvaged oak boat from the bottom of the Yuzhny Bug River, which experts date to the first millennium BC.

The Exchange's construction gave the Spit its present-day appearance. The shores were dressed in granite; stairways led down to the Neva, where huge stone spheres were installed on pedestals close to the water. The granite-lined paths descending to the Neva were not so much designed for promenading as for loading and unloading ships. If you go down to the water's edge, you'll see numerous champagne bottles. They derive from a local custom whereby newlyweds come to the Spit and break a bottle for good luck and future happiness.

The Rostral Columns

The 32-metre (105-ft) high **Rostralnye kolonny** ❸ (Rostral Columns) were built between 1805 and 1810 by de Thomon. Their name is derived from the Latin *rostrum*, which means the prow of a ship. The Romans decorated their triumphal columns with trophies of war, which included the sawn-off prows of Carthaginian ships, and these columns have a similar purpose. They are symbols of the glory of the Russian fleet.

The sculptures at the foot of the columns depict the rivers of Russia, which serve as major transport arteries. From left to right (seen from the Exchange), they are the Dnieper, the Volga, the Volkhov and the Neva. There are spiral staircases inside the columns that lead to metal basins on their tops. In the past they were used to light beacon fires. Today there are gas pipes in the basins, and 7-metre (23-ft) tall gas torches flame over the columns on holidays.

The ensemble on the Spit also includes the South and the North Bonded Warehouses on either side of the Exchange and the Customs House. The modest greygreen of their facades creates the required atmosphere of seriousness and serves as the background for the Exchange. The southern building has housed the

BELOW: Naval Museum.

Zoologichesky muzey ❹ (Zoological Museum; open daily 11am–5pm, closed Fri; entrance fee) since 1900.

The museum has over 40,000 animal species from all over the globe. Its collections consist of over 10 million specimens of insects, 185,000 specimens of fish, and 88,000 mammals. The stuffed mammoth, which was found in 1961 in the permafrost near Berezovo, which is thought to be 44,000 years old, as well as a baby mammoth found in 1977 near Magadan, are now in other museums but a exhibition recalls their excavation.* The top floor of the museum is entirely devoted to insects.

To the Literary Museum

Further along Makarova Embankment behind the North Warehouse is the former **Customs House**. Constructed in 1829–82, it is the youngest building here. The portico is decorated with the bronze statues of Mercury, Neptune and Ceres. The turret was used for observation and for making signals to ships arriving in port. Today, the house belongs to the Russian Literature Institute of the Academy of Sciences, also known as the **Pushkinsky dom** (Pushkin House).

The institute continued, in Soviet times, a collection that was started in 1905 as the **Literatorny muzey** ❺ (Literary Museum currently closed to the public; tel: 328 0502 for details). Today it is one of the foremost authorities on Russian literature. Over the years, it has gathered manuscripts, archives and first editions of the best-known works of Russian literature, plus collections of pre-revolutionary newspapers. There are also the personal libraries of several writers' including Pushkin's, the museum's first acquisition in 1905.

One section of the museum contains old handwritten and printed books, most of which were found as a result of book-finding expeditions. They are mainly holy books, written by hand and used for religious purposes by the peasants. Their

BELOW: the Zoology Museum and the Kunstkammer.

Map on page 202

abundance dispels the myth that the *raskolniki* (Orthodox Protestants) had no culture of their own, a belief that was widely endorsed in scientific quarters. The museum also has the manuscript of Archpriest Avvakum (17th century); this type of Magna Carta of the rebels against church reform is today cherished as a holy relic by the *raskolniki*. In the past few years, the staff of the museum has been working on documents which date to the 20th century. They are gathering what promises to become a unique collection of letters from the *Gulag* camps.

Famous scholars have worked at Pushkin House. One of its departments was headed by the late Dmitry Likhachev, Member of the Academy of Sciences and President of the Culture Fund who contributed the essay, *City on the Neva*, to this book *(see pages 102–103)*.

Early in 1990 Likhachev took a bold step. He threatened to leave the Academy if the city's party bosses did not authorise the long-promised work to conserve the Institute's manuscripts and rare books. Likhachev emphasised the urgent nature of the project because of a series of catastrophes that took place in the city between 1988 and 1990: fire in the library of the Academy of Sciences and the disastrous flooding in the Russian National Library. Each time, unique documents and books were either destroyed or endangered. Today, while the government provides little support, the Institute benefits from private sponsorship.

The Kunstkammer

From the Spit, let us head along University Embankment and marvel at its jewels. The first scientific establishment we encounter is the baroque house with the turret (No. 3), known today as the **Kunstkamera** ❻ (the Kunstkammer museum; open 11am–4.30pm, closed Mon and the last Thurs of the month; entrance fee) from the German *Kunst*, (art), and *Kammer* meaning (chamber).

The Kunstkammer was built between 1718 and 1734 in a subdued baroque style, for Russia's first museum of natural science and enjoyed the patronage of

Peter the Great. It also contained Russia's first public library and astronomical observatory. To create the museum, Peter issued a decree ordering all unusual and curious creations of nature to be brought to the capital.

Soon the tsar had quite a collection of curiosities. But the house where the collection was kept, and to which everyone was soon freely admitted, fell into decay. The upper part of the building, the turret, was destroyed by fire in 1742; two centuries later, in 1948–49, the turret was restored to its original form in accordance with the initial drawings.

Mikhail Lomonosov, the famous Russian scientist, worked in the building in 1741–65. Here this extraordinary polymath, born of peasant stock, conducted experiments in chemistry and physics, observed the stars, wrote verse, codified the rules of Russian grammar and studied minerals. Here, too, the Russian Academy of Sciences started its work. The hall where its members used to meet

RIGHT: the Lomonosov Museum.

(Lomonosov was the first Russian in the academy), has survived in its original form. There are three scientific establishments under one roof in the Kunstkammer: the **Muzey Antropologii i Etnografii** (Museum of Anthropology and Ethnography), which continues where the Kunstkammer left off; the **Etnografichesky Institut imeni Mikluho-Maklaya** (Mikluho Maklai Ethnography Institute) and the **Muzey M.V. Lomonosov** (Lomonosov Museum), dedicated to the work of the great polymath.

The museum of anthropology offers one of the largest exhibitions in the world. It is divided into subject collections, which describe, in the utmost detail, life on the Volga, in the Americas, Siberia and the Far East, Africa and Oceania. The collection includes costumes, household utensils, coins, weapons, tools and other objects used by various peoples in their everyday life. The round hall in the eastern gallery of the building invariably provokes the greatest interest. Here the anatomical specimens made by the famous Dutch pathologist, Frederik Ruysch, are on display. They include the so-called "monsters" – human and animal anomalies. There are Siamese twins, a two-faced man, a two-headed calf and enough assorted specimens to inspire a horror film. Certain objects from the collection caused such unhealthy interest that they were removed from display and transferred to the museum's storerooms several years ago. This fate befell the unusually long penis, which belonged to a guard who lived in Peter's day, and several similar items.

At the end of the 18th century, the needs of the Academy of Sciences outgrew the close confines of the Kunstkammer. Hence the new academy building, a fine specimen of strict classicism, was erected between 1783 and 1788 next door. It was designed by Giacomo Quarenghi. The central staircase of the academy is decorated by Lomonosov's mosaic panel, The Battle of Poltava. In 1934 the admin-

BELOW: outside the Kunstkammer.

Map on page 202

istrative bodies of the academy moved to Moscow, but the scientists got to keep the building, which now belongs to the St Petersburg branch of the academy.

Turning right here, along Mendeleyevskaya liniya, we come to the large grey building of the **Akademiya nauk ❼** (Academy of Sciences). Today, the library has approximately 9 million volumes (12 million if the collections of affiliates are added to the grand total). The library owns *The Apostol*, Russia's first printed book, which was published by Ivan Fyodorov in 1564, books from Peter the Great's personal library and the Lomonosov's student textbooks. Peter ordered the library to purchase copies of all books published in Russia. Fortunately, none of these rare editions were damaged in the fire that ravaged the building in 1988.

The Twelve Colleges

Also in Mendeleyevskaya liniya are the **Dvenadtsat kollegy ❽** (Twelve Colleges), a complex of interconnected buildings built in 1722–42, but which was occupied by the University in 1819. The main facade of the college an excellent example of Petrine baroque, is over 400 metres (1,300 ft) long and runs at a 90° angle to the Neva.

These buildings did not look as they did back in the early 18th century. There was no grille, and each college had a separate entrance with an arcade, according to Peter's instructions. The isolation of the buildings symbolised the independence of the colleges, which were granted a considerable degree of autonomy.

Even so, all the buildings were arranged in a single row, indicating that they were expected to pull one oar within the unified system of state administration. Peter's colleges were set up to replace Russia's numerous administrative bodies, known as *prikazy*. In their turn, the colleges gave way to ministries at the beginning of the 19th century. The reform of the administrative apparatus took place in the new building in Decembrist's Square, for the

BELOW: the Spit during the 18th century.

old building was already turning out future Russian intellectuals and dangerous free-thinkers.

Mendeleev's Museum

The university's research workers have glorified their *alma mater* by their world-famous work. One of the graduates was Dmitry Mendeleev (1834–1907) who lived and worked at the university between 1866 and 1890. Mendeleev discovered the periodic law of chemical elements. There is a museum in Mendeleev's apartment, the **Muzey Arkhiv D. I. Mendeleva** (Mendeleev Apartment Museum; open Mon–Fri 11am–4pm; entrance fee), which tells of his childhood and youth, about the way the periodic table came to the scientist in his sleep after a long and fruitless struggle to find the correct element order.

Mendeleev was aided, in the final stages of work on his system, by his love for the game of patience. The museum has the scientist's personal effects and the chemical devices that he designed – the scale for weighing liquid and gaseous substances, for example. Mendeleev's daughter, by the way, married the grandson of the university rector, the Symbolist poet Alexander Blok.

The university's has also seen Pavlov and Sechenov, Alexander Butlerov (the chemist), Pafnuty Chebyshev (the mathematician), natural scientists Vasily Dokuchayev and Kliment Timiryazev. It has also had its fair share of revolutionaries. Mikhail Butashevich-Petrashevsky, Nikolai Chernyshevsky, Dmitry Pisarev, Alexander Ulianov (sentenced to death for plotting a terrorist attack against Alexander III) and his younger brother Vladimir Ulianov (who took his graduation exams here and graduated *magna cum lauda*, with honours); Ulianov is better known today by his party pseudonym of Lenin.

Today, the University of St Petersburg is one of the largest educational centres in the country with over 20,000 students. It can no longer fit into the its original building, and occupies several other buildings not far away.

During Soviet times, the university was named in honour of one of Stalin's henchmen, former party secretary of the Leningrad Committee, Andrei Zhdanov. In the early 1990s, the students protested against this executioner and enemy of science and the arts, and Zhdanov's name was finally removed from the university. Zhdanov was one of the organisers of the notorious party decree concerning the *Zvezda* and *Leningrad* magazines (1948). He slandered the satirical writer Mikhail Zoschenko and the poet Anna Akhmatova, who was later elected an honorary doctor of Oxford University.

The Menshikov Palace

Two buildings away from the colleges, at No. 15 University Embankment, there is another house that dates to the earliest days of the city. It is the palace of the tsar's closest friend and advisor, and St Petersburg's first governor, Alexander Menshikov (1673–1729). In 1707, Peter presented the entire Vasilievsky Island to Menshikov as a gift. However, in 1714,

LEFT: the New Exchange Bazaar, part of the University of St Petersburg.

Map on page 202

when the tsar set out to create his administrative centre on the island, he took the island back. Menshikov nevertheless managed to build a palace for himself on the island between 1710 and 1714 using the architects Giovanni Fontana and Gottfried Schadel. At the time it was the only stone building in St Petersburg.

When Peter died in 1725 Menshikov fell into disfavour and was exiled. The Menshikov Palace, another example of Petrine baroque, was turned over to a military school – the First Cadet Corps. In the Soviet era, the building was given to the Hermitage Museum to house an exhibition entitled "Russian Culture in the First Third of the 18th Century".

In the 1970s, the decision was taken to restore the palace and it is now open to the public: **Menshikovsky dvorets** ❾ (Menshikov Palace; open Tues–Sun 10.30am–4.30pm; entrance fee). Much of the palace is now back to its original form. There are Roman and Greek statues in the niches of the main entranceway (Men-

shikov imported them from Europe in his desire to emulate Peter). The stairway grille bears the intertwined monograms of Menshikov and Peter. Then follows the secretary's quarters, decorated with Dutch landscapes and astronomical instruments.

Beyond, there are the palace halls, of which the first is decorated with Dutch tiles. Of the 25,000 tiles that had originally been used in the decoration of the palace, 1,500 have been restored by specialists who first had to discover the lost secrets of the Dutch masters. Next comes the bed chamber, Varvara's room (where the sister of Menshikov's wife lived), and the governor's favourite Walnut Study. The windows of the study face the Neva.

While restorers were working on the study they discovered a full-sized portrait of Peter in military uniform. Also on the wall of the study hangs Peter's mirror. Mirrors were a bold innovation in the 18th century. Before Peter's time everyday life in Russia was governed by a Russian Orthodox code of living known as

BELOW: Peter I's best friend: Alexander Menshikov.
RIGHT: Menshikov's Palace.

Domostroi, which expressly forbade people to look at themselves. It was therefore considered the height of bad manners to keep mirrors in the house.

The palace from which Menshikov was chased out after Peter's death soon became too small for the cadets, so another long building was added behind it in 1758–60. The building assumed its present form in 1938. In 1917, the First Russian Congress of Soviets took place here; the event was commemorated by the renaming of the former Kadetskaya Line as the Sjezdovskaya (Congress) Line.

In the **Rumanyantsevsky sad** (Rumaniantsev Park) beyond the Menshikov Palace and further down University Embankment, there is an obelisk commemorating the victory over the Turks in 1774. In 1779, architect Vikentiy Brenna installed it on the Field of Mars, but in 1818 Rossi recommended that it be relocated to its present position. Rossi made some alterations when he installed the monument. The site near the Cadet Corps was chosen because the Russian army that won the 1768–74 war was headed by Marshal Rumiantsev, a graduate of the school.

The Academy of Fine Arts

Behind the Rumaniantsev Park is the **Akademiya khudozhestv** ❿ (Academy of Fine Arts). The house was built in 1764–88 by Alexander Kornilov and Vallin de la Mothe for the Academy of Art. It is an excellent example of Russian classicism. The portico above the entrance is decorated with sculptures depicting Hercules and Flora.

"The Academy of the Three Most Noble Arts" (painting, sculpture and architecture) was founded in 1757. One of the building's architects was rewarded for his efforts – he went on to become a professor and later the rector of the Academy. Graduates of the Academy include Pyotr Klodt, Fyodor Shubin, Mark Antokolsky, architects Andrei Voronikhin, Andreyan Zakharov, Ivan Starov, Vasily

BELOW: shopping on Vasilievsky Island.

Map
on page
202

Bazhenov, the painters Dmitry Levitsky (who became famous by his portraits of aristocrats in the second half of the 18th and the early 19th century), Ilya Repin (whose most famous picture depicts Cossacks writing a letter to the Turkish Sultan), and Karl Bryullov, the painter of Italian scenes.

The Ukrainian poet and artist Taras Shevchenko spent the last years of his life (1858–61) at the Academy. He studied here after Bryullov's masterpiece *The Last Day of Pompeii* (which depicts the eruption of Mount Vesuvius and the imminent destruction of the ancient city) had been auctioned off to buy him, a serf, freedom from his master. A museum-studio of Taras Shevchenko's work was opened here in 1964.

In 1947, the Academy moved to Moscow. The Repin Institute and the Research Museum of the Academy stayed on, however. A **museum** (open Wed and Thurs 11am–5pm; entrance fee) displays graduation works collected over the years.

It also has a collection of copies of the world's great masterpieces, made directly from the originals by various artists who were masters in their own right. This unique educational aid was collected in the late 18th and early 19th century.

Church architecture

Just up the block from the Academy, on the corner of Bolshoy prospekt one can see the spire of the **Andreyevsky Sobor** (Cathedral of St Andrew), built in the 1760s. Across from it is the Andreyevsky rynok (St Andrew's market), which also dates from the end of the 18th century.

A little way down Bolshoy prospekt one comes to **Dom Savicheva** (No. 6/13), where Tanya Savicheva lived in 1941–42, and wrote a diary of her life in the blockade and how she witnessed her entire family die. Tanya died shortly after being evacuated from the city in 1942.

The island is rich in church architecture. Down at the far end of the embankment, past the most Leytenanta Shmidt

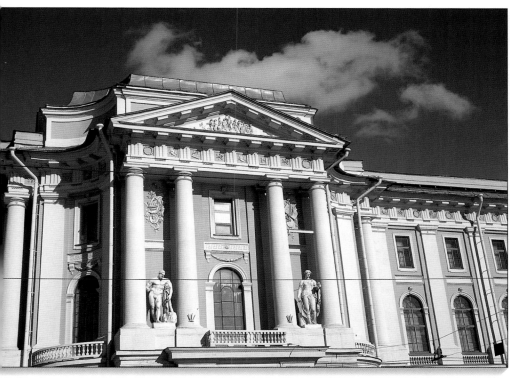

(Lieutenant Schmidt Bridge) is the Blagoveschenskaya Assumption Church, built in the distinctive Moscovite style in 1895–98 by the Kievo-Perchorsky Monastery. On the corner of the 6th line and Maly prospect, is the Blagoveschenskaya (Assumption) Church, also built in the Moscow style.

Moving quickly to the other side of the island, facing the Petrograd Side, the domed cupola of St Catherine's rises high in the sky. It was built in 1811–23, and was reputed to have one of the most impressive interiors, which were subsequently destroyed by the communists who turned the church into a warehouse.

On the nearby 1st Line, take a look at house No. 28 and you will see a plaque saying that the famous German archeologist Heinrich Schliemann lived there in the 1850s and 1860s. Schliemann, whom the tsar made an honorary Russian citizen, later found the legendary gold of Troy. At first, he offered the gold to the Hermitage Museum, but the Russian monarch refused because Schliemann had since remarried without being officially divorced from his Russian wife, and the self-righteous tsar didn't want anything to do with a polygamist.

Along the quay

Of the three moorings on the quay, the most remarkable one is near the Academy. In 1834, the ornamental girandoles and griffons were installed. At the turn of the century, the griffons disappeared under mysterious circumstances. Copies were restored to the mooring in 1959 made in accordance with surviving sketches.

Fame was brought to the place by its two **Egyptian sphinxes** of pink granite (from the famous Aswan Quarries). The sphinxes probably date to the era of the Pharaoh Amenhotep III (1417–1379 BC). The hieroglyphic inscription on one of the sphinxes says: "Son of Ra, Builder of Monuments, Who Rises to the Sky As the Four Pillars Which Hold the Vault of the Skies." The sculptor gave the sphinxes the

BELOW: the Church of St Catherine.

Map on page 202

face of the Pharaoh Amenhotep. They were buried by silt after a Nile flood and only found in 1820. Russia bought them from Egypt in 1831. It took a year for the 23-ton sculptures to travel to the city up the Neva. The time of their arrival in the capital is recorded in a Russian inscription that reads: "This sphinx from ancient Thebes in Egypt was delivered to the City of St Peter in 1832."

The sphinxes are separated from Lieutenant Schmidt Embankment by a bridge of the same name. Schmidt, a graduate of the Petersburg Naval College, led the mutiny on the battleship Ochakov of the Black Sea Fleet during the 1905–07 Revolution in Russia. The bridge was built in 1842–50. It was the first stationary bridge to connect Vasilievsky Island with the central part of the town. First called Blagoveschensky, it was later renamed Nikolayevsky. In 1937–38 the bridge was widened by 4 metres (13 ft) and restructured once more in 1975–76.

On Lieutenant Schmidt Embankment

the "academic relay" of the University Embankment continues. House No. 1 (1750, by Savva Chevakinsky) has 26 memorial tablets commemorating great scholars who lived there. Eighty academy members lived here during the 250 years of St Petersburg's history.

At No. 11 there is a museum (the **Pavlov Memorial Museum;** open by appointment only, tel: 323 7234 for details) in the former apartment of scientist and Nobel Laureate Ivan Pavlov (1890–1936) which contains books, personal possessions and photographs of Pavlov's experiments.

Further down the quay are the buildings of the Naval Cadet Corps (1796–98, by Fyodor Volkov), which are presently occupied by the **Vysha Voenno-morskaya shkola** (Higher Naval College). Named after Frunze it was Russia's first naval school. The college trained Admiral Fyodor Ushakov, the father of the Russian school of navy tactics, Admiral Pavel Nakhimov, the hero of Sevastopol in the

BELOW: sunset over the island.

Crimean war of 1854–55, and Admiral Mikhail Lazarev, who accompanied Faddei Bellingshausen on his 1820 Antarctic expedition.

The college, like just about every other place in the city, bears the traces of Lenin's energetic drive. In May 1917, he spoke here before an audience made up of members of the Petrograd Bolshevik Organisation and gave a public lecture entitled "War and Revolution"; a plaque recalls the historic event.

Another of the famed graduates of the college was Admiral Ivan Krusenstern (1770–1846), whose monument, erected in 1873 and designed Ivan Shreder, stands in front of the building on the Neva bank.

Krusenstern was later appointed director of the Cadet Corps. He commanded the first Russian round-the-world voyage in 1803–06. Krusenstern's observations during the voyage were an outstanding contribution to science, recognised by the several academic establishments in Russia, Germany, France and England

who elected him an honorary member. The 5.6-metre (18-ft) tall monument is inscribed: "To the first Russian to sail around the world, Admiral Ivan Fedorovich Krusenstern".

The Mining Institute

Between Lines 21 and 23, not far from Lieutenant Schmidt Embankment, is the building of the **Gorny institut ⓫** (Mining Institute), built by Andrei Voronikhin in 1801–11, though the Institute itself was founded in 1773. The entrance is adorned with sculptures which reflect the purpose of the college.

To the left is Cerberus, the three-headed dog, who guards the underworld, lying placidly near the feet of Pluto, the master of the dead. To the right is Hercules with Antaeus, the son of the Earth, symbolising the victory of reason over the chaotic forces of nature. It also contains mythological scenes symbolising the penetration of the secrets guarded by the bowels of the Earth and the use of their riches for the benefit of humanity.

The **Gorny Muzey** (Mining Museum; open Mon–Thurs and Sun 11am–5.30pm; closed last Thurs of the month; entrance fee) is as old as the Institute. Its collections offer a fascinating insight into the treasures of the Earth. There are thousands of minerals from 60 countries. Its unique items include a chunk of Ukrainian malachite weighing 1,054 kg (2,323 lbs), a Kazakhstani nugget of copper weighing 842 kg (1,855 lbs), a Ukrainian quartz crystal of 800 kg (1,800 lbs), an iron meteorite of 450 kg (990 lbs), and a palm tree that blacksmith Alexander Mertsalov fashioned from a strip of iron.

Alongside the institute is moored the icebreaker *Krasin* (open Tues–Sun daily; entrance fee), the world's only floating icebreaker museum. Launched in England in 1917 the ship was part of the international rescue mission to rescue Nobile's 1928 polar expedition. During World War II it took part in the historic convoy to Murmansk to ensure the safe delivery of supplies to the USSR. The ship's steam engine is still in working order and its lavish interior has been restored.

LEFT: Sphinx Quay. **RIGHT:** the Strelka.

Map on page 202

Map on page 220

THE VYBORG SIDE

This industrial district, once home to revolutionary ideas, contains a cemetery that commemorates the victims of the Leningrad Blockade and records a devastating part of the city's history

The Vyborg Side is the name given to the mainland area to the northeast of the Bolshaya (Greater) Nevka. Traditionally this was where the ordinary people of St Petersburg built their settlements. Subsequent generations of settlers built further away from the river and along the road to Vyborg. The road was divided into three sections in the old days (today they are all within the city limits and known as Bolshoy Sampsonievsky Prospekt, Engels Prospekt, and Vyborg Highway). Somewhat later, the nobility started to build summer houses there, followed by less noble but still rich people who built dachas.

In the second half of the 19th century, industrialists began to put up huge factories here, and the area now has one of the finest ensembles of factory architecture in Europe. Today, most of those factories stand idle and crumbling. But city fathers have plans to restore the Vyborg Side and turn it into a major business district, along the lines of London's Docklands area.

Revolutionary soil

Industrialists were attracted to the area by its considerable manpower resources. The Vyborg Side was turning into the district with the highest concentration of industrial production in the city, a major centre of metallurgy, machine-building and textile production.

Miserly wages and miserable working and living conditions fuelled discontent and made the working classes easy prey for Bolshevik agitators. Revolutionary groups and circles cropped up here and there among the workers who studied Marxism and propagated its ideas. The workers were told that they were the "leading class" and, as such, deserved a better life. The hitch was that this better life, they were told, had to be wrestled by force from the hands of the bourgeoisie.

In the days of the 1917 coup, and in the subsequent effort to defend the new regime, the workers of the Vyborg Side were the trump card of the Bolsheviks. Attempts to restore and improve the workers' quarter were made in the early 1920s; the party had to show how much it cared about the life of ordinary people.

In the end the project fizzled out. Only since the last war did large-scale construction of quality housing begin in the district. The area became fashionable in the 1960s, when local residents began to take pride in the fact that they lived in the centre of St Petersburg.

The areas to the north and to the east of the Neva were the focus of development. Many apartment blocks, shops, industrial

PRECEDING PAGES: flower sellers outside Finland station. **LEFT:** cemetery of the victims of the blockade. **RIGHT:** the industrial landscape.

enterprises and schools were built. Today, several major enterprises are located here: they include the Leningrad Optico-Mechanical Association, the Leningrad Metal Works which produces turbines for power stations, the Plastopolimer Corporation and the Svetlana Electronic Instrument Building Corporation. There are also large academic institutions such as the Forestry Academy and the Polytechnic Institute.

Around Finland Station

The most interesting areas of the Vyborg Side are **ploshchad Lenina**, the square in front of **Finlyandsky vokzal** ❶ (Finland Station), a part of Bolshoy Sampsonievsky Prospekt and the adjacent areas. The square in front of the station is a wonderful example of how even the most insignificant places could be made holy by the high priests of the new religion – Communism. The reason is that the square was fortunate enough to see Lenin's arrival from exile abroad.

In order to weaken Russia's resolve in the war, the Germans thought to inject the virus of revolution into the country. So they plucked Lenin, who like many other revolutionaries was caught off guard by how easily the monarchy collapsed, out of his comfortable life in exile in Switzerland, and sent him on a train to Finland.

From there he went to Petrograd in the small hours of 3 April 1917. Bolshevik sympathisers from among the workers, soldiers and sailors formed a welcoming crowd several thousand strong. Lenin scrambled onto an armoured vehicle bearing the inscription *Enemy of Capital*, which was used as a podium by assorted left-wing leaders to air their views. (Almost 75 years later, Boris Yeltsin would stand on a tank in Moscow to lead a new revolution that ended Communism in the country.) Lenin gave a short and fiery speech: he congratulated the audience for having accomplished the fall of the monarchy which, he said, opened the way for a genuine workers revolution.

LEFT: waiting for a train at Finland Station.

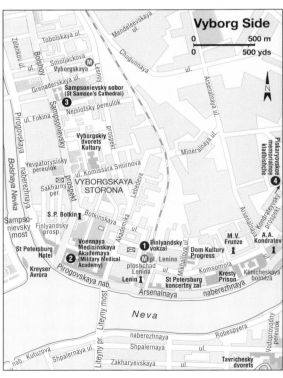

Map on page 220

When Lenin died in 1924, communist leaders gave his name to everything that could have one. The city on the Neva became one of this epidemic's first victims. It was followed by the square in front of the Finland Station.

In April 1924, the government decided to make sure that Lenin's speech would be remembered by everyone, not just those who had actually heard it. The lucrative order for a monument to Lenin went to sculptor Sergei Yevesev and two architects – Vladimir Schuko and Vladimir Gelfreikh, whose model won the contest. The dark-grey granite for the pedestal was delivered from the Onega Quarries. The statue was then cast at the Krasny Vyborzhets Works. The monument was initiated on 7 November 1926 and became the prototype for hundreds of thousands of similar statues and busts of Lenin which started to cover the USSR and many other countries.

To begin with, the overall shape of the square provided an awkward backdrop to the freshly installed monument. Some of the area were outright slums of the kind typically found near railway stations in those days. Gradually, however, the worst slums disappeared.

Today the focus of the square is Finland Station, which was redesigned in 1955. The central part of the old station was preserved and incorporated into one of the new buildings.

Near the boarding platform, under a glass cover, is another relic of the revolution: locomotive No. 293. Hugo Jalava (a Finn) brought Lenin (dressed as a coal hand) back into Russia on board the engine in October 1917; Lenin had fled the country, using the same locomotive, in August 1917.

The historic locomotive that played an important part in the revolution was presented to Russia by Finland in 1957. Though true capitalists, Finns still retain a fondness for Lenin because it was by his decree that the country gained its independence from Russia in 1918.

BELOW: statue of Lenin outside Finland Station.

The Military Medical Academy

Representatives of the medical profession occupy Akademika Lebedeva Street (named after the chemist Sergei Lebedev) and the right-hand side of Bolshoy Sampsonievsky Prospekt. Here stands the **Voennaya Medisinskaya Akademaya ❷** (Military Medical Academy). The main hall of the academy (Lebedeva Street No. 6) was built in 1798, in the same year the academy was founded simultaneously in St Petersburg and Moscow. It was originally called the Medico-Surgical Academy and was later given its present name. The academy is proud of its staff, whose members have included physiologists Pavlov and Sechenov, chemists Lebedev and Zenin, and Sklifosovsky, the surgeon.

Between 1841 and 1856, the academy's department of hospital surgery (one of the first in the world) was headed by Nikolai Pirogov who pioneered numerous medical innovations; he was one of the first to use ether for sedation during surgery and hypothesised about the existence of wound-infecting microbes. Pirogov's body, embalmed by his students, is in a sarcophagus in his former estate of Vishnya (now the village of Pirogovo near Vinnitsa in the Ukraine).

The Surgical Clinic

Bolshoy Sampsonievsky Prospekt links Lenin Square with the Vyborg Embankment. The modern complex of the St Petersburg Hotel, its facade turned to face the Neva, flanks the old buildings of the academy. On the even-numbered side of the avenue there are examples of the Constructivist style: Bartuchev built No. 14 in 1933, and No. 16, an electric-power substation, was built in 1927 by Schuko and Gelfreikh. On the other side of the avenue, the academy is flanked by the **Khirurgicheskaya Klinika** (Surgical Clinic; Soklov 1865–73). In the garden behind the central wing is a monument to a past President of the Medico-Surgical Academy, "Leib-Surgeon" Jacob Wylie (by sculptor Jensen and architect Staken-

BELOW: local transport with post-war charm.

Map on page 220

schneider, 1859). Wylie, who was of Scottish origin, built the clinic with his own money. In the garden on Botkin Street is a monument – to Hygeia, the goddess of health (1871, by Jensen) – and a fountain.

Downtown Vyborg ends here. Up ahead is the industrial area, the sugar factory (No. 24) and the **Russky Diezel** (Russian Diesel Factory), built by the Swedish immigrant Emmanuel Nobel in 1824 to produce naval mines. His son, Ludwig, organised the production of pig iron there in 1862, while another son who grew up in St. Petersburg, Alfred, made a fortune in oil in Baku in the south of the Russian Empire, and went on to create the prestigious prize that bears his name. At the far end of the avenue is the silhouette of the **Sampsonievsky sobor** ❸ (St Samson's Cathedral; open daily, entrance fee) belfry. In 1740 the secret wedding of Catherine the Great and Gigory Potyomkin took place here.

The **Kresty Prison**, about 800 metres (500 yds) to the east of Finland Station on Arsenalnaya naberezhnaya (Arsenal Embankment) was built during the reign of Catherine the Great. The prison became infamous during Soviet times when it was used to detain political prisoners.

Piskarevsky Cemetery

Situated on the outskirts of the city on the Vyborg Side is one of the city's most important sites: the **Piskaryovskoe memorialnoe kladbishche** ❹ (Piskarevsky Memorial Cemetery; open daily 10am–6pm), which was opened on 9 May 1960. To reach it we will have to take a taxi along Piskarevsky and Nepokoryonnykh prospekts. This memorial, designed by Vasiliev and Levinson, commemorates the victims of the blockade and was created between 1955 and 1960. It is an embodiment of the suffering that remains an important part of the city's memory to this day. The *Motherland* sculpture is the work of Isayeva and Taurit. The overall area of the cemetery is 26 hectares (64 acres). The length of the memorial wall is 150-metres (492-ft) and its height is 4.5 metres (15 ft). The poetry on the monument is by Olga Bergholts, who lived

through the blockade. Buried in the long lines of graves are the many victims of the blockade: some 640,000 people starved to death and more than 17,000 were killed by shells and air raids.

At the entrance to the cemetery are two **memorial halls** devoted to the Siege of Leningrad displaying documentary photographs and personal mementoes. One of the documents there is the diary of Tanya Savicheva, a schoolgirl, who recorded the deaths of all her family. Tanya herself was evacuated but she too died soon afterwards.

Another exhibit documents the "life line" over the frozen Lake Ladoga and the occasion when more than 1,000 vehicles and their drivers were lost while attempting to supply the city in the winter of 1941–42. Part of Olga Bergholts' poem reads:

So many beneath the eternal protection Of granite here lie, But you, who hearken to these stones, should know No one is forgotten, nothing is forgotten… ❏

BELOW: the memorial wall at Piskarevsky Cemetery.

Map on page 229

SOUTHERN SUBURBS

The southern suburbs of St Petersburg are a densely populated area but among the apartment blocks are some historical gems including the Moscow Triumphal Arch and the Chesma Church

Early in the 18th century, who could have imagined that the stretches of forest beyond the canal that served as the town's southern border would give way to huge residential areas? The area did, however, have the right credentials for development since the highways that linked St Petersburg with Narva, Moscow and Arkhangelsk, vital for the town's budding economy passed through it.

Originating along these routes, settlements started to grow outwards until the forests that once encircled St Petersburg on the south totally surrendered to apartment blocks in the second half of the 20th century. For some time the area, populated mainly by the working classes, was refused municipal status – the workers' barracks were cordoned off behind the Narva, Moscow and Nevsky Gates. Pickets of soldiers checked the credentials of everyone coming into or leaving the city.

While nearly every tour in downtown St Petersburg could be easily made on foot, some transport is necessary to get to the southern environs. So let us first take the Metro to **Narvskaya vokzal** (Narva Station) and then continue on foot along prospekt Stachek – a section of the old highway to Narva.

The Triumphal Gate

In front of the Metro station stands the only old building in the square – the **Narvskaya Triumfalnaya vorota** ❶ (Narva Triumphal Gate). Erected in 1814 to celebrate the arrival of the Russian Guards from defeated France, the original gates were made of wood (architect Quarenghi). Alexander I loved the gate from the moment he first laid eyes on it. He was very generous to the architect, bestowing an order and the title of honorary citizen on Quarenghi.

Quarenghi, by the way, was particularly proud of this ultimate honour – and for

good reason. In 1811, when Napoleon was preparing to invade Russia, he drafted Italians into his service. Napoleon's ally, the viceroy of Italy, ordered all Italians who were working in Russia back to Italy. Quarenghi refused – and was sentenced to death in his absence. Hence the pleasure with which the architect worked on the Triumphal Gate.

Ten years after the victorious return of the Russian army, the notorious climate all but destroyed the monument. The wooden gate was torn down and gave way to a stone structure (1817–34, by Vasily Stasov), which bore little resemblance to Quarenghi's original. Victory's chariot, which crowns the arch, was cast by Klodt and Pimenov. The statues on either side

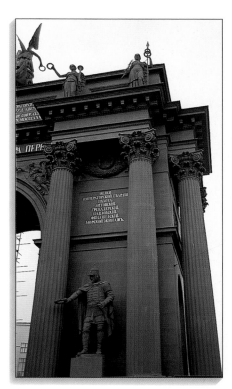

PRECEDING PAGES: sculpture at Victory Square. **LEFT:** bronze bust, Heroes' Avenue, Victory Park. **RIGHT:** detail of the Narva Gate.

of the arch depict old Russian folk heroes with laurels. In our day another of Stasov's original intentions was realised – a small museum will soon open its doors in the upper part of the arch. Its displays will be dedicated to the 1812 war.

On one side of the arch is the Gorky Community Centre. The constructivist structure was built in 1927. Its opening was timed to coincide with the 10th anniversary of the October coup. The hall of the centre, which seats 1,900, is a favourite place for amateur and professional troupes. A little later (1931), the Kirov Department Store, opposite the centre, was opened.

If you walk a few kilometers due west, you will come to the **port of St Petersburg**, which is Russia's second-largest port, and the largest on the Baltic Sea, annually handling over 30 million tons of cargo, most of it raw materials. The port is now being expanded and modernised to double its cargo capacity. Walking a bit further along prospekt Stachek, we come

to Kirovskaya plosh-chad ❷ **Kirov Square**, with its 50-metre (164-ft) high building, home to the District Soviet of People's Deputies. In the foreground we find the 15-metre/50-ft *Monument to Sergei Kirov* (the statue itself is 8 metres/25 ft tall), erected in 1938. In 1927, the statue adorned the entrance to the Soviet pavilion at the Paris World Exhibition. Its forcefulness and the perceptive way in which the artist grasped the energetic, wilful nature of the up-and-coming party bureaucrat earned it the honour of a silver medal.

The best place to end our tour of the area is in the **Sad 9 (Devyatovo) Yanvarya** (January 9th Park). Here, to the south of what is now the District Soviet building, the downtrodden inhabitants of the workers' quarter gathered on 9 January 1905 ("Bloody Sunday") to march towards the Winter Palace. The demonstration was met by army units near Narva Gate and in Dvortsovaya Square. The sophisticated beauty of the ironwork grille surrounding the park also merited the highest award at the 1901 Paris World Exhibition, after which it was promptly dismantled and removed to the park near the Winter Palace. Yet it blocked the view of the palace front and generally disagreed with the ensemble of the square. In 1919, it was once again removed to the position where we see it now.

Moscow Prospekt

To reach **Moskovsky prospekt** ❸ we shall again take the Metro to Sennaya ploshchad (Haymarket) where the 11-km (7-mile) road starts. It runs straight as an arrow along the Pulkovo Meridian.

The avenue branches out when it reaches Victory Square and continues straight to the south as Pulkovo (Pulkovskoe) Highway; this leads to the observatory and on to the Kiev Highway. Moscow Highway (Moskovskoe shosse) runs to the southeast, through the town of Pushkin. The avenue was designed in the 18th century as the road to Tsarskoe Selo, as Pushkin was then called, and appropriately christened Tsarskoselsky prospekt. Not far from Peace Square along Moscow

LEFT: a local tram.

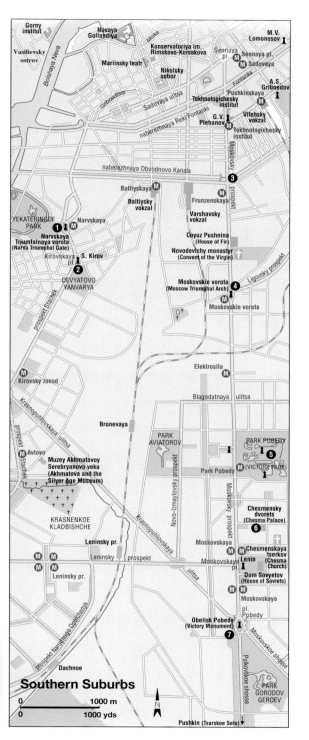

Southern Suburbs

0 ——— 1000 m
0 ——— 1000 yds

N

prospekt, there is an interesting place. No. 19 houses the **Gidromet institut** (Meteorological Institute), founded by Dmitry Mendeleev. The tower over the building has the largest – and, incidentally, most accurate – clock in town.

The Moscow Triumphal Arch

Taking the Metro again at the Tekhnologichesky institut Station, skip a stop and disembark at the Moscovskie vorota, (Moscow Triumphal Gate) Station. The **Moskovskie vorota ❹** (Moscow Triumphal Arch) was built by Vasily Stasov in 1834–38 to commemorate Russia's victory in the Turkish War of 1828–29 during the reign of Nicholas I. The monument is decorated with statues of Plenty, Glory and Victory (by Boris Orlovsky).

Parts of the gate are made of cast iron. A century after they were installed these parts suddenly found their way to the field of battle – they were used as tank traps at the southern approaches to the city in 1941. In 1958–60 the gate was restored.

Walking from the gate towards the centre, we find the **Coyuz Pushnina** (House of Fur, No. 98), where international fur auctions are held three times a year. Agents of the world's major fur-buying companies flock to these auctions to purchase some of the world's finest furs. Behind the Palace of Furs, away from the avenue, is the former **Novodevichy monastyr** (Convent of the Virgin), which has been handed over to the Orthodox Church and is slowly being restored to its former appearance.

We will now continue by Metro from Moscow Gate, passing the Elektrosila Station, and disembark at **Park Pobedy ❺** (Victory Park), founded to commemorate the end of World War II and laid out by volunteer labour. The central avenues are unerringly straight; the lesser paths wind underneath the trees.

In the Avenue of Heroes are bronze bust-size sculptures of those locals who were awarded the Gold Star (Heroes of the Soviet Union or of Socialist Labour). The fountain at the entrance has a pool diameter of 25 metres (82 ft), and a spring height 12 metres (39 ft); it is considered the city's largest. From the western edge of the park there is a view of the huge leisure and sports complex at its eastern end. People flock here not only for sports events: the place is a favourite venue for concerts by Russian and foreign pop groups. It also hosts large conferences, congresses and festivals.

Chesma palace and church

Walking along the avenue towards Pushkin, we find, on the left-hand side, the Chesma Palace and Church (1770, by Yury Felten). **Chesmensky dvorets** ❻ (Chesma Palace; closed to the public) was built as a stopover where the road-weary Catherine II could rest on her way between St Petersburg and her out-of-town residence.

The palace got its name from a victorious naval battle fought against the Turks in the Aegean Chesma Bay. The green frog on the palace's coat of arms refers to the site (known as Frog Swamp) where the palace, fashioned after a medieval castle with its turrets, moat and drawbridges, was built. For major receptions, the Green Frog – a set of china – was ordered from the Wedgwood porcelain company. The 592 pieces of the set bear 1,244 landscape scenes of England. Naturally, each piece also bears the symbol of the palace – the green frog. Today the palace is a retirement home for the elderly.

The **Chesmenskaya tserkov** (Chesma Church; open for services), one of the few neo-Gothic buildings in the city, was built between 1777 and 1780, also by Felten. Exactly two centuries after work on the church was started, the building was converted into a museum but it is now a place of worship again.

Moscow Square

Further along to the south on the avenue, not far away from the palace, is Moskovskaya ploshchad (Moscow Square). Here the eye is immediately caught by the 220-metre (720-ft) bulk of the **Dom Sovyetov** (House of Soviets)

BELOW: Chesma Church.

Map on page 229

and the huge statue of Lenin in the centre of the square. The House of Soviets was built by a group of architects headed by Noah Trotsky in 1936–41. It was designed with as much pomp as was humanly possible, following the architectural preferences of party bureaucrats. The **Monument to Lenin** (by the sculptor Mikhail Anikushin, architect Valentin Kamensky) was erected on the occasion of his 100th anniversary, as the inscription on the pedestal attests. The charismatic leader, with either a cap or a copy of *Pravda* (it is hard to say which) in hand, is depicted delivering one of his speeches.

Further to the south comes Victory Square with its grandiose **Obelisk Pobedy** ❼ (Victory Monument) to the heroic defenders of Leningrad (opened on 9 May 1975, the 30th anniversary of the victory against the Nazis). A 48-metre (157-ft) obelisk stands at the centre of a broken circle that symbolises deliverance from the blockade. Several groups of sculptures depict sailors, partisans, soldiers and volunteers. In the memorial hall under the monument, Shostakovich's *7th Symphony* sounds to the accompaniment of a metronome.

In the centre of the memorial hall is the *Bronze Book of Memory*, a chronicle of the blockade. The hall displays moving reminders of the privations suffered during the 900-day siege, as well as having screens which continuously show contemporary film footage, vividly recreating the appearance and atmosphere of the city at the time.Still further along the Pulkovo Highway there are several other structures of interest.

To the right, on Pulkovo Hill, is a pavilion, which is open on four sides. The granite pool inside is guarded by four sphinxes, which gave the place its name – the Four Witches. The Pulkovo Observatory, which we see on the right, is the country's astronomical centre.

In the world at large, the observatory is acclaimed for its pioneering experiments with computer-controlled telescopes. ❑

BELOW: Victory Park.

Map on page 236

PARKS AND PALACES IN THE SUBURBS

Many of the lavish imperial palaces and beautifully laid-out parks in the suburbs of St Petersburg can be easily reached by suburban railway and make worthwhile day trips

O ne of the shrewdest commentators to travel through Russia, the French Marquis de Custine, noted as early as 1839 that the architecture of St Petersburg was similar to that of Athens or Rome, but that the buildings were arranged in a completely different manner: you couldn't look up at them from below because they seemed to be sunk into the marsh. He also realised that St Petersburg was a city of facades, that buildings with antique porticos or churches might not be what they seemed from the exterior – behind a Greek temple you might easily find a Stock Exchange (Custine was talking about the main building of the Strelka ensemble on Vasilievsky Island, which now houses the Central Naval Museum).

So it has always been, but that grandiose experiment known as the Revolution made the city even worse: this city is almost the only place on earth where every name, and correspondingly every meaning, has been misplaced. Not one building in the city is used for the purpose for which it was built.

As a result the city seems rather like the set for a huge stage production which has ended, whose performers have sung their arias and gone and whose stage hands, of which there are very many, have emerged from backstage. They seem like the extras of a completely different play. This lack of correspondence between decorations and performances, between names and objects, constitutes the St Petersburg phenomenon.

This phenomenon is much less noticeable in the palaces, parks and estates in the suburbs of the city. There you will find the greatest possible harmony between past and present. The high and immortal art of the past neutralises and overshadows the squalor of modern life that we so often come across in downtown St Petersburg.

Peterhof

Situated 29 km (18 miles) to the west of the city is **Petrodvorets ❶** (Peterhof; grounds open daily; Great Palace open Tues–Sun 11am–5pm; other palaces and pavilions May–Sept Tues–Sun 11am–5pm, Oct–Apr Sat and Sun 11am–5pm; entrance fee), one of the most splendid and impressive country estates of the 18th and 19th century. In 1944 the town where it is located became officially known as Petrodvorets (Peter's Palace).

PRECEDING PAGES: winter at Pushkin.
LEFT: the Hall of Muses in Peterhof.
RIGHT: golden statue at Peterhof.

The southern shore of the Gulf of Finland has been populated by Russians for a very long time and was part of the territory of Novgorod. In 1617, however, it was seized by Sweden, thus depriving Russia of its Baltic coastline. Only the Northern War (1700–21), started by Peter I, restored to Russia its outlet to the sea. Peter often went there and a cottage was built for the tsar on the sea shore in 1705. The house was quite small – it had two rooms and was situated slightly to the west of the present-day park.

While the Northern War was in progress, Peter did not concern himself much with the niceties of interior decorating, but after the battle of Poltava (1709) and the naval victories at Gangut (1714) and Grengam (1720), he decided to build a town as a memorial to Russia's victory over Sweden, then its greatest rival, near the new capital. He also wanted Peterhof, in all its finery, to demonstrate the power and wealth of the Russian Empire.

During his trip to France at the end of the 17th century Peter had fallen under the spell of Versailles (the building of which, incidentally, cost France the entire annual income of its population, not to mention the deaths of 15,000 workers during its construction). Peter ordered a "palace and kitchen-garden" (as he called the park and garden) to be built, "better than the French king's at Versailles."

To build parks and gardens on damp clay soil on the shore of the Gulf of Finland (i.e. 12 degrees north of Paris) required drainage work, the removal of layers of clay and the transport of earth and fertilisers to the site by barge.

On Peter's orders tens of thousands of maples, lindens, chestnuts and fruit trees and bushes were brought to Peterhof from Europe. Floods and storms often destroyed the plantations, but they were replanted again and again. Ships brought building materials, fountain parts, wonderful statues, paintings and expensive damask fabrics to the estate. One archive document, for example describes the

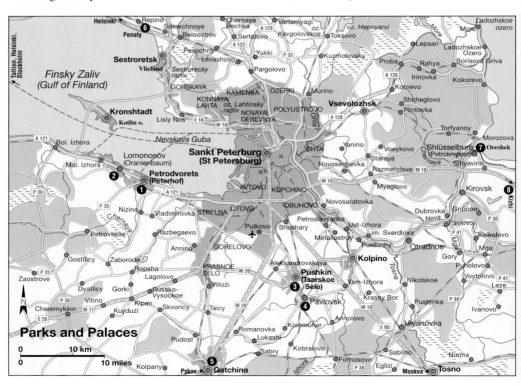

Parks and Palaces

Map on page 236

delivery of "12 lead statues denoting each of the months of the year"; another document records the delivery of a lead statue, "half-man, half-fish".

About 4,000 soldiers and serfs worked on the canal for the fountains alone. They suffered from the lack of proper living quarters and food, from the bitter cold and from the remorseless onslaught of infectious diseases which resulted in a high mortality rate. So, in this sense at least, Peterhof succeeded in surpassing Versailles.

Once the Northern War had ended Peter speeded up the construction work, taking part personally in the drawing up of plans and, according to his habit of putting the maximum amount of detail into each task, showing what and how he wanted things done. Here, for example, is just one quotation from one of his many orders: "Build a cart for Neptune and his four horses, from whose mouths water will flow in cascades, and put tritons on the ledges, so that it looks as if they are playing on horns, the tritons to be set in motion by

BELOW: Pavlovsk during the 18th century.

water, playing various water games." Peter not only thought up themes for groups of fountains, but also gave instructions for building ornamental paths. They were laid in such a way that not a single garden decoration was hidden from the sight of visitors. Peter chivied his craftsmen and ordered: "Appoint officers to keep an eye on every piece of work..."

Peterhof's fountains

The talented Russian architects Peter Yeropkin and Mikhail Zemtsov played a major role in the building of Peterhof in the initial stages, while its system of fountains, one of the world's greatest, was constructed under the supervision of Russia's first hydraulic engineer, Vassili Tuvolkov.

In 1715, together with Vassili Suvorov (father of the future military commander), Tuvolkov was sent to France "to the places where canals, docks and harbours were built, so that they could get a look at the machines and the like." Returning to Russia at the end of 1720, he began the

construction of hydraulic installations at such a fast pace that in eight months the first test-run took place to try out the fountains. The intricate piping system stretched from the so-called Ropsha Heights, 22 km (14 miles) away, and was appreciated by specialists as "a masterpiece of hydraulic art of the 18th century," while the beauty, grandeur and technically rational design of the fountains markedly surpassed that of the celebrated waterworks at Versailles.

In the following years such major Russian and West European architects and sculptors of the 18th century as Bartolomeo Carlo Rastrelli and his Russified son Varfolomei, Andrei Voronikhin, Mikhail Kozlovsky, Fyodor Shubin, Ivan Martos, Giacomo Quarenghi, Andrei Stakenschneider, Nikolai Benois and many others contributed to the creation of Peterhof's artistic appearance. With the help of these celebrated architects the Hermitage, Monplaisir Palace, Chateau de Marly and Bolshoy dvorets (Great Palace), as well as new fountains and a number of park buildings, were all completed. At the end of two centuries of construction work the famous Peterhof palace and park complex was finished, incorporating seven parks with a combined area of more than 600 hectares (1,500 acres) and more than 20 palaces and pavilions.

In 1734–35, Peterhof's largest fountain, Samson, was constructed at the base of the Grand Cascade. Peter wanted to immortalise the victory of Russia over Sweden in the form of the demigod Hercules "who wrestles with a nineheaded monster called the Hydra." But instead of Hercules a statue of the Biblical hero Samson, tearing open the lion's jaws, was put in the middle of the fountain.

This sculpture allegorically portrayed the victory of the Russian forces over the Swedes in the decisive battle of the Northern War at Poltava, a battle which took place on Samson Day, 27 June 1709. The lion symbolises Sweden. In the 18th century there were palisades all along the

BELOW: the South Parade, Grand Palace, Peterhof.

Map on page 236

canal, from the sea to the palace, with recesses in which fountains on the theme of Aesop's fables were built. The so-called Favourite Fountain, built on the principle of Segner's wheel, was also installed: the figures decorating this fountain portray a dog chasing ducks. The explanation for this fountain was as follows: "The favourite dog chases ducks in the water. Then the ducks tell him that he should not bother for he has the strength to chase them but not the strength to catch them." Many such humorous fountains adorn the avenues of Peterhof.

For two centuries the parks were out of bounds to the public. In the 18th century the guard at Peterhof was ordered "in no uncertain terms" to "make absolutely sure that the vulgar masses or, worse, beggars didn't wander around the garden and were not admitted under any circumstances."

After 1917, by special decree of the Council of People's Commissars, Peterhof's monuments were put in the care of the state, and on 18 May the first workers' excursion in the history of Peterhof passed through the halls of the Grand Palace carrying a red flag and revolutionary posters.

The visit to the palace by these 500 people marked the beginning of the Peterhof palace-museums; the gardens and parks of this wonderful area outside St Petersburg have became one of the favourite summer resting places of St Petersburgers and an obligatory stop for tourists from all corners of the globe.

The Great Palace destroyed

In September 1941, Hitler's invading forces managed to break through to Peterhof, which they occupied for 27 months. As a result, the Great Palace was destroyed, the fountains, statues, dams and sluices were wrecked and about 14,000 trees chopped down.

The restoration of Peterhof began as early as 1944. The restoration workers were helped by over 2,000 St Petersburgers every week, who went there on Sundays. They dismantled 300 dug-outs and bunkers, and filled in about 30 km (18 miles) of ditches and trenches. By June

1945 the Peterhof parks were open to visitors and the following spring the fountains were turned on.

The restoration work continued, however, for many more years. A new statue was erected in place of the figure of Samson, formerly at the base of the Grand Cascade but now stolen by Hitler's soldiers. Not far from Samson, at the crossroads of the Monplaisir and Marly avenues, had stood a bronze statue of Peter the Great erected in 1883 by the outstanding sculptor Mark Antokolsky. The Nazis stole this sculpture but it was recreated from a second copy kept in the Naval Museum in St Petersburg.

Restoration work

The restoration work at Peterhof was accompanied by extensive scientific research. For example, window glass, which in its external appearance does not differ from the few surviving ancient fragments, was made for the Monplaisir Palace with the help of the glass-working

department of the St Petersburg Technological Institute.

The walls of one of the rooms of the Monplaisir Palace – the Japanese room – were decorated with wooden panels with intricate drawings, formerly thought to be made by Japanese and Chinese craftsmen. These panels were used as firewood by the invaders, and it was only by chance that the restoration workers found three surviving panels in a nearby bunker built by the Nazis. It turned out that the panels were not, after all, the work of Oriental craftsmen, but rather of Russian icon-painters from the famous village of Palekh. Contemporary Palekh artists were able to recreate the works of their ancestors quite quickly.

By contrast, it took over 10 years to restore, from old photographs and drawings, the 2.5-metre (8-ft) shining golden bowl on the roof of the Great Palace, first put there more than 200 years ago but removed during the war. The list of such examples is endless.

The Grand Cascade

What do the large numbers of visitors who set off for Peterhof between spring and autumn on suburban trains, tour buses and, most popular of all, on hydrofoils, see? First and foremost, of course, they see the **Bolshoy kaskad** (Grand Cascade fountains; open May–early Oct 11am–5pm) running down from the foot of the Grand Palace to the edges of the Lower Park. The Grand Cascade ensemble is made up of 17 steps, 39 gilded bronze statues, 29 bas-reliefs and 142 spurts from 64 water jets. On the upper level of the cascade is the group of sculptures called Tritons Blowing into Sea Shells. The streams of water from these shells fall on to the exquisite Basket Fountain.

The steps of the cascade are adorned with sculptures of ancient gods and heroes, in order to emphasise the theme of Russia's victory in the Northern War. For example, the sculpture of Perseus with the head of Medusa in his hand and the bas-relief Perseus Saving Andromeda

BELOW: the Lower Gardens, Peterhof.

Map on page 236

from the Sea Monsters can be interpreted as an allegory of the liberation of the lands on the Baltic by the Russian army.

Several sculptures from the Grand Cascade serve as satirical allegories on the defeated Swedish king, Charles XII. One of these sculptures is The Frightened Actaeon, Running Away from His Own Dogs – an allegoric depiction of Charles XII, abandoned by his allies after the defeat. Another sculpture ridicules the king's love for himself – Narcissus, Turned into a Flower. Almost every sculpture of the Grand Cascade is imbued with various allegorical meanings.

The Lower Park

Less decorative, but still very interesting, are the cascades in the Lower Park, known as Golden Hill and Chess Hill. Wide avenues lead to the Monplaisir Palace, the Hermitage Pavilion, other cascades and the fountains known as Adam and Eve. The Great Fountains at the foot of the Golden Hill are of note – the water

bursts from them in jets of up to 30-cm (12-in) in diameter. Not by chance were they called Menagerie (Economic) in the past – these powerful streams are hollow.

The variety of fountains in the Lower Park is striking. Here you can see the water jets of the Roman Fountains and the Cup, the 505 jets of the Pyramid Fountain and dozens of others: the golden shroud of bell-shaped waterfalls at the foot of the gilded statues in the Monplaisir Garden and around the Marly Palace; streams of water pouring out of the mouths of dragons, dolphins and sea shells held by marine gods, water streaming smoothly over the squares of Chess Hill, through the marble and gilt of Golden Hill; seething waterfalls rushing down the steps of the Grand Cascade and flowing together towards the basin, over which a wide stream of water foams at a height of 20 metres (65 ft) from the lion's jaws being torn open by Samson. The jets of water shooting upwards, the gleaming of the gilded statues and the miraculous

**BELOW:
the Samson
fountain at
Peterhof.**

intertwining of streams, above which tiny droplets of water create rainbows, all combine to make a magnificent sight.

In the amount of water it uses, the variety of forms and the length of time the fountains are in operation, Peterhof is second to none in the world. Despite the fact that, in one working season, over 30,000 litres (6,600 gallons) of water are used every second, the fountains can work for 10 to 12 hours a day for up to five months a year. Peterhof is of course first and foremost about fountains, but there is more than this to see. This was the main country residence of the tsars, frequented especially in the 18th and early 20th centuries. For example, a few weeks before the outbreak of World War I, Raymond Poincare stayed here as a guest of Tsar Nicholas II.

There is, however, not just the one palace here. There are several dozen first-class buildings built in the 18th and 19th centuries, of which nine are now museums. The last two of these to be opened were the memorial museum of the international Benois family (whose members contributed greatly over three centuries to the artistic appearance of the town), and the museum of wax sculptures opened in the summer of 1990. The ambitious creators of this museum intended, eventually, to make it more lavish than Madame Tussaud's in London.

Peterhof can be reached by a special double-decker shuttle bus from the Baltiysky train station (metro Baltiyskaya), or by hydrofoil leaving twice hourly from the Dvortsovaya Embankment in from of the Hermitage.

Lomonosov

If you leave Peterhof and travel along the shore of the Gulf of Finland for another 10 km (6 miles) you will come to **Lomonosov** ❷ (open daily 11am–5pm, closed Tues and the last Mon of the month; entrance fee), once known as Oranienbaum, 40 km (25 miles) west of St Petersburg. This palace was founded in 1707 by Peter the Great's favourite,

BELOW: detail of a garden urn.

Map
on page
236

Alexander Menshikov, and renamed in 1948 in honour of "the father of Russian science", Mikhail Lomonosov, who opened a factory here in the middle of the 18th century.

It was often the case with the former pastry-cook, the dazzling Prince Menshikov, that his own residences significantly outshone the court of Peter the Great in size and splendour – as does the Menshikov Palace on the University Embankment in St Petersburg.

Similarly, the Oranienbaum Palace, built on the Izhora lands which he received as a gift from Peter I, turned out to be significantly bigger and more splendid than the palace built at Peterhof by the Russian tsar at the same time. Of course, the Peterhof palace was soon extended, and this main seashore residence of the tsar later overshadowed Oranienbaum, which remained in the possession of the tsar's distant relatives (specifically, the Mecklenburg-Streletskys).

However, Oranienbaum has at least one very important distinction – it was the only country palace in St Petersburg not to have been destroyed by the Nazis, and therefore it has been preserved in its original form rather than as a reconstruction.

The most important building at Oranienbaum is the **Bolshoy dvorets** (Grand Palace), built in 1710–25 by architects Gottfried Schadel and Giovanni Fontana, on the crest of the ridge along the shore. The building consists of a central section and side wings which were extended into octagonal pavilions. A church was situated in the western pavilion, while the eastern pavilion housed a Japanese hall. Terraces sloping down from the palace to the sea are adorned with elaborate balustrades and sculptures.

In front of the palace, on the empty shore of the Gulf of Finland, a Lower Park was built with fountains, statues, greenhouses and menageries. The strict geometrical planning of the park (the so-called regular style) was embellished with a man-made canal which, according to legend, was dug by 9,000 serfs in three days. The most significant buildings of the middle of the 18th century, when

Oranienbaum belonged to the husband of the future Catherine II, are the two-storey palace of Peter III, situated on the high right bank of the River Karost in the eastern part of the Upper Park, and also the Kamenny (Stone) Hall, the Opera House and the entire fortress of Peterstadt.

The final stage in the creation of the architectural ensemble at Oranienbaum was the construction, in 1762–68, of the famous Chinese Palace with its suite of ceremonial rooms, including the Hall of Muses, the Blue Drawing Room, the Bead Study, the Great Hall, the Lilac Drawing Room and the Great and Small Studies.

For two centuries visitors have been amazed by the fineness and exquisiteness of the interior decor: the murals and painted panels (the work of Stefano Torelli and Serafin Barozzi), the delicate stucco work, the embroidery and, finally, the parquet floors made of thin layers of maple, oak, ash, walnut, boxwood, larch, rosewood and mahogany. One of the most remarkable rooms in terms of artistic decoration is the

Bead Study, with its mosaic floor of coloured smalt (a glass-like alloy). This art, which is rooted in the ancient Orient, owes its revival to Lomon-osov. Unfortunately, however, only a part of this masterpiece has survived to be seen by visitors.

There is one more principal sight at Oranienbaum – the fine architecture of the white and blue Toboggan Hill (Katalnaya Gorka) in the northwestern section of the Upper Park. Such pavilions are purely Russian structures dating back to the 18th century when they formed one of the most popular attractions on public holidays. The design of the Oranienbaum buildings is severe and at the same time grand. This impression is created by the stepped silhouette of the buildings, the delicate colonnade on the ground floor, the smooth semi-circular cornices and slender, elegant dome.

Lomonosov takes one hour to reach by suburban train (don't be too shocked by the lack of comfort) from the Baltiysky train station at Baltiyskaya metro.

Pushkin

The foundation of **Pushkin** ❸, 25 km (16 miles) south of St Petersburg dates back to the beginning of the 18th century when royal country residences and summer cottages for nobles were being built around the growing capital. The first to be built here was the small country estate of Saari-Mois (meaning "elevated place" in Finnish) which comes out as Saarskaya Myza in Russian.

In 1710 Peter the Great presented the lands of this estate to his wife, the future Catherine I. From that time the place was called Saarskoye Selo, and after 1725, Tsarskoe Selo (Czsar's Village). In 1918, its name was changed again, for obvious reasons, to Detskoe Selo (Children's Village) and in 1937 the town was renamed yet again; it is now called Pushkin, in honour of the poet. Stone palaces with 16 front rooms were built for the first owners of Saarskaya Myza (on the site of the future Grand Palace). Serfs from the surrounding villages dug ponds, laid out gar-

BELOW: Catherine Palace at Pushkin.

Map on page 236

dens and built greenhouses and menageries – these were always included in tsars' country residences – where hunts were organised.

One of the most significant dates in the history of Tsarskoe Selo was the middle of the 18th century when this place became the main summer residence of the royal family (it remained so until 1917). In the 1740s and '50s, thousands of workers, serfs, soldiers and sailors extended and planned the parks and constructed the grandiose building of the **Yekaterininsky dvorets** (Catherine Palace; open daily 10am–5pm, closed Tues and the last Mon of the month; entrance fee), designed by the Russian architects Andrei Kvasov and Savva Chevakinsky.

The building was completed during the third quarter of the 18th century when the task was entrusted to the most outstanding architect of those days, Bartolomeo Rastrelli. As a result, a magnificent building was created, astounding the contemporary population by its beauty and exquisite form. The turquoise, white and gold facade, stretching for 306 metres (1,000 ft), is noted for its splendid decoration, the monumental rhythm of its columns and sculptures and its more than 200 types of stucco ornamentation.

The building is made even more grandiose by the large square in front of it, enveloped by two semi-circles of single-storey auxiliary buildings. The palace's golden suite of ceremonial rooms, including the world-famous Amber Hall, the Great Hall, the Picture Gallery, the Green Dining Room, the Lyons Parlour, the Blue Study, the Blue Drawing Room and the Maple Bedroom have all gone down in the history of art as matchless examples of Russian baroque architecture and for two centuries they have stunned visitors by their richness, originality, artistic scope and tastefulness. Second only in this respect to the Winter Palace in St Petersburg, the Catherine Palace is a valuable treasure house of decorative and applied art. But unlike the Hermitage, the Cather-

BELOW: towers of Catherine Palace.

ine Palace is still full of life. On New Year's Eve and during the summer months, organisations and wealthy individuals rent the palace to throw a full-fledged tsarist-style ball that costs up to $1,500 a plate.

By the beginning of the 19th century a few more dazzling buildings had appeared in Tsarskoe Selo: the Hermitage, intended for palace banquets, the Grotto Pavilion, the Island Concert Hall and other structures in the clear, severe, laconic style of Russian classicism which replaced the decorative forms of baroque.

Meanwhile the natural "landscape" style dominated in the planning of the famous ponds and the extension of the parks, which now cover 600 hectares (1,500 acres). At this time the Alexander Palace and Lyceum (from where Alexander Pushkin graduated in 1817), the Agate Rooms and the Cameron Gallery were built. Particularly striking is the great architectural brainchild of the outstanding architect Giacomo Quarenghi – the Alexander Palace, which was completed in 1796.

The famous historian Igor Grabar was to write a century later: "In St Petersburg and its suburbs there are palaces that are bigger and more regal than this one, but none can surpass the magnificence of its architecture. Suffice it to mention the mighty double colonnade joining the two wings of the palace. In terms of the artistic scope of its composition and the refinement of detail, this is a masterpiece of world architecture."

It is a great shame that for several decades no visitors have been allowed to see the interior of the **Aleksandrovsky dvorets** (Alexander Palace): until recently it was occupied by the military, and it is now under restoration.

The next most significant building after the Alexander Palace is the **Cameron Gallery**. The base of the building is made out of huge blocks of deliberately coarsely hewn grey stone, which form the ground floor. In stark contrast to this heavy foun-

BELOW: the gardens and the Agate Rooms at the Catherine Palace.

Map on page 236

dation the architect, Charles Cameron, built a light, airy gallery with pale, graceful colonnades and open sunny terraces.

Crowning the whole composition a wide staircase, with curved steps in the upper section, leads down to the Great Lake, uniting architecture and nature. On the high stone pylons on both sides of the staircase stand bronze statues of Hercules and Flora, made in 1786 in the Academy of Arts foundry and based on models by Fyodor Gordeyev. On the gallery's terraces there are 54 sculpted busts of ancient Greek and Roman statesmen, scientists, philosophers and mythological characters. These are first-class copies of the ancient originals.

Further building and finishing touches in the Tsarskoe Selo palace and park ensemble have brought us such masterpieces as the Triumphal Gates in honour of Russia's victory over Napoleon (architect Vassili Stasov), the Evening Hall (designed by Ivan Neyelov), the Granite Terrace (architect Luigi Rusca)

and the bronze *Girl with a Jug* (sculptor Pavel Sokolov). The rapid development of Tsarskoe Selo and its expansion into a sizeable town in the environs of the capital city were encouraged both by the natural desire of many members of St Petersburg's upper classes to be nearer to the imperial family in summer, and by the construction in 1836 of the first regular railway in Russia, linking the town with St Petersburg, on the one hand, and Pavlovsk, on the other.

A whole town quickly sprang up around the railway station, while the St Petersburg nobility built themselves summer cottages along the Pavlovsk highway. In 1887 a model water supply and sewerage system started functioning in Tsarskoe Selo and there was an electric power station – this was actually one of the first towns in Europe to be fully illuminated by electricity. Life was particularly animated here during the time of the last Russian emperor, Nicholas II. He always spent at least six months at a time here

BELOW: ironwork detail.
BELOW RIGHT: a classical sculpture in Pushkin.

with his family in the Alexander Palace, even in winter. Accordingly this palace is the largest of all the country residences around St Petersburg and the balls here overshadowed even those held in the Winter Palace.

The Empress Alexandra's favourite, Grigori Rasputin, was a frequent guest here (he was actually buried in the park here after his murder, but then removed from his grave by revolutionary soldiers). This is where Nicholas II lived as a private citizen, after his abdication, and it was from here that he and his family were taken into exile to the Urals, where they were villainously killed in 1918.

The town suffered terribly during World War II, for it found itself on the front line for nearly two years. Thousands of trees were chopped down, houses and pavilions were burned, bridges were destroyed, and much of the museum's treasures that were left after the evacuation were stolen. This includes the famous Amber Hall, which was untraceable, but which now being rebuilt from scratch by local craftsmen.

Pushkin takes 30 minutes to reach by suburban train from the Vitebsk train station at Pushkinskaya. Or one can take the No. 20 express mini-bus from the Moskovskaya metro station.

Pavlovsk

For many years after the foundation of the town of Tsarskoe Selo in the 18th century, the rulers of Russia used the forested area to the south as a hunting ground. In 1777, Catherine the Great made a gift of this area to her adult son Pavel so that he might build his country cottage there. The creation of the future park began shortly after this with the felling of trees, the clearing of thickets to make way for roads and paths and the draining of marshland.

With the arrival of the Scottish architect, Charles Cameron, plans were drawn up to construct a large palace and an enormous park that would occupy a territory of 600 hectares (1,500 acres) located 26 km (16 miles) to the south of St Peters-

BELOW: the flower garden and south facade at Pavlovsk Palace.

Map on page 236

burg. The result was to be a splendid example of the art of garden and park design and the most outstanding feature of **Pavlovsk** ❹ (palace and park open daily 10am–5pm, closed Fri and the first Mon of the month; entrance fee).

Work was intensified shortly after Pavel I came to the throne in 1796, when Pavlovsk received the status of a city and became the Tsar's official summer residence. V. Brenna was invited to replace Cameron as architect. His task was to make the palace and park larger and still more magnificent.

The third period of construction covers the first quarter of the 19th century when Pavlovsk park was given an artistic completeness akin to that of a landscape painting. Fruitful cooperation between Pietro Gonzaga, Carlo Rossi, Andrei Voronikhin and the reinstated Cameron fortified the expressive quality of the Pavlovsk landscape. With amazing skill and talent, they created a harmony between the buildings and nature and turned Pavlovsk into a priceless ensemble of park and garden art.

The compositional centre of this ensemble is the **Bolshoy dvorets** (Great Palace) which can easily be seen from all parts of the park. It is a high stone building crowned with a dome with 64 colonnades. The central block and one-story galleries leading off it to the side wings were designed by Cameron and built between 1782 and 1789. The construction of the square side blocks and the addition of front yard pavilions was completed in the 1790s by Brenna. Voronikhin began decorating the rooms of the palace in 1803 and Rossi added a library to the north westerly part of the palace in 1822.

The decorations and furniture of the palace rooms are of particular value. The architects used sculptures and paintings, marble, gilt and artistic fabrics to adorn the rooms. Most splendid of all are the Italian, Greek, Cavaliere and Throne Rooms, the War and Peace Rooms and the ceremonial northern and southern suites. When the Nazi occupying forces set fire to the palace much was destroyed. The rooms' architectural decorations, however, remained intact and the palace was once

again opened to visitors in the early 1960s.

Let us now, however, return to the **park**. Its beauty is unique. If the characteristic feature of 18th-century country residences, such as Peterhof, Yekaterininsky and Tsarskoe Selo, is their geometrically correct avenues and paths running through flower beds and the regularity of the trees planted at equal distances from each other, then Pavlovsk Park is distinguished by its beautiful landscapes that create pictures of nature in a natural setting.

The greater part of the park's avenues and paths have free curves and winding along them you can see not strategically pruned and symmetrically positioned lines of trees but freely growing flower beds and trees standing all alone, grouped in such a way as to display the natural beauty of their leaves and crowns. The reservoirs of Pavlovsk Park look like forest lakes with reeds at their banks, while the meandering river is like a quiet stream towards which silver willows incline. The wood-

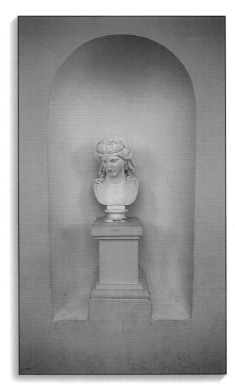

RIGHT: bust detail at the entrance of Pavlovsk Palace.

land park contains elk while, in the lilac thickets, the trill of the nightingale can be heard. Pavlovsk takes 35 minutes to reach by suburban train from the Vitebsk train station at Pushkinskaya metro station.

Gatchina

References to the village of **Gatchina ❺** (open Tues–Sun 10am–5pm; entrance fee) can be traced back to 15th-century manuscripts. At the beginning of the 18th century it was the site of the estate of Peter the Great's sister, Natalia, yet true fame came to Gatchina only after Catherine II came to the throne and presented it to her favourite, Grigory Orlov; he, together with his brothers, had played the most active part in bringing her to the throne while her husband, Peter II, was still alive.

From 1766 to 1772 Gatchina was made into a vast hunting park and a palace was built there by architect Antonio Rinaldi. In 1782 the palace and park ensemble, located 45 km (28 miles) from St Petersburg, and thus the furthest from the capital, came into the hands of Catherine II's son, Pavel I. Pavel duly created a military town-fortress in the Prussian style.

At the same time the palace itself was rebuilt according to the design of architect Brenna and took on the appearance of a medieval castle complete with moat and water, underground bridges and stone bastions. After Pavel's murder, life at Gatchina came to a halt and the palace, as we might say today, became an object of preservation. In 1881 it became the tsar's residence once again, with Alexander III staying there almost uninterruptedly for 13 years. After 1917 (or, as Anna Akhmatova used to say, "after what happened happened") Gatchina, like all other royal residences, was nationalised and became a museum.

There are many things well worth seeing at Gatchina concentrated around the **White Lake**, down to whose banks stretches a picturesque park that has been planted with much art. When its trees were planted the height to which they

BELOW: the Grecian Hall, Pavlovsk Palace.

Map on page 236

would grow was taken into account, as was the colour of the leaves and the time at which they would fall. Strange twisting paths, reservoirs, sunny glades and shady groves have given the park the appearance of untouched "naturalness," in contrast to the formal gardens with their straight avenues, carefully pruned tree tops, fountains and statues.

The **Upper Garden** is located nearby and is modelled on Italian gardens, which were traditionally arranged in terraces along the slopes of hills. Among the interesting buildings to be found in the park is the **Chesme obelisk**, which was erected in honour of the victory of the Russian fleet over the Turks in 1770. Also to be seen are the **Eagle Pavilion**, **Venus Pavilion** and the **Admiralty** where tiny warships were built to be sailed on Gatchina's lakes, the site of make-believe "sea battles" that included broadsides and onboard skirmishes. The palace building stands looking over the gardens and the entire park. According to the design made

out by Antonio Rinaldi, the author of the original project, the main facade was built facing the park with a wide staircase decorated with marble sculptures and five-angled towers.

Among the numerous well-preserved buildings in Gatchina, the **Prioratsky Palace of the Malta Order**, built by architect Nikolai Lvov in 1798, deserves special mention. That year Pavel I became patron of this order and was elected its grandmaster. The palace has the appearance of a medieval castle and it is interesting to note that it was finished in just three months. Lvov's method was to use wooden moulds which were filled with layers of clay and then compressed. The building has stood the test of time and proved the wisdom of its builder.

Gatchina can be reached by a one-hour suburban train ride from Baltiysky station.

Penaty

If you drive along Primorskoe Highway, you pass Ilya Repin's country estate,

BELOW: Penaty, Repin's country estate.

Penaty  (open daily 10.30am–4pm closed Tues; entrance fee). This is where the famous Russian painter lived from 1900 to 1930 and where he created many of his masterpieces, including *Pushkin's Examination* and *Bloody Sunday*. Today you can stroll through the park, visit his studio and living rooms, and get a good feeling for the style of living at the beginning of the century.

Penaty can be reached by a 50-minute suburban train ride from Finland station.

Shlüsselburg

The Neva, as anyone who visits St Petersburg will see, is a deep and full-flowing river. Yet not everyone knows that the Neva is, in fact, very short, beginning only 70 km (44 miles) to the east of St Petersburg where it flows out of Lake Ladoga, the largest lake in Europe.

In the middle of the Neva, at the point where it leaves Lake Ladoga, lies the small island of **Oreshek**  (open daily from 10am–5pm; entrance fee). Here, way

back in 1323, the citizens of Novgorod built a fortress as defence against the constant attacks launched by their northern neighbours.

In 1611, during the Time of Troubles, this region was seized by the Swedes and Oreshek became the Swedish fortress of **Noteborg**. It was only in 1702 that the Russians finally stormed the fortress, which Peter I duly renamed **Shlüsselburg** (Key Castle, from the German *Schlüsselburg*).

Six months later the foundations of St Petersburg were laid at the mouth of the river Neva. Key Castle, like the Peter and Paul Fortress around which the new Russian capital grew up, no longer played a role in deciding the military fate of the country and was turned (again like the Peter and Paul Fortress) into a prison for political prisoners.

Its location on a lonely island in the middle of a wide river with a fast current and its high fortress walls with watchtowers made this prison a most reliable place for confinement. In the course of its entire history no one ever managed to escape. Its proximity to the capital was considered by the government to be of a particular convenience.

In the 18th century the prisoners at Key Castle were mostly members of the royal family and representatives of the upper classes. During the reign of Peter I, Maria Alexeyevna, who had joined in the tsar's son's plot against his father, languished here in captivity for five years until she refused to accept food and died. After Peter's death his widow, Catherine I, had Peter's first wife, Evdokia Lopukhina, hidden away here.

Under Anna Ioannovna, Prince Golitsyn found himself in the fortress for advocating that the rights of the empress be curtailed. Ivan VI spent the last eight years of his confinement here until he was ultimately put to death, despite being innocent of any crime. Having been proclaimed tsar in his infancy, Ivan VI became the unfortunate pawn of palace intrigues before he was dethroned and thrown into a dark dungeon where he languished for 24 years.

LEFT: portrait of Repin.

Map on page 236

The 19th century increasingly witnessed the imprisonment of convinced opponents of autocracy. These included certain Decembrists, many members of the People's Will Organisation and large numbers of revolutionaries. Some of them, like Nikolai Morozov – landowner, revolutionary and scholar – spent more than 25 years in solitary confinement, while Valerian Lukasinsky, a Pole, languished under similar conditions for a total of 37 years.

After the February Revolution of 1917 all prisoners were liberated and the prison buildings burnt down. The ancient fortress once more acquired military significance during the siege of Leningrad in the Great Patriotic War (World War II).

Oreshek Island and the right bank of the Neva were in the full sense of the word a "key" to the Ladoga and it was through here that the only supply line to besieged Leningrad passed.

Today the small industrial town of **Petrokrepost,** officially named Shlüssel-burg, stands on both banks of the Neva. Since 1928 the island has housed a branch of the St Petersburg Museum of Political History. The suburban train for Oreshek leaves from the Finland station and takes one hour to reach its destination.

Kizhi

Reach the eastern coast of Lake Onega and you are already in **Karelia**, famous for its stern and magnificent northern beauty. Earlier it was called "subcapital Siberia," a reference to this region of peaceful birds, blue lakes, bubbling rivers and innumerable islands overgrown with woods.

Petrozavodsk, the capital of Karelia, is located approximately 300 km (190 miles) from St Petersburg on the most westerly bay of Lake Onega, the second biggest in Europe after Lake Ladoga.

Some 68 km (42 miles) from Petrozavodsk lies the island of **Kizhi** ❽, not the biggest but the most famous of all the 1,650 islands in Lake Onega. The name

BELOW: a wooden church at Kizhi.

of the island in Karelian means "playground." In heathen days celebrations took place here.

Later Kizhi became an ecclesiastical centre and in the 18th century, to commemorate the victory over the Swedes, the wooden **Churches of the Transfiguration** and of the **Protecting Veil of the Most Holy Mother of God** were built here.

In 1960, an open-air folk museum was created on Kizhi (open daily; entrance fee). Various buildings dating from the 14th to the 19th century were brought here from different parts of Karelia, including the ancient **St Lazarius Church** from Muromsky Island, houses from previous centuries, barns and an eight-sailed windmill.

In Russia wood has been and remains the most widely used of building materials. Unfortunately, because the life of wood is relatively short and because of frequent fires, many buildings have not survived until our own time. This makes

the museum-reserve on Kizhi even more unique, for here may be seen the great skill of local craftsmen who created the most wonderful masterpieces in wood with the most simple of tools.

The uniqueness of the buildings lies in the fact that they were built without nails. The craftsmen, moreover, used only the simplest tools – with a carpenter's axe and chisel they fitted the logs together in such a way that the solidity of the buildings was ensured. The most ancient of the preserved churches are reminiscent of peasant houses in that they both evolved from primitive timber shell-like structures (incidentally, this type of peasant hut still remains a fundamental feature of modern peasant life).

Later on, in order to create more space in their houses, they began to erect timber huts with numerous corners to them and, in this way, octagonal timber huts and churches with side altars and annexes appeared. In the 16th century churches with domed and tiered roofs appeared, consisting of a number of timber frames put one on top of the other and gradually diminishing in size.

The museum's main attraction is the 22-domed Church of the Transfiguration. Who exactly the builder was is not known. Legend attributes the glory to Nestor who, the story goes, threw his axe into Onega Lake when he had finished the construction work with the words: "This church was built by the master Nestor. There never has been and never will be anything like it evermore."

It was built in 1714 to celebrate the victory of the Russian army in the Northern War. At first sight the building seems a very complex one. Suffice it to say that it is as high as a 12-storey house. The church has survived in such a good state of repair because it was made out of especially tough, dry and resinous pine. It has no facade; to the octagonal timber structure four side altars are attached corresponding to the four points of the compass. To these, five tiers of cupolas are "threaded." The cupolas are of different sizes, something that lends the church its harmonious proportions. ❑

LEFT: statue at the Catherine Palace.
RIGHT: fountain at Peterhof.
FOLLOWING PAGE: detail of a door at the Catherine Palace.

Map on page 236

INSIGHT GUIDES

Travel Tips

Probably the <u>most</u> <u>important</u> TRAVEL TIP you will ever receive

Before you travel abroad, make sure that you and your family are protected from diseases that can cause serious health problems.

For instance, you can pick up *hepatitis A* which infects 10 million people worldwide every year (it's not just a disease of poorer countries) simply through consuming contaminated food or water!

What's more, in many countries if you have an accident needing medical treatment, or even dental treatment, you could also be at risk of infection from *hepatitis B* which is 100 times more infectious than AIDS, and can lead to liver cancer.

The good news is, you can be protected by vaccination against these and other serious diseases, such as *typhoid*, *meningitis* and *yellow fever*.

Travel safely! Check with your doctor at least 8 weeks before you go, to discover whether or not you need protection.

Consult your doctor before you go... not when you return!

SB
SmithKline Beecham
VACCINES

Produced as a service to public health

CONTENTS

Getting Acquainted

Area 6,563,000 sq. miles (17 million sq. km).
Population 146 million.
Politics The Russian Federation is a republic led by an elected president.
Political Parties More than 30 political parties have emerged in Russia since the break-up of the Soviet Union. They range from the pro-reform Union of Right Forces to the radical, ultra-nationalist "Liberal Democrats". Banned by Yeltsin in 1991, the Communist Party was reinstated in 1993 and immediately began to exert a considerable influence in the Russian Parliament.
Currency The rouble.
Languages The official language is Russian. Other languages spoken within the republic reflect the proportions of non-Russian ethnic groups.
Ethnic Groups Russians 82 percent, Tartars 4 percent, Ukrainians 3 percent, others 11 percent.
Religions 82 percent of all believers are Christians (primarily Russian Orthodox, but also Catholics, Baptists and Evangelists); the remainder are Muslims, Jews and Buddhists.
Natural Resources Crude oil, natural gas, coal, timber, manganese, gold, lead, zinc, nickel, potash, phosphates, mercury.
Agriculture Wheat, rye, oats, potatoes, sugar beet, linseed, sunflower seed, cotton, cattle, pigs, sheep.
Major Industries Mining, metallurgy, fuels, building materials, chemicals, machinery, aerospace.

City Profile

St Petersburg is on the same latitude as the southern part of Greenland and Alaska and consists of 72 islands separated by 65 rivers, channels and streams, totalling 160 km (100 miles) in length and spanned by 365 bridges, of which 20 are movable. It covers an area of 1,400 sq. km (540 sq. miles). Its population is now over 5 million and includes over 100 different nationalities and ethnic groups.

In St Petersburg there are some 30,000 weddings and 50,000 births per year; it has 1,455 health care institutions and is home to 41 institutions of higher learning, 450 research institutes and 2,500 libraries with over 150 million books and journals.

The city has 34 large stadiums and **Kavgolovo** 34km (22 miles) away has a 70-metre (230-ft) high ski-jump. There are more than 300 soccer fields and 1,700 basketball, volleyball and tennis courts.

The St Petersburg seaport is the country's largest and, even though the Baltic freezes over during winter, icebreakers keep the port open all year round.

St Petersburg's twin cities are: Bombay, Dresden, Göteborg, Turku, Gdansk, Le Havre, Manchester, Zagreb, Milan, Osaka and Rotterdam.

Government

On paper Russia has a constitution and a democratic parliamentary system. The federal legislature has two houses: the State Duma, the Lower House, where deputies serve two year terms, and the Federation Council, the Upper House, made of two representatives from each of Russia's 89 regions. Russia also has a Supreme Court and a Constitutional Court.

Despite this division of power, in reality, most political power is concentrated in the executive branch, in the hands of the president, and many political scientists say the country's leader rules as a czsar.

Russia is a Federation, with 89 constituent regions, each run by a governor. But the country is also divided into seven federal districts, each headed by a governor general whose authority supersedes that of the regional governor and who reports directly to the president. This system was created in 2000 by President Vladimir Putin to allow him to keep Russia's rebellious, and sometimes criminal, regional governors in check.

Economy

Russia has a free market economic system, but the state still intervenes heavily into the economic system, both officially and unofficially. The former concerns a myriad of onerous decrees regulating every aspect of business, while the latter concerns the enormous corruption that plagues Russia's state bureaucracy and world of business. The administration of President Putin has promised to wage war on both bureaucracy and corruption, but even the most optimistic forecasts say that significant change will only be seen by the middle of the decade.

Business Hours

Most stores in St Petersburg are open 10am–8pm, though in the city centre it is not difficult to find a 24 hour convenience food store. More and more businesses are working the entire day, foregoing closure at lunchtime. But many organisations, such as banks, do close for one hour, either between 1–2pm, or 2–3pm. Don't be shocked if service is not so courteous, but slowly sales personnel are being taught that the customer is most important.

Public Holidays

Besides the official state holidays below, Russians celebrate many other holidays. For instance, Russians celebrate the 'Old' New Year on 13 January, which is the New Year according to the pre-Revolution Gregorian calendar. Then in May, because of the proximity of three official days off, many people take a 10-day holiday, going to the country house to prepare for summer. In August, it seems the whole country shuts down, and it's difficult to find someone at his or her place of work. Many go to their country house, or visit relatives elsewhere in Russia.

- 1–2 Jan **New Year's Day**
- 7 Jan **Russian Orthodox Christmas**
- 8 March International Women's Day
- April Easter
- 1–2 May **Labour/Spring Holidays**
- 9 May **Victory Day**
- 12 June **Independence Day**
- 7 Nov **Day of Reconciliation**
- 12 Dec **Constitution Day**

Time Zones

St Petersburg time is GMT plus 3 hours. The same time is adopted nearly everywhere west of the Urals, although Western Ukrainians and the people of the Baltic states prefer to use the Mean European Time (GMT plus 1 hour) in their daily life to demonstrate their independence.

Religious Holidays

The most important religious holidays of the year include Christmas (celebrated by the Orthodox Church on 7 January) and Easter (a movable holiday celebrated in March–April).

Climate

St Petersburg has a maritime climate with cold winters -25°C/-13°F) and hot summers 30°C/86°F), the average temperatures, however, lie between 8°C/19°F) and 18°C/64°F). On 222 days the temperature rises above freezing and it rains an average of 126 days per year. Most precipitation is in August, and the least in March. The bathing season on the Gulf of Finland lasts from mid-June to the end of August when water temperatures are between 10°C (52°F) and 24°C (79°F).

Planning the Trip

What To Bring

ELECTRICITY

Electrical current in St Petersburg tourist hotels is normally 220 volts AC. Elsewhere in Russia it can vary. In some remote places you will also find 127 volts. Sockets require a continental type plug. It is best to have a set of adaptors with you. If your appliances depend on a supply of batteries, bring plenty with you, since they might not be available in Russia, even for hard currency.

What To Wear

Today St Petersburg is visited by many visitors who demonstrate all the caprices of fashion. Therefore the old guide book phrase, "when going to Russia, follow a modest and classic style of clothes" is outdated. You may dress as you would at home.

Coming to St Petersburg in the cold months (November to March) you should not be surprised to encounter temperatures as low as 30°C (-22°F). Waterproof shoes are a necessity in winter, since the traditional Russian frost is not as frosty anymore and is often interrupted by periods of thaw. For business meetings formal dress is obligatory. The dress code is as rigorously enforced as in the West and compliance with it is an important matter of status.

Entry Regulations

VISAS & PASSPORTS

A visitor to Russia must have a valid passport and a visa. The easiest way to obtain a visa is through a travel agent. A tourist visa is valid for between 10 and 90 days and varies in price, depending on how quickly it is needed. On the visa are the date and place of arrival and departure as well as the length of the trip. Changes are only possible in conjunction with an Intourist office. It is only possible to extend a trip to St Petersburg after arrival. In order to obtain a visa the travel agency will require a valid passport, visa application form, three passport photographs and, if you do not have an invitation from relatives or friends (see below), confirmation of hotel reservations. If you apply individually from an embassy or consulate, rather than through a travel agency, you should allow ample time, as it might take up to a month or so to check your papers.

According to the new regulations, this term can be shortened to 48 hours if an applicant is a business traveller or if he has a written invitation (telex and fax are also accepted) from a Russian host. However, it might take the Russian counterpart some time to have the invitation stamped by the local authority. If you go to Russia at the invitation of relatives or friends, you can get a visa for a private journey which presupposes that no hotel reservation is needed. Individual tourists should have their trip organised through their Russian hosts or a travel agency.

The visa is not stamped into the passport but onto a separate sheet of paper, consisting of three sections. The first part is removed when a person enters the country, the last is taken out when leaving it.

According to Russian law, everyone should carry his or her passport (Russians have an internal one) at all time. Foreigners also need to carry a visa. Some choose to carry photocopies of these in case they go missing, as indeed it is extremely difficult to replace your visa if lost or stolen. But police don't always accept photocopies as valid. Be careful of the police, especially at night, as they often swindle citizens and tourists.

Updates

While the rate of change has slowed in the decade after the collapse of the Soviet Union, there is still a greater amount of flux than in western Europe. The information in this book may become quickly outdated; for the most up-to-date information, you can access *St. Petersburg: The Guide* at www.spbguide.ru

CUSTOMS

When entering the CIS you will have to fill in a customs declaration which must be kept as carefully as a passport during the whole period of your stay on Russian territory. It must be returned to the customs office, along with another declaration, which you fill in on leaving the country.

Customs regulations have been revised several times in the past few years. Customs authorities want to find a compromise between conforming to international customs regulations in the epoch of openness and preventing the export of large batches of goods bought cheaply in Russian shops for resale in other countries.

The latest edition of the Russian customs regulations prohibits the import and export of weapons and ammunition (excluding approved fowling weapons and hunting tackle), and of drugs and devices for their use. It is prohibited to export antiquities and art objects except for those which the visitor imported to the country and declared on entry.

It is permitted to import free and without limitation: (1) gold and other valuable metals except for gold coins, whose import is prohibited

(2) materials of historic, scientific, and cultural value (3) articles approved by the licensees of V/O Vneshposyltorg (4) foreign currency and foreign currency documents (5) personal property except for computers and other technical devices (*see below*).

Limited Duty-Free Import

● Gifts. You are recommended not to have more than 10 units of an article if you want to escape time-consuming questions from customs officers. For more expensive items, such as electronic equipment, it is best to enquire about customs regulations prior to departure.

● Cars and motorcycles approved according to International Traffic Convention, no more than one unit per family, with the obligation to export the vehicle.

● Spare parts for the vehicles insured by the Russian international insurance company Ingosstrakh and approved by the documents of Ingosstrakh or Intourist (for other spare parts duty must be paid).

● Personal computers, photocopying apparatus, video-recorders, TVSat systems with the obligation to export (if the obligation is broken and the article is sold in Russia, duty must be paid).

● Alcohol (limited to persons over 21) spirits – 1.5 litres, wines – 2 litres.

● Tobacco (limited to persons over 16) 200 cigarettes or 200 grammes of tobacco per person.

Duty-Free Export

● Articles imported by the visitor.

● Foodstuffs in small amounts.

● Alcohol (over 21) spirits 1.5 litres, wines 2 litres per person.

● Tobacco (over 16) 100 cigarettes or 100 grammes of tobacco.

Some of the customs officers are indeed quite severe in their observation of these regulations. Therefore when you enter or leave the country you must expect a careful examination of all your luggage and you will be asked if any personal items are intended for sale in Russia (if the answer is yes, you will have to pay duty).

Money Matters

Foreign currency and other forms of currency such as travellers' cheques and letters of credit may be imported, but must be declared upon arrival on a customs declaration form. Currency taken out of the country must not exceed the amount shown on the import declaration. Officially documented but unspent roubles can be reconverted at the hotel exchange counter or at the Pulkovo 2 airport bank.

EXCHANGE

All major hotels have an official exchange counter where you can buy roubles with hard currency cash, traveller's cheques and credit cards. There are bureaux de change in many of the larger shops. You will be asked to present your passport and visa as well as your customs declaration where all your money transactions have to be recorded. You will need to present this form when leaving the country and you should, as with your passport, make sure not to lose it.

Hard currency can be obtained on an American Express card at the Grand Hotel Europe.

CREDIT CARDS

Most tourist-related businesses accept major credit cards. Hotels, restaurants and co-operative cafés that do so usually have a notice to this effect at the entrance. As well as American Express, Diners Club, Visa, Eurocard and Mastercard are also accepted.

LOCAL CURRENCY

Roubles come in both banknotes and coins. One rouble is equal to 100 kopeks. Details of current exchange rates are available from all bureaux de change.

THE BLACK MARKET

As everyone knows, dealing in convertible currency is against the law. It is true to say that no foreign national has yet been punished for violating currency regulations. As for the speculators, they do not even attempt to hide – in part because they know that their crime is difficult to prove. Even so, think twice before you agree to do business. Foreigners are often conned with money that has been withdrawn from circulation or through sleight of hand (money is counted as you watch, but only half of the agreed sum – at best – will make its way into your pocket).

Getting There

BY AIR

International airlines connect St Petersburg directly with 16 European countries. There are four weekly flights from London with British Airways and three weekly flights with Aeroflot. It is also possible to fly daily with Scandinavian Airlines via Stockholm or five times a week with Austrian Airlines via Vienna. There is a regular Aeroflot service between Moscow and St Petersburg.

International flights arrive at the **Pulkovo 2** Airport, which is 17 km (10½ miles) from the city centre. Pulkovo 2 is just 10 minutes by bus from the domestic airport Pulkovo 1. A shuttle bus service to the city centre is available. The **St Petersburg Air Terminal** is at Nevsky prospekt 7/9; buses for the airports leave from the nearby bus stop at Kirpichny pereulok 3.

Aeroflot operates internal flights linking St Petersburg with 105 cities in the CIS. Fares within the CIS are low, though flights have to be booked far in advance since there is a far greater demand than capacity. Check-in at Aeroflot counters starts three hours and ends 30 minutes before departure. Foreigners must pay for tickets in hard currency.

Foreign Airline Offices in St Petersburg:

British Airways: Malaya Konyushennaya ulitsa, 1, Tel: 329 2565
Delta Airlines: Bolshaya Morskaya, 36, Tel: 311 5819
Finnair: Kazanskaya ulitsa, 44, Tel: 326 1870
KLM: Voznesensky prospekt, 5, Tel: 325 8989
Luftsana: Voznesensky prospekt, 7, Tel: 314 4979

St Petersburg Aeroflot Offices:

Aeroflot Information, Tel: 293 9021; International Department, Tel: 314 6943. The **Central Aeroflot Office** is at Nevsky prospekt 7–9, Tel: 211 7980. Reservation for domestic flights: Aprelskaya ulitsa 5, Tel: 293 9021.

CIS Aeroflot Offices:

Moscow: 37, St Petersburg Highway, Tel: 155 0922.
Kiev: 66, Boulevard Shevchenko, Tel: 774 4223.
Minsk: 18/28, Karl Marx St, Tel: 224 232.
Yerevan: 2, Tumanyan St, Tel: 582 422.
Tbilisi: 2, Javakhishvily St, Tel: 932 744.
Vilnius: 21, Lenin Prospekt, Tel: 756 175.
Khabarovsk: 5, Amursky Blvd, Tel: 332 071.

Aeroflot's International Offices:

London: 69–72 Piccadilly. Tel: 020 7492 1756.
New York: 235 West 48th Street, NY 10036. Tel: (212) 245 1100

BY RAIL

Railway Terminal Information, Tel: 168 0111.
Within the European part of Russia railways are the most important means of passenger transportation. Railways connect St Petersburg with the largest CIS cities (Moscow, Kiev, Minsk) and Western European capitals. If you can spare the time you can travel in a comfortable first class sleeping car, the pride of the Russian Railways. From Central Europe the train takes two days to reach St Petersburg with a change of gauge at the junction with the railway system of the CIS. The Helsinki–St Petersburg route (departure 1pm, arrival 9pm) is the most popular rail route between the West and the CIS.

Travelling time from: Berlin: 33 hrs; Paris: 48 hrs; Warsaw: 22 hrs.

If you want to travel within Russia by train, there are transcontinental rail routes, such as those from Moscow to Vladivostok and from Moscow to Beijing, China. They demand an adventurous spirit and a week spent in the train contemplating the endless Siberian and Transsiberian (Baikal) landscapes. Food for the trip should be taken along since station buffet food is often not to the liking of weary travellers.

St Petersburg has five large stations: The **Baltic Station** with trains to the southern suburbs and Peterhof; the **Finland Station** with trains to Vyborg and Finland; the **Moscow Station**, with trains to Moscow, the northeast and the south of Russia; the **Vitebsk Station** with trains to the Ukraine and Belorussia, and to Pushkin and Pavlovsk; and the **Warsaw Station** with trains to Tallinn and Riga.

By Sea

St Petersburg can be reached by regular passenger ship from London, Bremerhaven, Helsinki, Copenhagen, Göteborg, Stockholm, Montreal and New York. Intourist and Morflot offices will provide detailed information about sea routes, schedules and bookings.

The **Sea Terminal** with the **Passenger Port** is on Vasilievsky Island and the **River Transport booking office** is at Rechnoy Vokzal, prospekt Obukhovskoy Oborony 195, Tel: 262 1318 (information), 262 5511 (booking office).

BY CAR

If you intend to visit St Petersburg by car you should first get in contact with Intourist as they have worked out a number of routes through the European part of Russia which can easily be negotiated with your own vehicle. The ideal route to St Petersburg is via Helsinki which can be reached comfortably by car ferry.

If you intend to continue within European Russia you can drive to Moscow, the Caucasus and the Black Sea, ferrying the car across to Yalta or Odessa and crossing the Ukraine to Slovakia or Poland. Details for this and other routes (across the Baltic States, Belorussia or Moldavia) can be found in the book *Motorists' Guide to the Soviet Union*, Pergamon Publishers Oxford, 1987. It gives details about fuelling stations, repair shops, overnight stops and emergency procedures.

Since crossing the border into Turkey is now possible, you can also exit or enter via Anatolia. Whether this route remains open, however, depends on the changing political conditions in the Caucasus.

Sovinterautoservice are the specialists for car travel in the CIS. They solve nearly every problem a foreigner is likely to experience on Russian roads. Write or phone for detailed information to Institutski pereulok 2–1, Moscow, Tel: (010 7095) 101 496; Malodyetskoselsky prospekt 24, St Petersburg, Tel: (010 7812) 292 5709 and 292 5763.

During the past few years marked changes have taken place in the quality of services along Russian roads. St Petersburg now has new service and repair stations for non-Russian cars. But you should still be cautious of the state of Russian roads. Diverting from the highways might get you into some unexpected adventures. It is now possible to do this at your own risk, but not necessarily advisable as accommodation and petrol stations are few and far between. We recommend that you organise

your journey through a recognised travel agency. Entry points to the CIS are: Brusnichnoe and Torfyanovka from Finland; Brest and Shegini from Poland; Chop when coming from Czechoslovakia and Hungary; and Porubnoe and Leusheny from Romania. You can also ship your car directly to St Petersburg.

Below are the main road routes to St Petersburg.

From Finland:
Torfyanovka–Vyborg–St Petersburg.

From Western Europe:
Brest–Minsk–Smolensk–Moscow and Chop–Uzhgorod–Lvov–Kiev–Orel–Moscow–St Petersburg.

Useful Addresses

RUSSIAN MISSIONS ABROAD

Australia: Griffis, 70 Canberra Ave, Canberra, Tel: 956 6408.
Canada: 285 Sharlotta St, Ottawa, Tel: 235 4341.
India: Shantipath Street, Chanakiapury, Delhi, Tel: 606 026.
Ireland: 186 Orwell Road, Dublin, Tel: 975 748.
New Zealand: Carory, 57 Messines Rd, Wellington, Tel: 766 113.
Singapore: 51 Nassim Road, Singapore 1025, Tel: 235 1834.
United Kingdom: 5, 13 & 18 Kensington Palace Gardens, London, Tel: 020 7229 3628.
USA: *Embassy:* 1125 16th Street, 20036 Washington DC, Tel: 628 7551, 628 8548, 628 6412. *Consulate:* 2790 Green Street, San Francisco, Tel: 922 6644.

Consulates

Canada: Malodetskoselsky Prospekt, 32, Tel: 325 8448
Germany: Furshtadtskaya ulitsa, 39, Tel: 327 3111
India: Ryleyeva ulitsa, 35, Tel: 272 1731
United Kingdom: Proletarskoy Diktatury ploshchad, 6, Tel: 325 6036
United States: Furshtadtskaya ulitsa, 15, Tel: 275 1701

LOCAL TOUR COMPANIES

Baltic Tours: Nekrasova ulitsa, 4, Tel: 273 2841
Arctur Travel: 6th Line, Vasilievskaya Island, 37, Tel: 327 7101, e-mail: arctur@sco.spb.ru
Escape Travel Ltd: Isaakiyevska ploshchad, 5, Tel: 311 5657
ADM: Ulitsa Marata, 9, office 30, Tel: 325 2233, www.adm.ru
Norvista: Kazanskaya ulitsa, 44, Tel: 326 1850
Russian Cruises, Kazanskaya ulitsa 42, Tel: 325 6120 www.russian-cruises.com Specialises in boat tours on Russia's rivers, as well as to the islands of Valaam and Kizhi.
Davronov Travel: Italyanskaya ulitsa, 17, 3rd Floor, Tel: 311 1629 www.davronov.da.ru Specialises in city tours, and trips to the suburban palaces, such as Peterhof and Pushkin, as well as other towns outside St Petersburg, such as Pskov and Novgorod.
Dassi: Nevsky prospekt, 82, Tel: 275 6019, e-mail: dassi@mail.rcom.ru
West Travel: Griboedov Canal, 12, Tel: 311 3519
MIR International Centre, 45 Voronezhskaya, St Petersburg, Tel: (812) 167 0831, Fax: (812) 167 1830.
The MIR agency can arrange inexpensive group travel, special interest tours, Russian language courses and international group exchange.

They are one of the new co-operatives who try hard to compete with Intourist. They can send out invitations for individual visas, arrange hotel and private accommodation, and make out-of-the-way travel arrangements. They have interpreters, hire out cars with or without drivers and organise symposiums. Their speciality is the organisation of individual trips to Russia, especially St Petersburg where they have their head office.

In St Petersburg they arrange for theatre tickets, restaurant reservations and individually guided city and museum tours.

INTOURIST OFFICES ABROAD

Delhi: Plot 6/7, Block 50-E, Njaja Marg Chanakiapuri, Tel: 609 145.
London: 219 Marsh Wall, Isle of Dogs, London EI4 9FJ, Tel: 020 7538 5902.
Montreal: 801 McGill College Ave, Suite 630, Tel: 849 6394.
New York: 630 Fifth Ave, Suite 868, Tel: 757 3884.
Sydney: Underwood House, 37–49 Pitt St, Tel: 277 652.

OTHER TRAVEL AGENTS

United States
Four Winds Travel, 175 Fifth Ave, New York, NY 10010.
Lindblad Travel Inc, 1 Sylvan Rd North, Westport, CT 06880.
Russian Travel Bureau Inc, 245 E. 44th St, New York, NY 10017.

United Kingdom
Interchange, 27 Stafford Road, Croydon, Surrey CRO 4NG, Tel: 020 8681 3612.
Progressive Tours, I2 Porchester Place, London W2 2BS, Tel: 020 7262 1676.
Voyages Jules Verne, I0 Glentworth Street, London NWI 5PG, Tel: 020 7486 8080.
Barry Martin Travel, I62 Regent Street, London WIX IRA, Tel: 020 7439 1271.
East West Travel, 15 Kensington High Street, London W8 5NP, Tel: 020 7938 3211.
Scotts Tours, 48a Goodge Street, London W1P 1FB, Tel: 020 7580 4843.

Practical Tips

Emergencies

SECURITY & CRIME

In the aftermath of the disintegration of the Soviet Union and the communist planned economy, newly won freedoms have combined with economic decline to produce a drastic increase in crime. This is particularly the case in the Russian metropolises of Moscow and St Petersburg.

Gone are the days when you could walk the streets of St Petersburg at night or leave your valuables unprotected in your hotel room. Criminals want their slice of the currency loaf.

Avoid private cabbies, who are certain to pester you with offers of their services in the international airport or at the hotel. Sometimes they take too much – everything you have, in fact. Be wary of the ladies of the night – many of them are just waiting for you to fall asleep. When you wake up, your things and money may be gone. Do not open your door to people you do not know.

St Petersburg is a beautiful northern city. It is particularly eye-catching between the end of May and the middle of July – the season of white nights. Even though you would be right to rely on the friendliness of the majority of the people you'll meet here – foreigners are still treated with particular respect in Russia – keep our advice in mind. Then your stay in the former Russian capital is certain to be a pleasant one.

Useful Numbers

Information: 008
Collision Ambulance (Skoraya pomoshch): 03
Assistance: 001
Directions within the city: 063
Gas Emergency (Sluzhba gaza): 04
Police (Militsia): 02
Police Task Force for Foreigners: 164 9787
Time: 060
Legal Counselling: 065
Aeroflot Information: 239 9021
Train Information: 168 0111
You will need to speak basic Russian to use these numbers.

SAFETY

Indeed, corrupt police officers are probably the only major worry a visitor to St. Petersburg will have. Best to stay further from them if you see them coming. Street crime is not very common in the centre, except for the pickpockets that work main arteries, such as Nevsky prospekt. Violent crime in the city is mostly connected to conflicts in the rough world of Russian business, and if you are only in the city for pleasure, there is little reason to worry about your physical safety.

Women should be aware that most Russian men can be aggressive, have little sense of proper behaviour, tend to see women as sexual objects, and what is considered to be sexual harassment in Anglo-American countries, is considered a normal way to meet a women in Russia.

Russian women, on the other hand, tend to be demure and rarely take the initiative to meet a man. If a woman in a restaurant or bar comes across as forward, however, there is a good chance she may be a prostitute, many of whom frequent places that foreigners tend to visit. There are many cases where prostitutes drug and rob their clients, so beware if you do use such services.

MEDICAL SERVICES

Visitors from the USA, Canada, European countries and Japan need no health certificate. It is a good idea to take your own medicines although there are chemists selling foreign medicines for hard currency and you can find most things you need.

The most common ailment is a mild stomach upset, but there is a more serious illness that can be picked up from drinking contaminated water containing the parasite *Giardia lamblia*. It is thus advisable to drink either boiled tap water or bottled mineral water. But don't be too alarmed by the "Leningrad water disease". It won't kill you, though it can make life unpleasant. Ask your doctor what you should take with you as recommended treatment.

The following are polyclinics which also stock foreign medicines:
American Medical Centre: Serpukhovskaya ulitsa, 10, Tel: 326 1730. Way overpriced medical care from Russian doctors.
Euromed Clinic: Survorovksy prospekt, 60, Tel: 274 9320. Quality medical care at reasonable prices.
International Clinic: Dostoyevskogo Ulitsa, 19, Tel: 320 3870; Quality medical care at reasonable prices.

Dental Services

American Medical Centre: Serpukhovskaya ulitsa, 10, Tel: 326-1730. Overpriced care from Russian dentists.

Tipping

Although the former Soviet Union was a Socialist state for 70 years, tipping, one of the capitalist sins, was always an accepted practice. Waiters, porters, taxi drivers, especially in Moscow and St Petersburg, have always appreciated tips. As anywhere in the West, 10 percent is the accepted rule. However, do not tip guides, interpreters or other Intourist personnel.

If you want to show your gratitude they will appreciate a small souvenir or gift.

Religious Services

Russian Orthodox: Cathedral of the Trinity, ploshchad Alexandra Nevskovo; Cathedral of St Nicholas, ploshchad Kommunarov; Cathedral of the Transfiguration, ploshchad Radischeva; Vladimir Church, Vladimirskaya ploshchad.
Catholic: The Catholic Church, Kovensky pereulok 7.
Baptist: The Baptist Church, 29a Bolshaya Ozernaya ulitsa.
Mosque: Mechet, 7 Kronversky prospekt.
Synagogue: The Synagogue, 2 Lermontovsky prospekt.

Postal Services

Main post office (Glavny Pochtant): Pochantskaya ulitsa 9 (9am–9pm, Sundays 10am–8pm); every large hotel has a post office with facilities for basic postal services. Other post offices usually open at 10am, but routine postal services are available at reception in the larger hotels between 8am–10pm. There is no new official postal tariff and it is advisable to check charges at an Intourist office.
Westpost: Nevsky prospekt, 86, Tel: 327 3092, Open Mon–Fri 9.30am–8pm. American-owned postal service that delivers to Europe and America in about a week for $2–$3 a standard letter.
Fedex: Griboedov Canal, 16, Tel: 327 0480 or 299 9071
TNT: Sofiiskaya ulitsa, 14, Tel: 118 3330

Telecommunications

Central telephone and telegraph office: Pochantskaya ulitsa 9. For a pay phone the token must be inserted before dialling. If you hear a bip-bip tone during the conversation insert another token. In the past, visitors had to book international calls in advance. Now, if you don't enlist the services of a hotel, it is possible to call abroad direct

from a private phone. Dial 8 +10 + the international code: Australia 61; France 33; Germany 49; Japan 81; Netherlands 31; Spain 34; United Kingdom 44; US and Canada 1. If calling St Petersburg from abroad be warned that the lines are not very good and are very busy. The international direct dial code for St Petersburg is 7-812.

Photography

Photographic equipment is easily obtained and there are quick film-developing services. Most hotels sell photographic equipment. Generally speaking, taking photographs in galleries, museums and exhibitions is permitted, though often at a hefty charge. You should not take photographs of military installations or from aeroplanes and it is also not recommended to take them from the train. The interpretation of what constitutes a military installation rests with the officials. You will have to be cautious and if possible ask your guide or interpreter before you take a picture of a bridge, a railway station, an airport or anything else that might be seen as a security object.

Travelling with Kids

Unless your children are interested in the high culture that the city has to offer, there is not much for them to do. Even locals bemoan the fact that on weekends there are few places to take children except for a walk in the park, or in the forest when the weather is warm. Amusement parks are often small and decrepit, though there is a highly regarded puppet theatre. Few travellers bring children under 18.

Gay Travellers

Since the change in Russia's legal system in the mid-1990s that abolished Soviet-era prohibitions on homosexuality, the city's gay community has come above ground and gained more acceptance. There are several openly gay and lesbian clubs, and society is more tolerant than it was just five years ago. Some say that a gay lifestyle is even fashionable in the city and common among prominent government officials and business leaders.

Travellers with Disabilities

It is strongly recommended that disabled travellers do not travel alone. In general, Russian society is not sympathetic to the plight of the disabled, and has a long way to go to improve their ability to be active members of society.

The city and Russia is quite difficult for disabled travellers to get around, though progress is slowly being made. The Russian Museum, for instance, recently installed equipment to allow those in wheelchairs to go upstairs. But most places do not have the means to accommodate those in wheelchairs. Likewise, the transport system provides no assistance, and it is even difficult to rent a car or van that would have such capacity.

Etiquette

Don't be surprised by Russians' rudeness, near lack of public manners and don't expect a Russian to apologise if he happens to bump into you accidentally on the street. Also, car drivers can be one of the most dangerous encounters for a foot-bound traveller. Even if you have a green light, they may not stop and may beep and shout at you to get out of the way.

Russians tend to be an unpredictable and emotional people (though of all Russian cities, the people of St Petersburg tend to be the most reserved), who sometimes appear to be angry, screaming and yelling. Often it is just the normal way they speak to each other, and one need not be alarmed. But if a Russian is indeed angry, their mood can just as easily change to joy and laughter. Don't worry about Russian

mood swings. Despite, their public rudeness, Russians are quite demanding and snobbish when it comes to etiquette at the home and at work, and one must be careful not to offend. Russians can be very kind, sometimes too much so, in the home and on a personal level. For instance, you should take off your shoes and put on slippers. Failure to eat and drink what your host offers will be taken as a grave offence.

Russians don't like small talk, as is common in the West, and don't be surprised if they ask you some questions Westerners find quite personal, as well as make comments in that vein. For instance, a young woman, aged 27, might be questioned why isn't she married with children. Likewise, feel free to act the same way toward your Russian acquaintance or friend. They won't be offended, but rather enjoy the chance to talk in depth, and not just about the weather.

Getting Around

Public Transport

The Metro dazzles with the beauty of its stations, particularly those that were built in the 1950s. But the initial rapture quickly disappears at the sight of the crowds which cram into the cars like the proverbial sardines. And the Metro will not necessarily take you anywhere you want to go. The extensive network of surface transport – buses, trolleys and trams – can also let you down, even though the fares are still very cheap by Western standards.

If you are alone in town, you may find it hard to find your way, particularly if you have to travel far. You also have to bear in mind that in St Petersburg, as indeed all over Russia, transport does not run in accordance with a rigid schedule, and you may have to wait a while. So it may be best to take a taxi and be ready to give a large tip.

TAXIS

If you're looking to save money and feel confident negotiating in Russian or sign language, a *chastnik*, or private car, is the best deal. Most Russians travel this way, and if you're travelling during the day and in the centre, it is safe and sometimes even interesting, should your driver be an aspiring poet or unemployed nuclear scientist trying to make ends meet. At night and during long trips beyond the city centre, however, most people think twice about whom they hitch a ride from.

But if money is not a problem, and one feels uncomfortable doing as the Russians do, there are a number of taxi services to choose from.

Taxi Blues: Ulitsa Krasnovo Tekstilshika, Tel: 274 3786

Peterburg Taxi: Tel: 068, www.taxi068.spb.ru

Konnyushenny: Konnyushennaya ploshchad, 2, Tel: 313-7600, or 312-0022; open 24 hours

CAR HIRE

Official car hire agencies can be quite expensive, and many travellers understandably prefer not to drive in a foreign city. Hiring a private car and driver is the best way to get around town with the least amount of hassle. Many foreign tourists choose this option. If you have friends or acquaintances in town, ask them to find a driver; a fee of about $50–$70 a day is more than enough.

Hertz: Pulkovo 1 and 2, Tel: 324 3242

Executive Car: 2nd Line, Vasilievsky Island, 35, Tel: 327 7256

Rolf: Vitebsky prospekt, 17, Tel: 327 0660

Service Stations

In St Petersburg there are service stations that are used to dealing with foreigners at: 5 Pervaya Staroderevenskaya ulitsa, Tel: 233 6930. Open 8am–8pm and at 69 prospekt Kosmonavtov, Tel: 299 6302. Open 8am–9pm.

Parking

Parking is free where there is no prohibiting sign. Protected parking is available at Isaakiyevskaya ploshchad, next to the Astoria Hotel, on the Vyborg side, at 5 Pervaya Staroderevenskaya ulitsa.

Rules Of The Road

Russia is a signatory to the International Traffic Convention. Rules of the road and road signs correspond in general to international standards. The basic rules, however, are worth mentioning.

● Traffic drives on the right.

● It is prohibited to drive a car after consuming even the smallest amount of alcohol. If the driver shows a positive alcohol test, the consequences may be very serious. It is also prohibited to drive a car under the effect of drugs or strong medicines.

● Drivers must have an international driving licence and documents verifying their right to drive the car. These papers must be in Russian and are issued by Intourist.

● Vehicles, except for those rented from official travel agencies such as Intourist and Mir, must carry the national registration code. All must have a national licence plate.

● The use of the horn is prohibited within city limits except in emergencies.

● The use of seat belts for the driver and front seat passenger is compulsory.

● The speed limit in populated areas (marked by blue coloured signs indicating "town") is 60 kph (37 mph); on most arterial roads the limit is 90 kph (55 mph). On

highways different limits apply and these are shown on road signs.

● You can insure your car in Russia through **Ingosstrakh**, the national insurance company.

THE METRO

The most convenient local transport is St Petersburg's Metro. Construction started before the war and was completed in 1955. All the major hotels have Metro stations marked "**M**", nearby.

On 15 November 1955, the first Metro line was opened from Uprising Square (now Znamenskaya ploshchad) to Avtovo, covering some 11 km/7 miles. Now the lines total 60 km/38 miles, and trains run at speeds of 40 kph (25 mph); during the rush hours trains arrive at intervals of 1½ minutes.

The signs and underground maps with lighted routes make it possible to find the right direction quickly, as long as you can read Cyrillic letters. The cost of a one-way ticket is subject to rapid inflation. Tokens are bought at the ticket office and are fed into the automatic barriers. The Metro runs from 5.30 to 12.30am.

There are four lines in operation: The **Moskovsko-Petrogradskaya Line**, the **Kirovsko-Vyborgskaya Line**, the **Nevsko-Vasileostovskaya Line** and the **Pravoberezhnaya Line**.

The stations were built in many architectural styles. Some of the most impressive are: Avtovo, Kirovsky Zavod, Narvskaya, Baltiskaya, Znamenskaya Ploshchad and Ploshchad Muzhestva on the Kirovsko-

Bridge Closing Hours

One of St Petersburg's most unique and beautiful sights is the raising of the bridges. But it can also cause great inconvenience and one must schedule one's nightlife around the bridges if you don't wish to be stuck in one part of town. If you are, and need to cross the river, the city has kindly

allowed Dvortsovy Bridge to close for about 30 minutes to let traffic pass. The sight of the 3am bumper-to-bumper traffic jam of cars trying to cross the bridge is also something to see.
Bridge closing hours are:
Lt. Schmidt, 1.40–4.55am
Liteyny, 1.50–4.40am

Troitsky, 1.50–4.50am
Dvortsovy, 1.35–2.55am, and then again from 3.15–4.50am
Okhitinsky Bolshoy, 2–5am
Volodarsky, 2–3.45am, and then again 4.15–5.45am
Birzhevoy, 2.10–4.50am
Tuchkov, 2.10–3.05am, and then again 3.35–4.45am

Ride through the **past** in a **trishaw** and be welcomed into the **future** by **lions.**

Live it up!

For the time of your life, live it up in Singapore! Explore historic back lanes and shop in malls of the future. Take part in a traditional tea ceremony at a quaint Peranakan house, then tee off for a birdie at one of our challenging golf courses. Spice things up with some hot Pepper Crab and unwind in a world-class spa. Join a Feng Shui Tour to harness positive energy and later channel it into a night on the town. Come to Singapore and catch the buzz and excitement of Asia's most vibrant city.

Singapore NEW ASIA

www.newasia-singapore.com

For more information, mail to: Singapore Tourism Board, Tourism Court, 1 Orchard Spring Lane, Singapore 247729 or Fax to (65) 736 9423.

Name: _____ Address: _____

_____ Email: _____

Holiday villas beyond indulgence.

BALEARICS ~ CARIBBEAN ~ FRANCE ~ GREECE ~ ITALY ~ MAURITIUS
MOROCCO ~ PORTUGAL ~ SCOTLAND ~ SPAIN

If you enjoy the really good things in life, we offer the highest quality holiday villas with the utmost privacy, style and true luxury. You'll find each with maid service and most have swimming pools.

For 18 years, we've gone to great lengths to select the very best villas at all of our locations around the world.

Contact us for a brochure on the destination of your choice and experience what most only dream of.

INTERNATIONAL
CHAPTERS

Toll Free: 1 866 493 8340
International Chapters, 47-51 St. John's Wood High Street, London NW8 7NJ. Telephone: +44(0)20 7722 0722
email: info@villa-rentals.com www.villa-rentals.com

Vyborgskaya Line. On the Moskovsko-Petrogradskaya Line, the Park Pobedy station actually has no boarding platform but is equipped with a "horizontal lift".

Nevsky prospekt and Petrogradskaya are impressive for their optimal use of space. The Nevsko-Vasileostrovskaya Line brings you from the Pribaltiyskaya Hotel to Nevsky prospekt. At the Gostiny Dvor station there is no surface station; the exits lead directly into the department store. At Ploshchad Alexandra Nevskogo the exit leads into the Moskva Hotel.

The transfer stations, where you can change from one line to the other are **Gostiny Dvor**, **Znamenskaya Ploshchad**, **Tekhnologichesky Institut**, **Sadovaya/Ploshchad Mira**, **Vladimirskaya/Dostoyevskaya** and **Ploshchad Alexandra Nevskogo**.

Street Glossary

ulitsa (Ul.) = street
ploshchad (Pl.) = square
pereulok (Per.) = lane, small street
naberezhnaya (Nab.) = embankment
most = bridge
ostrov = island
Vasilievsky ostrov = Vasilievsky Island
Petrogradskaya Storona = Petrograd Side

BY BUS AND TRAM

Services run from 5.30am to midnight. Prices change just about every week.

BY BOAT

From May to October it is possible to view the city from a steamer on the Neva (departure point: Senate's Square, the Palace or the embankment by the Summer Garden) or a river trip to Peterhof (departure point: Palace Embankment at the Hermitage).

On Foot

Anyone lucky enough to be in St Petersburg for the *White Nights* should (one *Night* when half the city inhabitants seem to be on the street) take the following walk: from Dvortsovaya ploshchad (Palace Square) along Millionnaya ulitsa (Millionaire's Street) to Zimnyaya Kanavka (Winter Canal), then left to Dvortsovaya Naberezhnaya (Palace Embankment), along to Dvortsovy most (Palace Bridge) and across the Neva to Birzhevaya ploshchad (Stock Exchange Square) on the Strelka spit. Thanks to the unique lighting of the White Nights, from this spot, the breathtaking view over one of the most beautiful parts of the city spot is doubly impressive.

At other times of the year, St Petersburg is an excellent city to explore on foot with many of its principal sites grouped around Nevsky prospekt and the Palace Embankment. Another bonus of walking is that it gives visitors an opportunity to take in the detail of the city's outstanding architecture.

Where to Stay

Choosing a Hotel

The ever increasing stream of tourists, with about 2.5 million foreigners visiting in 2001, is flowing into a small and constant supply of hotel space. It is almost impossible to find rooms during the peak months of June and July.

The city has about 130 private and state owned hotels with 32,000 beds, but less than half meet the standards of visitors from developed countries. Only one full-fledged hotel, the four-star SAS Radisson, has opened in the city since the early 1990s.

In April 2001, the city governor, Vladimir Yakovlev, took notice of the problem, and hastily pushed through legislation supporting the construction of more hotels by 2003. About 90 hotel projects, many of which are badly-needed, affordable, three-star hotels, have been approved by city hall. But in Russia, approving plans on paper is one thing; reality another.

Some visitors get around the hotel problem by sailing into St Petersburg on a cruise liner. These do indeed bring the majority of foreign tourists into the city during the summer.

LUXURY

Astoria
Bolshaya Morskaya, 39
Tel: (812) 313 5757
In the US call toll free, 1-800-223-6800, and in the UK, call toll free, 0800-181123
Fax: (812) 313 5133
e-mail: reserv@astoria.spb.ru
www.rfhotels.com
Centrally located on St Isaac's Square with a view of St Isaac's

Cathedral, a double goes for $250–$400 a night. **$$$**

Grand Hotel Europe
Mikhailovskaya ulitsa, 1
Tel: (812) 329 6000
Fax: (812) 329 6001
e-mail: res@ghe.spb.ru
www.grand-hotel-europe.com
Centrally located near the Russian Museum just off of Nevsky prospekt, the city's main avenue, a double goes for about $300–$400 a night, and more luxurious suites are available. **$$$**

Sheraton Nevsky Palace
Nevsky prospekt, 57
Tel: (812) 275 2001
Fax: (812) 301 7323
e-mail: bc@sheratonnevskij.ru
Centrally located on the city's main street, a double at this luxury hotel costs $300 a night, and more luxurious suites are available. **$$$**

Radisson SAS Royal Hotel St. Petersburg
Nevsky prospekt, 49/2
Tel: (812) 322 5000
Fax: (812) 322 5001
www.radissonsas.com
Centrally located on the city's main street, the average double room is about $290, and more luxurious suites are available. **$$$**

MEDIUM-PRICED

Angleterre
Bolshaya Morskaya, 39
Tel: (812) 313 5009
In the US call toll free, 1-800-223-6800, and in the UK, call toll free, 0800-181123.
Fax: (812) 313 5059
e-mail: reserv@astoria.spb.ru
www.rfhotels.com
This is owned by the same company as the Astoria, and is in an adjacent building, but is cheaper. Centrally located on St Isaac's Square with a view of St Isaac's Cathedral, a double is about $200 a night. **$$**

Pribaltiiskaya Hotel
Korabelstroiteli ulitsa, 14
Tel: (812) 356 0263
Fax: (812) 356 0094
e-mail: market@pribaltiyskaya.ru
www.pribaltiyskaya.ru

This hotel has a great view on the Gulf of Finland, but is far from the city centre. A double costs about $160 a night. **$$**

Deson Ladoga
Shaumyana prospekt, 26
Tel: (812) 528 5202 or 528 5393
Fax: 528 5448
e-mail: dladoga@bcltele.com
www.deson.lek.ru
This hotel, located across the river from Smolny Cathedral, is inconveniently located if you don't have a car. Room for two is $130 a night. **$$**

Rand House Bed and Breakfast
Grivtsova Ulitsa, 11; apt 83
Tel. (812) 310 7005.
www.randhouse.ru
Well-run, clean, and efficient, American-owned bed and breakfast in the city centre off of the Griboyedov Canal, costing between $50 and $70 per double per night (4 rooms).

BUDGET

Hotel St Petersburg
Pirogovskaya naberezhnaya, 5
Tel: (812) 542 9411
Fax: (812) 248-8002
e-mail:postmaster@spbhotel.spb.su
This hotel has a great view on the river in the city centre, but it has not been renovated since Soviet time. A double costs about $100 a night. **$**

Hotel Moskva
Alexandra Nevskoo ploshchad, 2
Tel: (812) 274 0020
Fax: (812) 274 2130
e-mail: business@hotel-moscow.ru
www.hotel-moscow.ru
This hotel is also located on the river, but further away from the centre, near the Alexander Nevsky Lavra. A double costs about $100 a night. **$**

Neptune Hotel and Business Centre
Embankment Obvodny Canal, 93A
Tel: (812) 324 2000
Fax: (812) 324-4611
email: hotel@neptune.spb.ru
www.neptune.spb.ru

150 rooms; $100 single; $140 double. **$**

Pulkovskaya Hotel
Pobedy Square, 1
Tel: (812) 123 5732 or 123 5814
Fax: (812) 264-6396
e-mail: sale@pulkovskaya.ru
Close to the airport and quite comfortable, this hotel is favoured by many Western tour groups. A double costs about $120 per night.**$**

Russ Hotel
Artilleriyskaya ulitsa, 1
Tel: (812) 273 4683
Fax: (812) 279 3600
email: hotelruss@m.astelit.ru
This hotel has little to write home about, with poor service and substandard rooms; best avoided unless there are no other vacancies. A double costs about $70 per night. **$**

Sovetskaya Hotel
Lermontovsky prospekt, 43
Tel: (812) 329 0182
Fax: (812) 251 8890
e-mail: hotel@sovetskaya.com
www.sovetskaya.com
This hotel lives up to its name, quite Soviet in decor and service, but some rooms have been renovated to Western standards. A quality double costs about $120 per night. **$**

Oktyabrskaya Hotel
Ligovsky prospekt, 10
Tel: (812) 277 6330 or 277 6255
Fax: (812) 227-2618
e-mail: hotel@spb.cityline.ru
This hotel has also renovated some rooms, and is tolerable by Western standards. A double costs $70 per night. **$**

Matisov Domik
Pryazhka Embankment, 3
Tel: (812) 219 5445
Fax: (812) 219 7919
This hotel is located on the very fringe of the city centre, not far from the shipyards. A double costs about $70 a night. **$**

Youth hostel accommodation can be booked and paid for in advance when ordering a visa. Staff at the hostels are friendly and there is

Camping

Camping Site
Klenovaya ulitsa 9, Repino.
Olgino Motel and Camping Site
(Intourist)
Primorskoe Shosse 5
Tel: (812) 238 3551

usually an English-speaker present.
The rooms generally take four to
five people, but a double room can
be booked if you are prepared to
pay extra. The youth hostel at St
Petersburg provides breakfast.
St Petersburg International Hostel
3rd Sovietskaya ulitsa, 28
Tel: (812) 329 8018
e-mail: ryh@ryh.ru
www.ryh.ru
This American-run hostel offers
cheap, clean and efficient rooms
for about $50 a night in a room for
two. **$**
International Hostel Holiday
Arsenalnaya Embankment, 9
Tel: (812) 327 1070
Fax: (812) 327 1033
e-mail: info@hostel.spb.ru
www.hostel.ru
This hostel is near the Finland train
station, not far from the city centre,
$35 in a room for two. **$**

Apartments

Many St Petersburgers like to rent
out their apartment for hard
currency. This can be a very
personal and inexpensive way of
staying in the city for a longer
period and of avoiding the high
Intourist hotel charges. Such private
accommodation can be arranged
through the MIR International
Centre.
Pulford Real Estate
Tel: (812) 325 6277
Fax: (812) 320 7561
e-mail: pulford@mail.wplus.net
www.pulford.com
An apartment costs about $80 per
bedroom per night, and is perhaps
the most affordable option in the
city for a fine level of comfort.
Alina Suslova
Thaikovskovo 81
Tel: (812) 296 1865

e-mail: suslova@mail.ru
www.hotelspb.narod.ru
Eighty sq metre (96 sq yard), three-
room private apartment in the city
centre near the Tauride Palace,
recently renovated.
Dr Oleg Melnikov
Tel: (812) 272-5519
Mobile: (812) 939-2561
Eighty sq metre (96 sq yard),
private apartment in the city centre
near Letny Sad, recently renovated;
costs $80 per couple.
Anastasia Ivanova
Tel: (812) 312 1073
Fifty sq. metre (60 sq. yard) luxury
private studio, in top security
building, with view on Field of Mars
in city centre, $100 per night for
entire apartment; $150 in peak
season in June and July.

Home Stays

Interchange, a UK-based tour
company specialising in travel to
Central and Eastern Europe,
offers the opportunity to stay
with English-speaking Russian
families in St Petersburg. You
provided with your own room,
breakfast and dinner and use of
shared family facilities. Home
stays are a wonderful
opportunity to experience cosy
Russian domesticity and home
cooking. For more details
contact:
Interchange, Interchange House,
27 Stafford Road, Croydon,
Surrey CR0 4NG.
Tel: 020 8681 3612; email:
interchange@interchange.uk.com

Eating Out

What To Eat

The Russians love hearty meals.
For breakfast there is a choice of
bread, coffee with milk, tea with
lemon, or cocoa, sour cream,
yoghurt, milk pudding, soft-boiled
eggs or omelettes, hot sausages or
tefteli (meat balls), butter and
marmalade. The main meals
consist of three or four courses. On
offer for the first course are egg
dishes, sliced meat or sausage,
aspic (with meat, mushrooms or
fish), cucumber, prawns, fish
salads, brawn, various kinds of fish
or black caviar. This is followed
by soup.
Popular from the selection available are: *shchi* (cabbage soup),
borscht (beetroot and meat soup
with sour cream), *rassolnik* (kidney
soup with gherkins), meat ball
soup; in summer also: *botvinya*
(cold soup with smoked fish, radish,
beetroot and cucumber) or
akroshka (cooked meat, smoked
sausage, hard-boiled eggs, finely-
sliced onion and fresh cucumbers
with *kvas*, served ice-cold). For the
main dish there is a choice of beef
and pork joints, chicken, duck,
game, mushroom dishes, fish (eg
salmon, sturgeon, pike-perch,
sterlet) with potatoes, beet,
cucumbers, vegetables, salad, etc.
For dessert there are cakes, biscuits, semolina or buckwheat *bliny*
(pancakes) with sweet sauces, curd
or apples, stewed fruit, *kisyel* (a
dish made from fruit juice or fresh
berries, dried fruit and potato flour).
Russian cooking is enriched by
the different regional specialities
from the former Soviet Union, many
of which are available in St
Petersburg. Favourite Ukrainian
dishes include *galushki* (pastry with

a meat or curd cheese filling) and *varenyky zvyshneyu* (curd dumplings with red cherries served with sugar and sour cream). Chicken Kiev (or Kiev Cutlet), known throughout the world, is prepared with different spices and garlic. Loved by everyone in the Ukraine is *salo* (salted raw lard spiced with garlic) served with black bread. *Kolbasa* (different kinds of smoked sausages) is very also popular.

With perestroika Georgian food came to the rest of the former USSR (served at restaurants like the traditional Kavkaz in St Petersburg). The Georgian cuisine is famous for its *shashlik*, *tsyplyata tabaka* (roast chicken), *basturma* (specially fried meat), *suluguni* (salted cheese) and *satsyvi* (chicken). It can be served with *lavash* (special kind of bread) or with *khachapuri* (roll stuffed with cheese).

In St Petersburg you can also find restaurants serving Armenian-Turkish *dolma* dishes (minced meat in tomatoes, cucumbers, paprika etc), as well as *chebureki* (meat pasties) from the Crimea and *pelmeny* (ravioli) from Siberia. Central Asian cuisine is represented by pilaws or rice dishes.

Table Reservations

Please note the phone numbers below also double as fax numbers, but if one wants a reservation it is better to call. Since only a small portion of the local population can afford to go regularly to restaurants, plenty of space is always available and reservations are rarely needed, except during the peak season of June and July.

Where To Eat

With the great selection of fine restaurants today in the city, it's hard to imagine that not long ago, in the mid-1990s, visitors had almost no decent eating option outside their hotel. The city now has the full range of cafes and restaurants, from quick and cheap

to luxurious, that one would expect from any European capital. Finding those restaurants is not always easy, and requires knowing the location ahead of time and having a good map. There is no central restaurant strip as in most major cities.

One of the best restaurants in town is simply called **Restoran**, (Tamozheny pereulok, 2; tel: 327 8979), just across from the Museum of Anthropology (Kunstkamera). It is fast becoming St Petersburg's most fashionable and stylish dining venue. Restoran's sleek and cold simplicity, with elements of pre-1917 Russian tastes, was designed by one of Russia's leading interior designers, Andrei Dmitriev.

Just across the street from Restoran is another fine restaurant, the **Old Customs House**, (Tamozheny pereulok, 1; tel: 327 8980) which is Russian owned, but British-managed. Though expensive, it is a very pleasant and comfortable experience. Around the corner, one will find, the popular restaurant and dance club, **Academia** (Birzhevoy proezd, 2; tel: 327 8942). This place is quite fashionable with the city's young and rich. The pizza is quite good.

Tinkoff and Brasilia are other hot spots for the young and affluent crowd. **Tinkoff** (Kazanskaya ulitsa, 7; tel: 314 8485) is Russia's only micro-brewery, featuring several types of dark and light beers. There's live entertainment, usually jazz or blues, on the weekends. **Brasilia** (Kazanskaya ulitsa, 24) features Latin-style food and exotic cocktails in a sexy, stylish atmosphere. Another hot spot with the city's youth is **Decadence** (Admiralteisky Embankment, 12; tel: 312 3944). Though many fashionable young people go here, the crowd is mixed, with people of all ages and backgrounds. There's live acid jazz in the early evenings.

For those looking for something a bit quieter and pensive, check out **Cafe Idiot** (Moika River Embankment, 82; tel: 315 1675)

where one can borrow chess and backgammon sets and sip the city's finest cappuccino all night long.

If you'd like to try the cuisine of the other nations which populate the former Soviet Union, it's best to go Georgian, and head on over to the Petrograd Side for a visit to **Salkhino** (Kronverksky prospect, 25; tel: 232 7891). This is by far the best Georgian food in the city, and it's almost like visiting the owner's home. Her name is Ketino, and she easily mixes and socialises with customers. And so it's no surprise that there is a regular following, including many of the city's leading personalities.

If you're looking for fine Ukrainian cuisine, pay a visit to **Shinok** (Zagorodny prospekt, 13; tel: 311 8262), which also features live music in the evenings. If you're looking for Old World charm, **Staroe Cafe** (the Old Cafe) makes for a very romantic evening and good Russian cuisine. Though **Staroe Cafe** (Fontanka Embankment 108; tel: 316 5111) has only four tables, it seems there is always one table free. The decor features genuine antiques from the late 19th century, and walls and ceilings deliberately damaged to give them the smell of years gone-by. After 7pm, a piano player hits out some tunes.

For one of the most unusual and memorable restaurant experiences, go to **Russkaya Ribalka** (Primorsky Park Pobeda, 2nd south pond; tel: 235 2395), where you must first catch your own fish before they cook it. This restaurant, which has its own pond in a city park, works all year long, and in the winter, you can go ice fishing.

For a quick bite at a bargain basement price, try **Blinny Domik** (Kolokolnaya ulitsa, 8 tel: 315 9915), which has the city's best *bliny* as well as art exhibits and live piano music. There are also a number of bistros such as **Laima** (Nevsky prospekt, 30/16 tel. 315-5545) where you can get a full dinner of grilled chicken or broiled fish for $4.

Restaurant Listings

RUSSIAN & EUROPEAN CUISINE

Restoran, $$$
Chic decor and fine Russian cuisine.
Tamozheny pereulok, 2
Tel: 327 8979

Tinkoff, $$$
Trendy place for youth, with sushi, pizza and American-style salads.
Kazanskaya Ulitsa, 7
Tel: 314 8485

Troika, $$$
Russian cuisine and folk show, catering to tourists.
Zagorodny prospekt, 27/21
Tel: 113 5343
res@mail.ru

Austeria, $$$
Atmosphere of early St Petersburg, with fine Russian and European cuisine.
Peter and Paul Fortress
Tel: 238 4262

Russkaya Ribalka, $$$
One of the city's most enjoyable fish venues. You catch the fish in the pond, and they cook it.
Primorsky Park Pobeda,
2nd south pond
Tel: 235 2395

Borsalino, $$$
Considered to be the finest European cuisine in St Petersburg
Anglettere Hotel
Bolshaya Morskaya, 39
Tel: 313 5115

Count Suvorov, $$$$$
One of the few places that serves exotic Old Russian dishes, such as bear meat.
Lomonosova ulitsa, 26
Tel: 315 4328

Staroe Cafe, $$
Cozy, with four-tables, and live piano music in evenings.
Fontanka Embankment, 108
Tel: 316 5111

1913, $$$
Perhaps the finest Russian cuisine for the price.
Voznesensky prospekt, 13/2
Tel: 315 5148

Old Customs House, $$$$
Fine Russian and European cuisine in an historic interior.

Tamozheny pereulok, 1
Tel: 327 8980

Zolotoi Vek, $$
Provides fine Russian cuisine at reasonable price. Located just off Nevsky prospekt.
Malaya Sadovaya, 3
Tel: 314 3556

Price Guide

$$$$$–$100 + per couple
$$$$–$70 to $100 per couple
$$$–$40 to $70 per couple
$$–$25 to $40 per couple
$–less than $25 per couple

Academia, $$$
Upscale hangout with dancing club for well-off and stylish youth.
Birzhevoy proezd, 2
Tel: 327 8942

Da Vinci, $$$
Russian cuisine in flashy, neon club.
Malaya Morskaya, 15
Tel: 311 0173

The Noble Nest, $$$$$
The city's most expensive and elite location with czsarist grandeur.
Dekabristov ulitsa, 21
Tel: 312 3205

Na Zdorovye, $$$
Fine Russian country cooking in folksy atmosphere.
Bolshoy prospekt 13
Tel: 232 4039

Senat Bar, $$$$
Chief hangout for the swinging crowd, better known for its women than food.
Galernaya 1
Tel: 314 9253

St Petersburg, $$$
Fine Russian cuisine.
Kanala Griboedova 5
Tel: 314 4947

Valhalla, $$$
A hearty Russian dinner on Nevsky prospekt for those looking for a rowdy night out.
Nevsky prospekt 22
Tel: 311 0024

Kameya, $$$
Russian cuisine in quiet, elegant atmosphere, off the beaten track.
2nd Sovetskaya, 21
Tel: 277 5542

Kotletnaya, $$
Fine Russian cuisine in parody on Soviet interior.
Kazanskaya 34/7
Tel: 318 4050

Shinok, $$$
Excellent Ukrainian food served in villagey interior.
Zagorodny prospekt, 13
Tel: 311 8262

Bliny Domik, $
Cheap, great Russian food with artsy atmosphere.
Kolokolnaya ulitsa, 8
Tel: 315 9915

Laima, $
Modern bistro.
Nevsky prospekt, 30/16
Tel: 315 5545

AMERICAN

California Grill, $$$
Standard American burgers and salads.
Nevsky prospekt 176
Tel: 274 7470

Payment

Nearly all places accept major credit cards, but it's a good idea to have the cash on hand just in case the credit card machine is out of order, which is not that uncommon.

CHINESE

Golden Dragon, $$
Dekabristov ulitsa 62
Tel: 114 8441

Golden Dragon By the Zoo, $$
Fine Chinese cuisine in quiet, charming atmosphere.
Kronverksky prospekt 61
Tel: 232 2643

JEWISH/KOSHER

Sem Sorok, $$$
Bolshaya Samsonievsky, 108
Tel: 246 3444

Shalom, $$$
Ulitsa Koly Tomchaka, 8A
Tel: 327 5475

Price Guide

$$$$$–$100 + per couple
$$$$–$70 to $100 per couple
$$$–$40 to $70 per couple
$$–$25 to $40 per couple
$–less than $25 per couple

CAUCASIAN

Salkhino, $$$$
Excellent food and displays
Georgian art for sale.
Kronverksky prospekt, 25
Tel: 232 7891
Kavkaz Bar, $$$$
Exotic Caucasian interior and fine
shish kebabs.
Karavannaya ulitsa 18
Tel: 312 1665
Kolhida, $$$
Nevsky prospekt 176
Tel: 274 2514

ITALIAN

Mama Roma's, $$
A step above the typical pizzeria.
Karavannaya ulitsa 3
Tel: 314 0347
Rossi's, $$$
Standard Italian fare, not highly
recommended.
Mikhailovsky ulitsa 1
Tel: 329 6000
Patio Pizza, $$
The best pizza in town, plus other
Italian dishes.
Nevsky prospekt 182, and
Nevsky prospekt 30
Tel: 314 8215
Pizzacato, $$
Also very good pizza, but it's in the
basement.
Bolshaya Morskaya, 45
Tel: 315 0319

MISCELLANEOUS

Brasilia, $$$
Dishes appear to be something
between Latin and Russian, but
certainly good.
Kazanskaya Street, 24
Tel: 320 8777

Federic Fellini, $$$
Decked out in themes from Fellini
movies; food is so-so.
Malaya Konyushennaya 4
Tel: 311 5078
Caravan, $$$
Excellent Central Asian food in motif
interior.
Voznesensky prospekt
Tel: 310 5678
Bistro Garcon, $$$
Fine French cuisine in cosy Parisian
setting.
Nevsky prospekt, 95
Tel: 277 2467

What to Drink

In the drinks line, the big restau-
rants stock: tea; mineral water;
fruit juices; beer; vodka;
Georgian dry wines; Ukrainian
dessert wines; Moldavian;
Azerbaijani; Armenian and
Georgian cognac, Crimean
sparkling wine, and so on. During
the summer *kvas*, a light, fer-
mented drink made out of dried
black bread with yeast and
raisins, is offered for sale on the
street. World-famous of course is
Russian vodka. There are various
kinds and the best are:
*Stolichnaya, Zolotoye Koltso,
Starorusskaya* and *Sibirskaya*.
Soviet champagne is also
excellent, if you can try the dry
Sukhaye variety.

VEGETARIAN

Cafe Idiot, $
Moika River Embankment, 82
Tel: 315 1675

BARS, PUBS AND BEER HALLS

Mollie's Irish Pub
Rubinshteyna ulitsa, 36
Tel: 319 9768
Football Bar
Karavannaya, 28
Tel: 314 8468
Sports Bar
Marata ulitsa 36
Tel: 113 2442

Kazemat
Peter and Paul Fortress
Tel: 238 4541
Bristol Cellar
Nevsky prospekt 22
Tel: 311 7490
Rotunda Bar
Bolshaya Morskaya, 39
Tel: 210 5837
Tribunal Bar
Dekabristov ploshchad 1
Tel: 311 1690
Swinging club favoured by
foreigners and Russian girls looking
to meet foreigners.
James Cook
Shvedsky pereulok, 2
Tel: 312 3200
Fine restaurant and coffee house.
Korsar
Bolshaya Morskaya, 14
Tel: 318 4184
Hip student bar and club.

COFFEE HOUSES

James Cook
Shvedsky pereulok, 2
Tel: 312 3200
Fine restaurant and coffee house.
Ideal Cup (Idealnaya Chashka)
Nevsky prospekt, 15
Tel: 315 0927
Nevsky prospekt, 112
Tel: 275 7140
Pushka Inn
Moika River Embankment, 14
Tel: 314 0663

Hotel Cafeterias

There are also cafeterias in the
large restaurants, where it is
possible to buy sandwiches,
other small snacks, cakes,
pastries as well as the usual
choice of drinks.

Attractions

Classical Music and Theatre Venues

Theatres and concerts almost always begin at 7pm, unless it's a matinee or special event. It is customary and considered good manners to hand in your coat when visiting museums or the theatre.

Capella
Moika River Embankment, 20
Tel: 314 1058
Ticket office open noon–7pm.
Mariinsky Theatre
Teatralnaya ploshchad, 1
Tel: 114 1211
Ticket office open 11am–8pm.
Mussorgsky Opera and Ballet Theatre
Arts Square 1
Tel: 314 1949
Ticket office open 11am–8pm.
The Conservatory Opera Hall
Teatralnaya ploshchad 3
Tel: 312 2519
Ticket office open 11am–7pm.
The Shostakovich Philharmonic
Mikhailovskaya ulitsa 2
Tel: 110 4257
Ticket office open 11am–8pm.
The Alexindrinsky Theatre
Ostrovskogo ploshchad 2
Tel: 110 4103
Ticket open 11am–8pm.
Hermitage Theatre (ballet, opera and chamber music)
Hermitage Museum
Dvortsovaya Embankment, 34
Tel: 279 0226; 272 9682
Ticket office open 11am–6pm.
The Bolshoi Drama Theatre
Fontanka Embankment
Tel: 310 0401
Ticket office open 11am–6pm.
The Maly Drama Theatre
Rubinshteyna ulitsa 18
Ticket office open from noon–7pm.

The Alternative Theatre Station
The Five-Year House of Culture
Ulitsa Dekabristov, 25
Tel: 114 2027
Komissarzhevskaya Drama Theatre
Italianskaya ulitsa, 19
Tel: 311 0849
Ticket office open noon–7pm.
Baltiysky Dom Theatre
Alexandrovsky Park, 4
Tel: 232 3539
Ticket office open noon–7pm.
Performances begin at 7pm.
Mironov Russian Enterprise Theatre
Bolshoy prospekt, 75
Tel: 346 1670
Ticket office open noon–7pm.
Nikolaevsky Art Centre
Palace of Labour
Truda ploshchad 4
Tel: 311 7110
Features Russian folk dance and music shows. Ticket office open 11am–6pm. Performances begin at 7pm and at 9pm.
The State Circus
Fontanka Embankment, 3
Tel: 210 4198
Ticket office open 11am–7pm.
Matinee begins at 11am and 3pm; evening performances are at 7pm.
The Bolshoy Puppet Theatre
Nekrasova ulitsa, 10
Tel: 273 6672
Ticket office open 11am–7pm.
Performances at 11.30am and 2pm.

Art Galleries

Borei Art Gallery
Liteiny prospekt 58
Tel: 273 3693

Buying Art

The past few years have seen a boom in the type of art which has never had anything to do with "socialist realism". Theatre and especially painting, has just emerged from the underground. Artists who were banned are now openly exhibited; on Nevsky there are hundreds of hitherto undiscovered paintings. Some artists have already found a way to sell their works in the West. Others will gladly sell their paintings for several hundred roubles. Bear in mind that such paintings may cost several thousand dollars in Western Europe. Naturally, the streets are full of cheap stuff – moons over ponds, imitation icons, portraits of rock stars and naked women – but you may also run into something interesting.

Exhibitions of local and foreign artists, painting, graphics, photographs and installation. Open noon–8pm.
Gisich's Private Art Gallery
Fontanka 21
Tel: 314 4380
E-mail: gisich@pisem.net
www.gisich.com
Visits by appointment only.
SPAS
Moika River Embankment 93
Tel: 311 4260
Exhibitions of paintings. Open 11am–6pm.
Palitra Gallery
Malaya Morskaya 5
Open 11am–7pm.
Mikhailov Gallery
Liteyny prospekt 53
Tel: 272 4848
Open 11am–8pm.

Festivals

St Petersburg spends a good part of the year in cold and darkness, so when the short summer comes with its radiant White Nights, the locals let loose with an intensity rarely seen elsewhere in Europe. In June, the city centre throbs around the clock as people rush to take part in dozens of cultural events in palaces, theatres, and museums.

Since the fall of the Soviet Union, St Petersburg has witnessed a cultural boom, with an explosion of festivals from art and music to film.

The central attraction of the White Nights is the festival of the **Stars of the White Nights Festival**, sponsored by the Mariinsky Theatre, which every June features

Beer Festival

The annual **St Petersburg Beer Festival** brings nearly half a million beer enthusiasts, mostly young people, out on to the central streets and squares in mid June. In the 1990s, St Petersburg became Russia's equivalent of Milwaukee, the United States' beer capital, and the country held its first beer festival here in 1996. During the festival, beer lovers can try up to 40 types of Russian beer, such as Baltika and Nevskoye, and leading Russian pop stars perform at concerts held on Palace Square.

a host of Russian and international stars in opera and ballet. Tickets cost between $50–$100 and reservations can be made online at the theatre's web site: www.mariinsky.ru, but one must come in person to the theatre box office at Teatralnaya Ploshchad to purchase them. Little sister to the Mariinsky's White Nights festival is the **Annual Chamber Music Festival**, "Palaces of St Petersburg", organised by chief conductor of the Moscow Chamber Orchestra, Konstantin Orbelian, and violinist Mariya Safariants. Featuring international and Russian singers and musicians, among which are those from the Mariinsky Theatre and the St Petersburg Philharmonic, it also runs the entire month of June but is organised on a much smaller scale, with quartets and soloists performing in the close and intimate quarters of small palace theatres, such as the State Hermitage Theatre, which was the personal theatre of the tsars and tsarinas; the State Russian Museum's Mikhailovksy Palace; the Yusupovsky Palace; the Marble Palace; as well as the Catherine, Peterhof and Gatchina Palaces, all three located in the city's suburbs.

St Petersburg's cultural life is certainly steeped in classical arts and culture, but it continues to develop on the popular level. On 27

May, **City Day**, the city commemorates its official founding by Peter the Great in 1703. A flood of parade floats and revellers dressed in costume stream down Nevsky Prospect, the city's main avenue, to Palace Square next to the Hermitage.

The carnival continues on the first weekend in June with street festivities at the **International Tsarksoe Selo Carnival** in the central square of Pushkin, the tsarist-era summer residence which is a 30-minute train or bus ride from St Petersburg. The event includes a wide range of festivities, among which are contests and competitions such as Best Carnival Costume, Best Cake, the Carnival Parade, and the "cutting of the neckties", a ritual by which the city's bureaucrats are unceremoniously defrocked of their power for one day.

Cinema

Cinemas open at 9am or 10am and show films all day long. The entrance fee is between 3 and 7 roubles. Up to 4pm tickets are sold at half price.
Avror, 60 Nevsky prospekt.
Baltika, Vasilievsky Ostrov 34 Sedmaya Linyia.
Khodozhestvenny, 67 Nevsky prospekt.
St Petersburg, 4 Potemkinskaya ulitsa.
Moskva, prospekt Gaza.
Nevsky, 4 Narodnaya ulitsa.

Nightlife

Nightclubs

Clubs usually have a cover charge, which varies between $3 and $20 depending on the day and whether or not a top group may be playing.
Akvatoria
Vyborgskaya Embankment 61
Tel: 245 2030
Top city disco, with entertainment centre, including bowling and billiards. Cover charge of around $10.
Captain Morgan
Bolshoy prospekt (P.S.), 61
Tel: 230 7151
Casino and club for the young, wealthy crowd.
Club 69
2nd Krasnoarmeiskaya ulitsa, 6
Tel: 259 5163
The city's leading gay club, with go-go strip show and dark room.
Decadence
Admiralteysky Embankment, 12
Tel: 312 3944
Small, cosy, top-notch club for city's glamorous youth; tough door policy for Russians – to keep bandits out – while almost no problem for foreigners.
Dostoevsky Art Bar
Vladimirsky prospekt, 15
Tel: 310 6164
Rocking club with live music.
Golden Dolls
Nevsky prospekt, 60
Tel: 110 5570
Erotic nightclub with topless waitresses who do whatever you want, for money of course; cover charge of around $20.
Konyushney Dvor
Griboedova Canal, 5
Tel: 315 7607
Swinging scene for students and yuppies; strip shows daily; $3 cover charge.

London
Chorny Reki Embankment, 41
Tel: 327 1567
www.londonclub.spb.ru
Sophisticated dance club for
upscale crowd.

Luna
Voznesensky prospekt, 46
Tel: 310 3628
Upscale, rich crowd, with cover of
about $20.

National Hunt
Malaya Morskaya, 11
Tel: 311 1343
Swinging student and yuppie scene.

Plaza
Admiral Makarov Embankment, 2
Tel: 323 9090
City's top club, for the glamorous
crowd; cover $10 to $20.

Sinners (Greshniki)
Griboedova Canal, 28
Tel: 318 4291
Gay club.

Tribunal
Dekabristov ploshchad, 1
Tel: 311 1690
Swinging ex-pat crowd looking to
meet local girls.

Casinos

Plaza
Admiral Makarov Embankment, 2
Tel: 323 9090
City's top club, for upscale,
glamorous crowd; cover
$10–$20.

Astoria
Malaya Morskaya ulitsa, 20
Tel: 313 5020

Conti
Kondratyevsky prospekt, 44
Tel: 540 8130

Premier
Nevsky prospekt, 47
Tel: 315 7893

Taleon Club
Moika River Embankment, 59
Tel: 312 5373

Jazz Clubs

Since Soviet times, St Petersburg
has had Russia's most vibrant jazz
scene, and more and more jazz
clubs open every year.

Jazz Philharmonic Hall
Zagorodny prospekt, 27
Tel: 164 8565
Sophisticated venue with
mainstream and dixieland jazz.

JFC Jazz Club
Shpalernaya ulitsa, 33
Tel: 272 9850
Relaxed venue with all forms of jazz
and Latin nights.

Jimi Hendrix Club
Liteyny prospekt, 33
Tel: 279 8813
Lively venue with live bands every
night.

Quadrat
Bolshoy prospekt, 83
(Petrograd Side)
Tel: 315 9046

Shopping

Business Hours

Many small shops have a one-hour
lunchbreak sometime between noon
and 5pm. Larger shops are continuously open Mon–Sat between 7am
or 9am and 8pm or 9pm; certain
food stores might be open until
10pm. Book shops and other
speciality shops open around 10am
or 11am and are open until 7pm or
8pm, with a break usually between
2pm and 3pm. On Sundays all
shops, with the exception of some
food stores, are closed.

What To Buy

SOUVENIRS

Though the city economy is growing
and has greatly diversified since
Soviet times when it was entirely
dependent on the military-industrial
complex, there are few high-quality,
speciality items for tourists to buy.
If you want something besides the
usual trinkets of Russian dolls and
lacquer boxes, try the **Lomonosov
Porcelain Factory**, (LFZ), Europe's
third oldest porcelain factory.
Founded in 1743 as the Imperial
Porcelain Factory by Empress
Elizabeth to provide the tsarist
court with high quality porcelain,
the factory makes fine porcelain at
prices much less than major
European manufacturers.
LFZ has stores at:
Vladimirsky prospekt, 7
Tel: 113 1513
Open daily 10am–8pm.
Obukhovskoy Oboruni prospekt,
151 (factory outlet)
Tel: 560 8544
Open Mon–Sat 10am–7pm
Visits to the factory and its
wonderful museum can also be

arranged, but by appointment only.
Tel: 560 8301.

St Petersburg Doll Museum
Has an exhibition and sale of
handmade dolls and doll-making
materials.
Kamskaya ulitsa, 8
Tel: 327 7224

Where To Buy

Retro Antiques
Hotel Astoria
Bolshaya Morskaya ulitsa, 39
Tel: 315 9673
Fine antiques from a reputable
dealer.

Babushka Souvenirs
Lt. Schmidt Embankment, 33
Tel: 327 9823
Truly one of the finest assortments
of quality Russian souvenirs, in
contrast to the sometimes dubious
trinkets sold at outdoor markets
such as the one near the Church on
the Spilled Blood.

Heritage
Nevsky prospekt, 116
Tel: 279 5067
Standard Russian souvenirs.

Peterburg
Nevsky prospekt, 54
Tel: 311 4020
Standard Russian souvenirs.

Benetton
Nevsky prospekt, 72
Tel: 272 9856
Branch of the European clothing
store.

Gostiny Dvor
Nevsky prospekt, 35
The city's largest department store
containing dozens of small boutiques
where you can find everything from
food to clothing and appliances open
every day from 9am–9pm.

DLT
Bolshaya Konnyushennaya, 21
Large department store with nearly
everything on sale open every day
10am–9pm.

Gianni Versace
Nevsky Prospect, 39
Tel: 314 1492
Designer clothing.

Tatyana Parfionova
Nevsky prospekt, 51
Tel: 113 3669
www.parfionova.ru

Clothing by a top St Petersburg
fashion designer.

Tom Klaim
Nevsky prospekt, 88
Tel: 275 4827
Clothing by a leading Moscow
fashion designer.

MARKETS

There are 16 so-called collective
markets where farmers sell fruit,
vegetables and other food products
from different regions in Russia.
The biggest and best include:
Kuznechny, Kuzneschny pereulok 3;
Andreyevsky, Vasilievsky ostrov, 18
Bolshoy prospekt; **Nekrasovsky**, 52
ulitsa Nekrasova; **Sytny**,
Petrogradskaya Storona, 3/5
Sytninskaya ploshchad; **Oktyabrsky**,
Moskovsky prospekt 4b.

FUR SHOPS

Lena
Nevsky prospekt, 50
Tel: 311 7169; 312 3234
Open daily, 10am–9pm.

Rot Front
Zagorodny prospekt, 22
Tel: 321 5722
Open Mon–Fri, 11am–7pm, Sat.
11am–6pm, Sun noon–6pm.

Soyuz Pushnina (the House of Fur)
Moskovsky prospekt, 98
Tel: 298 7601
Open Mon–Fri 10am–8pm, Sat–Sun
11am–5pm.

Buying Antiques

Antiques (items produced before
the 1958) and pieces of
contemporary art can only be
taken out of Russia with an
export licence from the Ministry
of Culture, Griboedova Canal,
107. The office is open Mon–Fri
11am–2pm.

Sport

Sports Centres

St Petersburg, like most Russian
cities, has few public sport centres
where one can play basketball,
tennis, or go for a swim. There are
literally a handful of places because
interest is low and sports are not
promoted by the state. In their
spare time, Russian men, for
instance, prefer to sit with friends to
drink and smoke. It is such habits
that contribute to the average male
mortality rate of 59 years. Still, the
city is in the midst of a fitness boom
as young successful professionals
are more and more concerned about
their appearance and health. Most
turn to fitness centres to lift weights
and attend aerobic classes. Since
most work on monthly membership,
if you're in for a short visit, it might
be best to enquire at any of the
major hotels.

Fitness Factory
ulitsa Razyezzhaya, 21
Tel: 346 8033
Open Mon–Fri 7am–11pm, Sat–Sun
10am–9pm. Small but upscale
fitness centre that sells monthly
passes for about $100.

Galaxy Sport Club
Petrovsky Stadium, Petrovsky ostrov
Tel: 119 5741
Small but upscale fitness centre
that sells monthly passes only for
about $60.

Planet Fitness (3 branches)
Kazanskaya ulitsa, 37
Tel: 315 7175
Grand Hotel Europe
Mikhailovskaya, 1
Tel: 329 6597
Robespera Embankment, 12
Tel: 275 6201

Gloria Tennis Club
Kuznetsovksaya ulitsa 25
Tel: 298 3410

Open daily 8am–11pm. Two tennis courts in pleasant atmosphere.

SKA Swimming Pool
Litovskaya ulitsa, 1
Tel: 542 0162
Open daily 6.30am–10.30pm. The city's 50 metre swimming pool. For a swim, you need a doctor's certificate of good health to get in.

Natasha Club
Alexandra Nevskovo ploshchad, 2A
Tel: 277 4191
Swimming pool, solarium, sauna and massage.

Palm Golf
ulitsa Professora Popova, 47
Tel: 234 5547
Mini-golf course. Open 6am–6pm.

Windsurfing Club
Morskaya Embankment, 15
Tel: 355 6126

Saigon Paintball Club
Aptekrsky pereulok, 16
234 0117

St Petersburg Shooting Range
Sredny prospekt, 83
Tel: 321 3013

Carting Recreational Centre
prospekt Stachek, 45a
Tel: 183 6984

Language

Language Tips

Modern Russian has no established and universally used forms of salutation. The old revolutionary form "*tavárishch*" (comrade), still used among some party members, lacks popularity among the rest of the population. Alternatives include: "*Izviníti, skazhíte pozhálsta…*" (Excuse me, tell me, please…) or "*Izviníti, mózhna sprasít…*") or "*I ozhálst*" (Excuse me, can I ask you…).

If you want to sound original and show your understanding of the history of courteous forms of greeting, you can address a man as *gospodin* (sir), and a woman as *gospozha* (madam). Many people want to restore these pre-Revolutionary forms of address in modern Russian society.

If you know the name of the father of the person you are talking to, the best and the most neutral way of addressing them is to use either *gospodin/gospozha* together with the relevant paternal name. English forms of address – Mister/Sir or Madam/Miss – are also acceptable.

You will hear the common parlance forms *Maladan heelavék!* (Young man!) and *Dévushka!* (Girl!) directed toward a person of any age, and also *Zhénshchina!* (Woman!) to women in the bus, in the shop or at the market. These forms should be avoided in conversation.

Transliteration

There are four systems of transliteration of Russian words into English (*see The Transliteration of Modern Russian for English*

Language Publications by J.T. Shaw, the University of Wisconsin Press, 1967). If necessary, the systems can be combined so that one letter or a group of letters is transliterated according to one system and the other according to another. To transliterate some Russian letters, English letter combinations are used:
ж = zh, x = kh, ц = ts, ч = ch, ш =sh, щ = shch, ю = yu, я = ya, ë = yo. The Russian letter combination кс is transliterated both as *ks* and as *x* Russian letters are transliterated (with a few exceptions) in a similar way: й, ы = y, e, ë = e.

To transliterate Russian soft sign between the consonants and before no-vowel, the apostrophe is used, or the soft sign is ignored, as before vowels. The transliteration of nominal inflections has a number of peculiarities: ый, ий = y, ие, ье = ie, ия = ia.

If the traditional English spelling in names differs from their letter-by-letter transliteration they are mostly translated in their English form: Moscow (city), but river Moskva.

The genetive inflections in the names of streets and other objects are translated according to their pronunciation, and not their spelling: площадь Горького, (*ploshchad' Gór'kogo*) = pl. Gorkovo in this book. The transliteration in this section shows the way to pronounce Russian words and therefore does not correspond exactly with their spelling.

The city maps and their captions use Russian words and abbreviations: ul. (*úlitsa*) means street; per. (*pereúlok*) – lane; prosp. (*prospékt*) – avenue; pl. (*plóshchad'*) – square; *alléya* – alley; *bul'vár* – boulevard; *magistrál* – main line; *proézd* – passage; *shossé* – highway; *spusk* – slope.

The Russian system of writing out house numbers is as follows *prosp. Kalinina 28* (*28 Kalinin Avenue*).

English/Russian

From a linguistic point of view, Russian belongs to the Slavonic branch of the Indo-European family of languages. English, German, French, Spanish and Hindi are its relatives.

It is important when speaking Russian that you reproduce the accent (marked here before each stressed vowel with the sign ') correctly to be understood well.

Historically Russian can be called a comparatively young language. The evolution of the language to its present form on the basis of the spoken language of Eastern Slavs and the Church-Slavonic written language is thought to have occurred between the 11th and 14th centuries.

Modern Russian has absorbed a considerable number of foreign words. Very few tourists will be puzzled by Russian words such as *telefon, televizor, teatr, otel, restoran, kafe, taxi, metro, aeroport*.

What intimidates people making their first acquaintance with Russian is the Cyrillic alphabet. In fact the alphabet can be remembered easily after a few repetitions and the difference with the Latin alphabet is only minimal. An understanding of the Russian alphabet permits one to make out the names of the streets and the shop signs.

The Russian (or Cyrillic) alphabet was created by two brothers, philosophers and public figures Constantine (St Cyril) and Methodius, both born in Solun (now Thessaloniki in Greece). Their purpose was to facilitate the spread of Greek liturgical books to Slavonic speaking countries.

Today the Cyrillic alphabet with different modifications is used in the Ukrainian, Belarusian, Bulgarian and Serbian languages, among others.

The Alphabet

The first two columns printed below show the printed letter in Russian upper and lower case. The third column shows how the Russian letters sound and the fourth column shows the name of the letter in Russian.

А	а	**a**, archaeology	**a**
Б	б	**b**, buddy	**be**
В	в	**v**, vow	**v**
Г	г	**g**, glad	**ge**
Д	д	**d**, dot (the tip of the tongue close to the teeth)	**de**
Е	е	**e**, get	**ye**
Ё	ё	**yo**, yoke	**yo**
Ж	ж	**zh**, composure	**zhe**
З	з	**z**, zest	**ze**
И	и	**i**, ink	**i**
Й	й	**j**, yes	**jot**
К	к	**k**, kind	**ka**
Л	л	**l**, life (but a bit harder)	**el'**
М	м	**m**, memory	**em**
Н	н	**n**, nut	**en**
О	о	**o**, optimum	**o**
П	п	**p**, party	**pe**
Р	р	**r** (rumbling – as in Italian, the tip of the tongue is vibrating)	**er**
С	с	**s**, sound	**es**
Т	т	**t**, title (the tip of the tongue close to the teeth)	**te**
У	у	**u**, nook	**u**
Ф	ф	**f**, flower	**ef**
Х	х	**kh**, hawk	**ha**
Ц	ц	**ts**, (pronounced conjointly)	**tse**
Ч	ч	**ch**, charter	**che**
Ш	ш	**sh**, shy	**sha**
Щ	щ	**shch**, (pronounced conjointly)	**shcha**
ъ		(the hard sign)	
Ы	ы	**y** (pronounced with the same position of a tongue as when pronouncing G, K)	**y**
ь		(the soft sign)	
Э	э	**e**, ensign	**e**
Ю	ю	**yu**, you	**yu**
Я	я	**ya**, yard	**ya**

Useful Words and Phrases

Numbers

1	*adín*	один
2	*dva*	два
3	*tri*	три
4	*chityri*	четыре
5	*pyat'*	пят´
6	*shes't'*	шесть
7	*sem*	семь
8	*vósim*	восемь
9	*d'évit'*	девять
10	*d'ésit'*	десять
11	*adínatsat'*	одиннадцать
12	*dvinátsat'*	двенадцать
13	*trinátsat'*	тринадцать
14	*chityrnatsat'*	четырнадцать
15	*pitnátsat'*	пятнадцат´
16	*shysnátsat'*	шестнадцать
17	*simnátsat'*	семнадцать
18	*vasimnátsat'*	восемнадцать
19	*divitnátsat'*	девятнадцать
20	*dvátsat'*	двадцать
21	*dvatsat' adin*	двадцать один
30	*trítsat'*	тридцать
40	*sórak*	сорок
50	*pidisyat*	пятьдесят
60	*shyz'disyat*	шестьдесят
70	*s'émdisyat*	семьдесят
80	*vósimdisyat*	восемьдесят
90	*divinósta*	девяносто
100	*sto*	сто
200	*dv'és'ti*	двести
300	*trísta*	триста
400	*chityrista*	четыреста
500	*pitsót*	пятьсот
600	*shyssót*	шестьсот
700	*simsót*	семьсот
800	*vasimsót*	восемьсот
900	*divitsót*	девятьсот
1,000	*tysicha*	тысяча
2,000	*dve tysichi*	две тысяч и
10,000	*d'ésit' tysich*	десятьтысяч
100,000	*sto tysich*	сто тысяч
1,000,000	*milión*	миллион
1,000,000,000	*miliárd*	миллиард

Pronouns

I/we
ya/my
я/мы

You
ty (singular, informal)/
vy (plural, or formal singular)
ты/вы

He/she/they
on/aná/aní
он/она/они

My/mine
moj (object masculine)/
mayá (object feminine)/
mayó (neutral or without marking the gender)/
maí (plural)
мой/моя/моё/мои

Our/ours
nash/násha/náshe/náshy (resp.)
наш/наша/наше/наши

Your/yours
tvoj etc. (see My)
vash etc. (see Our)
твой/ваш

His/her, hers/their, theirs
jivó/jiyó/ikh
его/её/их

Who?
khto?
Кто?

What?
shto?
Что?

Greetings & Acquaintance

Hello!
zdrástvuti (neutral, and often accompanied by shaking hands, but this is not necessary)
Здравствуйте!

zdrástvuj (to one person, informal)
Здравствуй!

alo! (by telephone only)
Алло!

priv'ét! (informal)
Привет!

Good afternoon/Good evening
dóbry den'/dobry véchir
Добрый день/Добрый вечер

Good morning/Good night
dobrae útra/dobraj nóchi (= Sleep well)
Доброе утро/Доброй ночи

Goodbye
dasvidán'ye (neutral)
До свидания

ciao! (informal)
Чао!

paká! (informal, literally "until")
Пока!

Good luck to you!
shchislíva!
Счастливо!

What is your name?
kak vas (tibya) zavút?/kak váshe ímya ótchistva? (the second is formal)
Как вас (тебя) зовут?/Как ваше имя и отчество?

My name is.../I am...
minya zavut.../ya...
Меня зовут...Я...

It's a pleasure
óchin' priyatna
Очень приятно

Good/excellent
kharashó/privaskhódna
хорошо/отлично

Do you speak English?
vy gavaríti pa anglíski?
Вы говорите по-английски?

I don't understand/I didn't understand
ya ni panimáyu/ya ni pónyal
Я не понимаю/Я не понял

Repeat, please
pavtaríti pazhálsta
Повторите, пожалуйста

What do you call this?
kak vy éta nazyváiti?
Как вы это называете?

How do you say...?
kak vy gavaríti...?
Как вы говорите...?

Please/Thank you (very much)
pazhálsta/(bal'shóe) spasíba
Пожалуйста/(большое) спасибо

Excuse me
izviníti
Извините

Getting Around

Where is the...?
gd'e (nakhóditsa)...?
Где находится...?

bathroom
vánnaya
...ванная

bus station
aftóbusnaya stántsyja/aftavakzál
...автобусная станция/автовокзал

bus stop
astanófka aftóbusa
...остановка автобуса

airport
airapórt
...аэропорт

railway station
vakzál/stántsyja (in small towns)
...вокзал/станция

post office
póchta
...почта

police station
...milítsyja
...милиция

ticket office
bil'étnaya kássa
...билетная касса

market place
rynak/bazár
...рынок/базар

embassy/consulate
pasól'stva/kónsul'stva
...посольство/консульство

Where is there a...?
gd'e z'd'es'...?
Где здесь...?

currency exchange
abm'én val'úty
...обмен валюты

pharmacy
apt'éka
...аптека

(good) hotel
(kharóshyj) atél'/(kharoshaya) gastínitsa
...(хороший) отель/(хорошая) гостиница

restaurant
ristarán
...ресторан

bar
bar
...бар

Metro station
mitró
…метро

service station
aftazaprávachnaya stantsyja/aftasárvis
…автозаправочная станция

newsstand
gaz'étnyj kiósk
…газетный кноск

public telephone
tilifón
…телефон

supermarket
univirsám
…универсам

department store
univirmák
…универмаг

hairdresser
parikmákhirskaya
…парикмахерская

jeweller
yuvilírnyj magazin
…ювелирный магазин

hospital
bal'nítsa
…больница

Do you have…?
u vas jes't'…?
У вас есть…?

I (don't) want…
ya (ni) khachyu…
Я (не) хочу…

I want to buy…
ya khachyu kupít'…
Я хочу купить…

Where can I buy…
gd'e ya magú kupít'…
Где я могу купить…

cigarettes
sigaréty
…сигареты

wine
vinó
…вино

film
fotoplyonku
…фотоплёнку

a ticket for…
bilét na…
…билет на…

this
éta
…это

postcards/envelopes
atkrytki/kanv'érty
…открытки/конверты

a pen/a pencil
rúchku/karandásh
…ручку/карандаш

soap/shampoo
myla/shampún'
…мыло/шампунь

aspirin
aspirn
…аспирин

I need…
mn'e núzhna…
Мне нужно…

I need a doctor/a mechanic
mn'e núzhyn dóktar/aftamikhánik
Мне нужен доктор/автомеханик

I need help
mn'e nuzhná pómashch'
Мне нужна помощ́

Car/plane/trains/ship
mashyna/samal'yot/póist/karábl'
машина/самолёт/поезд/корабль

A ticket to…
bil'ét do…
билет до…

How can I get to…
kak ya magu dabrátsa do…
Как я могу добраться до…

Please, take me to…
pazhalsta atvizíti minya…
Пожалуйста, отвезите меня…

What is this place called?
kak nazyváitsa eta m'ésta?
Как называется это место?

Where are we?
gd'e my?
Где мы?

Stop here
astanavíti z'd'es'
Остановите здесь

Please wait
padazhdíti pazhalsta
Подождите, пожалуйста

When does the train [plane] leave?
kagdá atpravl'yaitsa poist [samalyot]?
Когда отправляется поезд (самолёт)?

I want to check my luggage
ya khachyu prav'érit' bagázh
Я хочу проверить багаж

Where does this bus go?
kudá id'yot état aftóbus?
Kuda idöt qtot avtobus?

How much does it cost?
skól'ka eta stóit?
Сколько это стоит?

That's very expensive
eta óchin' dóraga
Это очень дорого

A lot, many/A little, few
mnóga/mála
много/мало

It (doesn't) fits me
eta mn'e (ni) padkhódit
Это мне (не) подходит

I have a reservation
u minya zakázana m'esta
У меня заказана комната

I want to make a reservation
ya khachyu zakazát' m'esta
Я хочу заказать место

A single (double) room
adnam'éstnuyu (dvukhmestnuyu) kómnatu
одноместную (двухместную) комнату

I want to see the room
ya khachyu pasmatrét' nómer
Я хочу посмотреть номер

Key/suitcase/bag
klyuch/chimadán/súmka
ключ/чемодан/сумка

Money

I want to exchange currency (money)
ya khachyu abmin'át' val'yutu (d'én'gi)
Я хочу обменять валюту (деньги)

Do you accept credit cards?
vy prinimáiti kridítnyi kártachki?
Вы принимаете кредитные карточки?

Can you cash a traveller's cheque?
vy mózhyti razminyat' darózhnyj chek?
Вы можете разменять дорожный чек?

What is the exchange rate?
kakój kurs?
Какой курс?

Eating Out

Waiter/menu
afitsyánt/minyu
официант/меню

I want to order...
ya khachyu zakazat'...
Я хочу заказать

Breakfast/lunch/supper
záftrak/ab'ét/úzhyn
завтрак/обед/ужин

the house speciality
fírminnaya blyuda
фирменное блюдо

Mineral water/juice
minirál'naya vadá/sok
минеральная вода/сок

Coffee/tea/beer
kófe/chai/píva
кофе/ чай/пиво

What do you have to drink (alcoholic)?
shto u vas jes't' vypit'?
Что у вас есть выпить?

Ice/fruit/dessert
marózhynaya/frúkty/disért
мороженое/фрукты/десерт

Salt/pepper/sugar
sol'/périts/sákhar
соль/перец/сахар

Beef/pork/chicken/fish/shrimp
gavyadina/svinína/kúritsa/ryba/kriv'étki
говядина/свинина/курица/рыба/креветки

Vegetables/rice/potatoes
óvashchi/ris/kartófil'
овощи/рис/картофель

Bread/butter/eggs
khleb/másla/yajtsa
хлеб/масло/яйца

Soup/salad/sandwich/pizza
sup/salát/butyrbrót/pitsa
суп/салат/бутерброд/пицца

A plate/a glass/a cup/a napkin
tar'élka/stakán/cháshka/salf'étka
тарелка/стакан/чашка/салфетка

The bill, please
shchyot pazhalsta
Счёт, пожалуйста

Delicious/Not so good
fkúsna/ták sibe
вкусно/так себе

I want my change, please
zdáchu pazhalsta
Сдачу, пожалуйста

Time

What time is it?
katóryj chas?
Который час?

Just a moment, please
adnú minútachku
Одну минуточку

How long does it take?
skól'ka vrémini eta zanimáit?
Сколько времени это занимает?

Hour/day/week/month
chas/den'/nid'élya/m'ésits
час/день/неделя/месяц

At what time?
f kakóe vrémya?
В какое время?

This (last, next) week
eta (próshlaya, sl'édujshchiya) nid'elya
эта (прошлая, следующая) неделя

Yesterday/today/tomorrow
fchirá/sivód'nya/záftra
вчера/сегодня/завтра

Sunday
vaskris'én'je
воскресенье

Monday
panid'él'nik
понедельник

Tuesday
ftórnik
вторник

Wednesday
sridá
среда

Thursday
chitv'érk
четверг

Friday
pyatnitsa
пятница

Saturday
subóta
суббота

The weekend
vykhadnyi dni
выходные дни

Signs & Inscriptions

вход/выход/входа нет
fkhot/vykhat/fkhóda n'et
Entrance/exit/no entrance

туалет/уборная
tual'ét/ubórnaya
Lavatory

Ж (З)/М (М)
dlya zhén'shchin/dlya mushchín
Ladies/gentlemen

зал ожидания
zal azhidán'ya
Waiting hall

занято/свободно
zánita/svabódna
Occupied/free

касса
kassa
booking office/cash desk

медпункт
mitpúnt
Medical services

справочное бюро
správachnae bzuro
Information

вода для питья
vadá dlya pit'ya
Drinking water

вокзал
vakzál
Terminal/railway station

открыто/закрыто
atkryta/zakryta
Open Closed

запрещается/опасно
zaprishchyaitsa/apásna
Prohibited/danger

продукты/гастроном
pradúkty/gastranóm
Grocery

булочная/кондитерская
búlachnaya/kan'dítirskaya
Bakery/confectionery

закусочная/столовая
zakúsachnaya/stalóvaya
Refreshment room/canteen

самообслуживание
samaapslúzhivan'je
Self-service

баня/прачечная/химчистка
bánya/práchichnaya/khimchístka
Bath-house/laundry/dry cleaning

книги/культтовары
knígi/kul'taváry
Books/stationery

мясо/птица
m'ása/ptítsa
Meat/poultry

овощи/фрукты
óvashchi/frúkty
Green-grocery/fruits

универмаг/универсам
univirmák/univirsám
Department store/supermarket

Further Reading

History

Catherine the Great, by J.T. Alexander. Oxford University Press, 1989.
Stalin, Man of Contradiction, by K.N. Cameron. Strong Oak Press, 1989.
History of Soviet Russia, by E.H. Carr. Pelican, 3 vols, first published 1953.
A History of the Soviet Union, by G. Hosking. Fontana/Collins, 1990.
The Making of Modern Russia, by L. Kochan and R. Abraham. Penguin, 1983.
The Blackwell Encyclopaedia of the Russian Revolution, ed. by H. Shukman. Blackwell, 1989.
St Petersburg, by Solomon Volkov, Simon & Schuster, 1995.
From Leningrad to St Petersburg, Robert Ortung, 1996.
Sunlight at Midnight, by W. Bruce Lincoln, Basic Books, 2000.

Politics

Voices of Glasnost, by S. Cohen and K. van den Heuvel. Norton, 1989.
The Other Russia, by Michael Glenny and Norman Stone. Faber & Faber, 1990.
Perestroika, by M.S. Gorbachev. Fontana, 1987.
Towards a Better World, by M.S. Gorbachev. Richardson and Steirman, 1987.
Glasnost in Action, by A. Nove. Unwin Hyman, 1989.
Against the Grain, by Boris Yeltsin. Jonathan Cape, 1990.

Biography & Memoirs

The Making of Andrei Sakharov, by G. Bailey. Insight Penguin, 1990.
Alone Together, by Elena Bonner. Collins Harvill, 1986.
An English Lady at the Court of Catherine the Great, ed. by A.G. Gross. Crest Publications, 1989.

On the Estate: Memoirs of Russia Before the Revolution, ed. by Olga Davydoff Bax. Thames & Hudson, 1986.

Into the Whirlwind and *Within a Whirlwind*, by Eugenia Ginzburg. Collins Harvill, 1989.

In the Beginning, by Irina Ratush-inskaya. Hodder & Stoughton, 1990.

Ten Days that Shook the World, by John Reed. Penguin, first published 1919.

The Gulag Archipelago, by Alexander Solzhenitsyn. Collins Harvill, 1988.

Russia: Despatches from the Guardian Correspondent in Moscow, by Martin Walker. Abacus, 1989.

Art

A History of Russian Painting, by A. Bird. Phaidon, 1987.

Russian Art of the Avant Garde, by J.E. Bowlt. Thames & Hudson, 1988.

New Worlds: Russian Art and Society 1900–37, by D. Elliot. Thames & Hudson, 1986.

The Kremlin and its Treasures, by Raimann. Phaidon, 1989.

Russian Art from Neoclassicism to the Avant Garde, by D.V. Sarabianov. Thames & Hudson, 1990.

Street Art of the Revolution, by V. Tolstoy, I. Bibikova and C. Cooke. Thames & Hudson, 1990.

The Art of Central Asia. Aurora Art Publishers, 1988.

Folk Art in the Soviet Union. Abrams/Aurora, 1990.

The Hermitage. Aurora, 1987.

Masterworks of Russian Painting in Soviet Museums. Aurora, 1989.

Travel, Geography & Natural History

First Russia, Then Tibet, by Robert Byron. Penguin, first published 1905.

Caucasian Journey, by Negley Farson. Penguin, first published 1951.

Sailing to St Petersburg, by Roger Foxall. Grafton, 1990.

The Natural History of the USSR, by Algirdas Kynstautas. Century Hutchinson, 1987.

Portrait of the Soviet Union, by Fitzroy McLean. Wwidenfeld and Nicolson, 1988.

Atlas of Russia and the Soviet Union, by R. Millner-Gulland with N. Dejevsky. Phaidon, 1989.

The Big Red Train, by Eric Newby. Picador, 1989.

The USSR: From an Original Idea by Karl Marx. Faber & Faber, 1983.

Journey into Russia, by Laurens van der Post. Penguin, first published 1964.

Among the Russians, by Colin Thubron. Penguin, first published 1983.

Ustinov in Russia, by Peter Ustinov. Michael O Mara Books, 1987.

The Nature of the Soviet Union: Landscapes, Flora and Fauna. Mokslas Publishing 1987.

Russia. Bracken Books, 1989.

USSR: The Economist Guide. Hutchinson Business Books, 1990.

Literature

The Russia House, by John le Carré. Coronet, 1990.

The Brothers Karamazov; The Idiot, by F. Dostoevsky.

Doctor Zhivago, by Boris Pasternak.

Children of the Arbat, by A. Rybakov. Hutchinson, 1988.

And Quiet Flows the Don; The Don Flows Home to the Sea, by Mikhail Sholokov.

War and Peace; Anna Karenina, by Leo Tolstoy.

Other Insight Guides

Insight Guide: Russia and *Insight Guide: Moscow* complement this

book as part of the same series. Other Insight Guides with the equally high-quality pictures and detailed information cover The Baltic States, Eastern Europe, Norway, Sweden and Finland.

Insight Pocket Guide: Moscow is part of the series designed for short–break visitors, with a host author setting out special itineraries to help you make the most of a short visit.

Compact Guide: St Petersburg is a fact-packed portable guide with text, pictures and cross-referenced maps.

Insight FlexiMap: St Petersburg combines clear cartography with essential information about the city and has a laminated finish that makes the map durable and exceptionally easy to fold.

ART & PHOTO CREDITS

APN 66
Bogdanovich 18, 20, 34, 89
Cephas 81
Fritz Dressler 1, 22, 54, 56, 57,
64/65, 69, 74, 85, 90, 91, 103,
116, 117, 118, 119, 120, 121, 125,
130, 136, 139, 148, 155, 156/157,
158, 162, 166, 167R, 168, 171,
172, 178/179, 183, 186, 189, 190,
192, 200, 204, 218, 219, 222,
224/225, 235, 239, 241, 242, 243,
244, 245, 251, 254, 255
Alain Le Garsmeur 19, 79, 144
Govorukhin 21, 25, 29, 36, 42, 46,
96, 98
Gudenko 6/7, 8/9, 10/11, 12/13,
16/17, 24, 27, 28, 32/33, 35, 37,
38, 39L/R, 41, 43, 44, 45, 77, 88,
92, 95, 102, 104/105, 106/107,
108/109, 122/123, 129, 154, 180,
185, 207, 209L, 237, 253
Clare Griffiths 99, 163, 164R
The Hermitage, St. Petersburg
152
Robert Harding Picture Library 82R
Hans Höfer 133, 169L, 256
Jim Holmes/Apa back cover left,
spine
Michael Jenner 76
Jürgens 30, 31, 32/33, 48, 49, 51,
86/87, 93, 94, 97, 196, 215
Wilhelm Klein 50, 187, 247R

Knop 26, 40, 68
Fred Mawer 75
MIR Agency USA 82L
Anna Mockford & Nick Bonnetti/Apa
front flap top & bottom, back cover
centre, bottom & right, back flap top
& bottom, 2/3, 3B, 4/5, 4B, 5B, 14,
52/53, 55, 58, 59, 60, 61, 62/63,
67, 70, 71, 72, 73, 80, 100, 101,
104/105, 106/107, 108/109, 110,
113, 124, 128, 131, 132, 134, 135,
137, 138, 140, 141, 143, 145, 146,
147, 149, 150, 151, 153, 159,
164L, 165, 167L, 170, 173, 174,
181, 188, 193, 194, 195, 197,
198/199, 201, 203, 205, 206, 208,
209R, 210, 211, 212, 213, 214,
216/217, 221, 223, 226, 227, 228,
230, 231, 238, 240, 246, 248, 249,
250
State Russian Museum, St.
Petersburg 175L/R, 176, 177
Shablovsky 23, 232/233, 234, 247L
Shone/Contrast 220
Jon Spaull/Apa 84
Stin/Firsov 78
Robert D. Tonsing/White Tiger 83

Map Production Laura Morris
© 2002 Apa Publications GmbH & Co.
Verlag KG (Singapore branch)

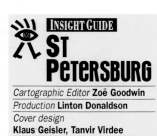

INSIGHT GUIDE
ST PETERSBURG

Cartographic Editor	**Zoë Goodwin**
Production	**Linton Donaldson**
Cover design	
Klaus Geisler, Tanvir Virdee	
Picture Research	
Hilary Genin, Britta Jaschinski	

Index

Numbers in italics refer to photographs

66 I was first drawn to the Insight Guides by the excellent "Nepal" volume. I can think of no book which so effectively captures the essence of a country. Out of these pages leaped the Nepal I know – the captivating charm of a people and their culture. I've since discovered and enjoyed the entire Insight Guide series. Each volume deals with a country in the same sensitive depth, which is nowhere more evident than in the superb photography. 99

Sir Edmund Hillary

St Petersburg Metro

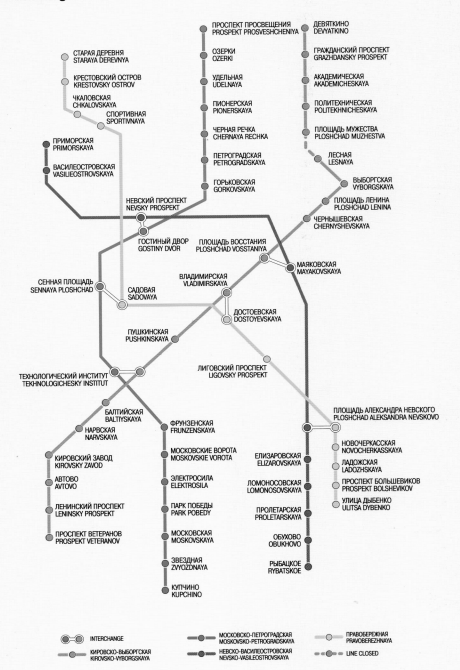